energy
FOR DEVELOPMENT

energy
FOR DEVELOPMENT:
AN INTERNATIONAL CHALLENGE

Prepared for the North-South Roundtable
of the Society for International Development

John Foster, Efrain Friedmann, James W. Howe,
Francisco R. Parra, David H. Pollock
with a foreword by Maurice F. Strong

PRAEGER

PRAEGER SPECIAL STUDIES • PRAEGER SCIENTIFIC

Published in 1981 by Praeger Publishers
CBS Educational and Professional Publishing
A Division of CBS, Inc.
521 Fifth Avenue, New York, New York 10175 U.S.A.

ⓒ 1981 North-South Roundtable (SID)

123456789 145 987654321
Library of Congress Catalog Card Number: 81-8683
Printed in the United States of America

The views expressed in this publication are those of the
authors and do not necessarily represent those of the
North-South Roundtable of the Society for International
Development or of the Overseas Development Council, its
directors, officers, or staff.

FOREWORD

It was not so long ago that the voices of those who warned of an impending energy "crisis" were unheard and unheeded. Now the mood has changed dramatically. Energy is decried by many as the source of all the economic and financial ills of both the industrialised "North" and the developing "South". That the energy issue is a critical and important one for the entire world community is undeniable. But the present tendency to ascribe to energy the blame for most of our current ailments would be as wrong and misguided as the apathy and skepticism that characterised the attitudes existing before the advent of the energy crisis. Sharp increases in oil prices and potential shortages of supply have indeed produced major impacts on the economies and the prospects of virtually all countries. They have produced a shift of economic power and comparative advantage that is unprecedented both in its dimensions and its speed.

This dramatic shift towards one group of oil-rich developing countries is fundamentally altering the world's political and economic balance. While this has moved the international economic order towards the kind of changes all developing countries have been seeking, it has also created new burdens for the energy-deficient countries, particularly the poorest, and given rise to new needs for international action. The consequences for the oil-deficient industrialised countries, the oil-importing developing countries and the oil-exporting countries will have a profound effect on the future of each of these groups. On the one hand it sharpens the differences and potentials for conflict among them; on the other hand, it makes the need for understanding and cooperation more urgent and compelling than ever.

The rapid evolution of the sense of "crisis" surrounding the energy issue has been accompanied by a great deal of mis-information, misunderstanding, and emotion. In this climate, it has proven extremely difficult to mount the kind of constructive and objective dialogue which is needed to facilitate international agreement on the issues. Indeed, attempts to date to negotiate these issues at the international level have been ominously unsuccessful. They have floundered largely on the unwillingness of the industrialised nations to link negotiations on energy with a serious consideration of the demands of the developing countries for a more just and equitable "new international economic order," and on the insistence of both oil-exporting and oil-importing developing countries that energy issues can only be effectively addressed within this broader context.

In the meantime, the sense of crisis has yielded a proliferation of energy studies. While these have been helpful, they have also showered the public with such a plethora of facts and viewpoints that they have tended to add to the confusion. More importantly, most of these studies have been carried out in the Western industrialised countries and have been biased towards the perspectives and interests of these countries. There is as yet very little broad understanding of the interests and concerns of the oil-exporting countries and the acute plight of the oil-importing developing countries. And there has still been far too little recognition of the real need and importance of viewing the energy issue, and dealing with it, as an integral part of the complex of issues which affect relations between the industrialised and developing countries--the North and the South.

It is against this background that the North-South Roundtable of the Society for International Development (whose activities are described at the end of this volume) has established an Energy Roundtable to help bridge the gaps in information and understanding which have thus far prevented the establishment of effective dialogue and negotiations on these issues. It is designed to assemble the best available information, analyses, and opinions concerning energy as it affects each of the principal groups of nations-- industrialised, oil-exporting, and oil-importing developing nations--and the relations among these nations which bear on the prospects for peace, security, and prosperity for the entire world community.

It is not the intent of the Roundtable to produce a single solution to these issues, but to provide the kinds of information, understanding, and ideas out of which solutions may be fashioned. It is not a forum for official negotiations; but it is designed to undergird and support the processes of official dialogue and negotiations and to feed information and ideas into this process. It is not another energy study; but it draws upon virtually all of the principal energy studies that have been produced recently, and has had the benefit of contributions from many of the authors of such studies. It is not intended to argue the case for any single group of nations; yet it accepts a special obligation to bring out the perspectives of the developing countries, both oil-exporting and oil-importing, because there has been far too little understanding and appreciation of the interests and concerns of these countries by the industrialised world.

The Report is a product of the first phase of an ongoing process of dialogue which the North-South Energy Roundtable has initiated. It presents the views of the authors, expressed in their personal capacities, rather than any consensus reached in the Roundtable, even though these views have developed after several intensive discussions in Roundtable meetings.

The second phase is envisaged as a series of in-depth dialogues organised by the Roundtable. These would take place in a variety of fora in both industrialised and developing countries as well as international institutions. It would involve small teams of experts in dialogue with policy-makers. It would be designed to give the policy-makers the benefits of the information and viewpoints assembled by the Roundtable and at the same time add to the insights and knowledge available to the Roundtable.

In the third phase of the process a final document would be produced, incorporating the results of the entire process. But this final report, like the framework report, will represent only a portion of the fruits of this process. The most important contribution of the Energy Roundtable will be the common base of knowledge and understanding, which will be developed throughout the exercise in the process of inter-action among experts and policy-makers representing a broad and diversified range of experience and interest. It is in this continuous nurturing of understanding and dialogue which undergirds and facilitates the processes of policy-making at the national level and of formal negotiations among nations at the international level.

This initiative originated at the meeting of the North-South Roundtable in Colombo, Sri Lanka in August 1979. Overall coordination of the project has been the responsibility of its Steering Committee, which I have the privilege of chairing. A number of meetings have been held involving people from all regions of the world representing a wide variety of experience in the field of energy, economic and social policy, governments, international organisations, and private industry. Important contributions were made by a number of others. All participants contributed in their personal capacities. To all I would like to express my deep gratitude.

I would like to record our special thanks to Mahbub ul Haq, Chairman of the North-South Roundtable, whose leadership and commitment have made this project possible; also to John Foster, Francisco R. Parra, James W. Howe, David H. Pollock, and Efrain Friedmann for their indefatigable work in preparing this report. And none of us would have been able to function without the gracious and efficient support of Khadija Haq who, as Director of the Roundtable Secretariat and its principal organising genius, pulled it all together.

I would also like to record our gratitude for the financial support provided, in cash and in kind, from a number of sources, government and private, and in particular the generous support of the Government of Sweden, the Atlantic Richfield Company, Petro-Canada, the Overseas Development Council, and the International Energy Development Corporation.

Maurice F. Strong
October 1980

CONTENTS

Page

FOREWORD .... M.F. Strong v
List of Charts xi
Abbreviations and Acronyms xii
Overview Summary xiii

INTRODUCTION .... J. Foster 1

I.   THE GLOBAL ENERGY SCENE .... J. Foster 5
     1. Energy and Development 5
     2. Global Energy Prospects 13
     3. Oil 16
     4. Energy Other Than Oil 38
     5. Natural Gas 39
     6. Coal 41
     7. Nuclear Energy 44
     8. Hydroelectricity 48
     9. Geothermal Energy 48
    10. Other Renewable Forms of Energy 49
    11. Conclusion 55

II. THE PARTIES INVOLVED.................................. 57
     1. Oil-Importing Developing
        Countries .... J. W. Howe 57
     2. Oil-Exporting Developing
        Countries .... F. R. Parra 96
     3. Industrialised Countries .... J. Foster 120
     4. Convergences and Conflicts ..... D. H. Pollock and
                                         J. W. Howe 142

III. GLOBAL OPPORTUNITIES 161
     1. Managing the Remaining Decades of Oil 161
        Development of Oil and Gas in
        the OIDCs .... F. R. Parra 161
        Energy Efficiency and
        Conservation .... J. Foster and
                                       J. W. Howe 173
     2. Managing the Transition
        Oil to Other Sources .... J. Foster and
                                        J. W. Howe 183
     3. Meeting the Energy Needs of
        Developing Countries .... J. W. Howe 193
     4. Improved International
        Cooperation on Energy .... J. W. Howe 202

IV. A FRAMEWORK FOR ENERGY POLICIES IN OIL-IMPORTING
     DEVELOPING COUNTRIES .... E. Friedmann 205
     1. External Supply Options 205
     2. Domestic Supply Options 210
     3. External Assistance Needs 232

Footnotes and Bibliography 241
About the North-South Roundtable and the
     Society for International Development 254

List of Charts

Page

1. World Consumption and Production of Commercial Primary Energy, 1979 6

2. Secondary Energy Consumption by End-Use, 1976 8

3. Secondary Energy Consumption by Type, 1977 11

4. World: Consumption of Commercial Primary Energy, 1960–1979 14

5. World: Oil Consumption, 1979 17

6. World Production of Crude Oil and Natural Gas Liquids, 1960–2000 22

7. World Ultimate Recoverable Resources 26

8. World: Oil Trade, 1960–1979 28

9. World: Estimated Oil Imports, 1980 32

10. Oil-Importing Developing Countries: Estimated Oil Imports, 1980 34

11. Payments Balance on Current Account, 1973–1980 77

12. OIDC Current Account Deficits, 1973–1990 80

13. Developed and Developing Countries: Geophysical Activity, Seismic Party-Months, 1970–1978 163

14. Developed and Developing Countries: Number of Wildcat Wells Drilled, 1970–1978 164

15. Developed and Developing Countries: Rigs Active, 1971–1980 167

16. Petroleum Basins of the World (Map) 215

Abbreviations and Acronyms

CIEC   Conference on International Economic Cooperation
CPE   Centrally planned economy
DAC   Development Assistance Committee of the OECD
DRE   Decentralised renewable energy
ECLA   Economic Commission for Latin America
ECSC   European Coal and Steel Community
EEC   European Economic Community
G-77   Group of 77
IAEA   International Atomic Energy Agency
IDA   International Development Association
IDB   Inter-American Development Bank
IEA   International Energy Agency
IMF   International Monetary Fund
LDC   Less developed country
LNG   Liquefied natural gas
NGL   Natural gas liquids
NIEO   New international economic order
NSERT   North-South Energy Roundtable
NSRT   North-South Roundtable
OAPEC   Organisation of Arab Petroleum Exporting Countries
ODC   Overseas Development Council
OECD   Organisation for Economic Cooperation and
          Development
OIDC   Oil-importing developing country
OPEC   Organisation of Petroleum Exporting Countries
OXDC   Oil-exporting developing country
RD&D   Research, development, and demonstration
SDR   Special drawing rights
SID   Society for International Development
UNCTAD   United Nations Conference on Trade and Development
UNDP   United Nations Development Programme
UAE   United Arab Emirates
UNICEF   United Nations Children's Fund

b/d   barrel per day
cfd   cubic feet per day
o.e.   oil equivalent
tce   metric ton of coal equivalent

OVERVIEW SUMMARY

The North-South dialogue has encountered many setbacks, but a new attempt is currently being made to revive it, this time within a United Nations framework of global negotiations, the corner-stone of a Third Development Decade. This is just the latest in a long series of international efforts to resolve the problems of North-South relations.

The issue of natural resources has been at the forefront of developing countries' efforts to improve their concept of the international economic order. During the 1970s, oil-exporting developing countries (OXDCs) acquired increased bargaining strength, which has led to enormous changes in petroleum arrangements. No other natural resource has yet turned out to be as strategic to the world as oil, which has become a catalyst in the movement towards an improved international order.

This basic framework report is predicated on the existence of a new consensus between the parties involved, even though the international system faces a host of difficulties. One of the failures of the past has been a dialogue of the deaf. What will help is a clearer exposition of perspectives and a fuller understanding of each party's objectives and policy options. Nations can make greater progress towards achieving energy security and do so at less cost if they treat the problem as a global one, resolvable through cooperative international action, rather than solely a unilateral or bilateral one.

I. THE GLOBAL ENERGY SCENE

Energy and Development

Energy is one of the most important inputs in the process of development. Human material progress and the use of non-human energy have gone hand in hand. Consequently, there is proper concern whether energy (especially oil and woodfuels) will be available in adequate supply and at prices which will allow progress to continue.

World energy problems are not confined to oil, though oil is a preoccupation because of a) its finite nature and the need to conserve its use and develop alternative energy sources, b) its impact on balance of payments, international financial flows, inflation, and economic growth, c) dangers of supply disruptions, and d) its importance as the prime form of commercial energy in developed and developing countries alike. It is the single largest primary commodity by value entering into world trade.

Nor are world energy problems confined to commercial forms of energy. These are the ones mainly used in industrialised countries and in the modern and urban sectors of developing countries. But equally crucial are the problems of societies based on non-commercial energy. Some 60% of the world's population are rural and mostly rely on traditional energy fuels. The fuelwood crisis and other constraints on living standards are a fact of life for the majority of the world's population.

The present world energy prospect can be viewed as a virtual stagnation in the overall trade of oil, and little growth in traditional energy sources. These constraints point to a future transition to the accelerated development of alternative energy sources and, equally important, to increased efficiency in energy use. Much of the world's population is faced with a threefold energy problem: i) obtaining enough traditional energy, ii) shifting to better-quality fuels and, iii) making the transition to more plentiful energy sources than oil.

Oil

Oil has been a key input to economic growth in industrialised and developing countries alike. The remarkable growth in its consumption until 1973 was facilitated by the extraordinary increase in production and low-cost exports from OPEC countries, particularly in the Middle East. Since then oil has entered a high-cost era. Its growth has moderated greatly, reflecting the downturn in economic activity in industrialised countries, substitution of other energy forms, and increased efficiency in energy use.

There are now only a few countries where oil production is large and still clearly expanding, and in none is it thought likely to exceed by much their national objectives: China, Mexico, North Sea, Iraq, and a few developing countries. There are a number of other developing countries where output is smaller but expanding. Four of the most important OPEC producers do not wish to produce at capacity and are reluctant to undertake further large-scale expansion: Iran, Kuwait, Saudi Arabia, and the UAE. Undoubtedly the most contentious issue between industrialised and OPEC countries would be the rate of development and production in the few countries where there is large potential for expansion.

Exploration in oil-importing developing countries (OIDCs) had been picking up in recent years. A large number can reasonably expect to become medium to small producers.

Throughout most of 1980s and during the 1990s, oil demand is likely to be constrained by supply availability, though this must be understood in the context of production limits for political and economic reasons in some major oil-exporting countries.

Higher oil prices have improved the economic viability of exploitation of small fields, enhanced recovery, exploration in high-cost areas such as polar and deep water, heavy oil, tar-sand, and oil shale deposits, and fields with poor reservoir characteristics. In many countries small fields will be found well into the next century. Their cumulative impact may be great, and their support to economies including OIDCs will be significant.

The prospects for international oil trade during the next two decades appear to be at best a continuance of their present levels, unless incentives can improve prospects for OXDC output.

A particular uncertainty is the extent to which the Soviet Union/Eastern European bloc may move from being a net exporter to a net importer of oil. It would be prudent to plan on this prospect, though there are many unknown variables which could ameliorate it.

We find a great concentration of oil imports into a relatively few OIDCs. The upper middle-income countries import the lion's share. Thus, for many countries their oil imports are minuscule in relation to world trade. But to each of them, these imports could be a heavy burden.

If the prospects for the next two decades are truly for an increasing constraint on international oil trade, then national oil trade, and if OIDCs are to just even have a modest increase in their trade, then the industrialised countries will import no more oil than at present, and quite likely less. This is recognised by them in the formulation of their oil import targets.

Oil prices are generally expected to continue rising in real terms during the next two decades. For example, the World Bank now postulates a 3% p.a. increase as an illustrative hypothesis. Of course, price projections are no more than illustrative. In no way can they have precision, and the uncertainties are huge. There could be some alleviation of pressure on prices if steps in oilimporting countries to moderate oil import demand are successful. Conversely, there could be more severe price pressures, if future world energy supplies turn out to be less than hoped.

Though the international oil market could ease up in the short term, it still does not appear prudent to plan on such an outcome for the long term. Oil importers are precariously dependent on just a few export sources. There is vulnerability from reliance on physical concentration of large-scale export facilities. There is little flexibility in the supply system.

Natural Gas

Natural gas is likely to make an increasing major contribution to world energy supplies. It will be an important transitional fuel. It could be the fastest growing energy source in developing countries as well as elsewhere. Expansion of the local gas usage should be the main policy aim. But where the domestic market is limited, exports by pipeline or liquefied natural gas (LNG) may be advantageous.

In recent years pricing, financial, economic, technical, and environmental reasons led to the delay or cancellation of many LNG projects. In particular, their high cost has made for a relatively low price netback for gas at the wellhead. Hence petroleum-producing countries have typically pursued other uses for natural gas or have flared it. Today's oil prices have greatly improved the economic viability of LNG projects. They have also improved those of other high-cost sources of energy, and investment decisions will have to be justified in relation to other energy opportunities.

The potential for deep conventional gas may be great. It could be one of the world's major fossil fuel sources when oil begins to be depleted in the next century. A major deterrent has been the high costs of exploration and development. The Middle East could have giant deep gas deposits, but these horizons are unlikely to be tested until oil reserves are more drastically depleted. A comprehensive survey of energy resources must also include unconventional gases, much of which is not yet explored. They include gas dissolved in water, natural gas from coal-beds, gas from Devonian shales, gas from tight sands, and gas hydrates.

Coal

The world's resources and reserves of solid fuels are huge, much larger than those of oil and gas. There are many countries which are believed to have untapped and unassessed coal reserves. Africa and South America have only sporadically been examined for coal. Worldwide, a large production base exists which could be expanded, if markets were developed. There are great opportunities in both industrialised and developing countries. The key to resource development lies with government policies to encourage such exploitation.

A critical issue for the expansion of coal use is its acceptability to end-users. Particularly in developed countries, unresolved questions on environmental issues have typically not been adequately covered: for example, strip-mining, air-pollution, acid rain, and CO_2 accumulation in the atmosphere. There are also constraints in recruiting miners and engineers, lead-times, and considerable investment costs. Nevertheless, a large increase is expected in output and, even more so, in international trade.

Nuclear Power

The present outlook for nuclear power is very mixed. France and the Soviet Union are greatly expanding its development, while in a number of industrialised countries its development continues to be retarded by public concern, safety, economic, and financial issues. The number of developing countries which can handle the technology and have a large enough electricity sector is relatively limited. Elsewhere, most developing countries are going slow in their approach towards nuclear power at this time.

Fear of weapons proliferation has made supplier countries cautious in supplying technology and fuels. In return, recipient countries are concerned about the principle of retaining sovereignty over their national policies. This raises questions of how far existing international agencies can adequately establish nuclear safeguards, and how far supplier countries should go in balancing the political and strategic risks in relations with recipient countries.

Hydroelectricity

Hydroelectric power is expected to continue growing during the next two decades. New sites are becoming harder to come by in most industrialised countries other than Canada and Norway. But there are still huge opportunities in developing countries. The use of small-scale hydro plants is also seen to increase greatly, as has happened in China.

Other Renewable Forms of Energy

Interest in renewable energy has much increased with the continued rise in oil prices. The technologies for some forms of renewable energy are mature, for others are promising and being developed for commercialisation, and for others are under research and development and have long-term possibilities. Issues regarding these energy forms will be addressed closely in the UN Conference on New and Renewable Sources of

Energy in August 1981 in Nairobi.   In developing countries,
interest has particularly focussed on decentralised and small-
scale applications in rural areas.   A key problem for OIDCs is
the need for energy in food production and household use.
This requires more effort to improve technologies for use of
biomass, particularly fuelwood and charcoal.   There has been
significant development of processes for large-scale production of ethanol from carbohydrates such as sugar and starchy
roots.   An outstanding program is the one in Brazil.   Biogas
is also receiving much interest; it has been promoted extensively in China.   Solar energy in its many varieties, wind
power, and methanol all have significant potential.

II.   THE PARTIES INVOLVED

1.   Oil-Importing Developing Countries

The developing countries consume much less commercial energy than industrialised countries, but their energy
consumption is increasing at a faster pace.   Their use of
energy varies greatly among greatly among countries.   There is
also great inequality within each country between cities and
countryside, and even within cities between the modern sector
and urban slums.   The rural peoples and those in the urban
slums rely upon traditional sources of energy such as wood,
crop residues, animal power, and charcoal.

Energy waste abounds in the South as well as in the
North but for different reasons.   In the South it is due to
inefficient practices and equipment.   In rural areas, there is
waste in the use of fuel for cooking and in the making of
charcoal.   The cure is to provide the funds and expertise to
improve efficiency.

At least 73 countries depend on imports for 100% of
their oil needs.   There is thought to be a great deal of oil
in the OIDCs.   Some geologists believe that much oil yet
undiscovered may be on or offshore the developing countries.
Yet the drilling rates are low in relation to the oil-
producing industrialised countries.   Outside help is needed to
find and produce their own fossil fuels, to improve efficiency
in energy use, and to adopt new and more plentiful substitutes
for oil.   OIDCs will need help to pay for essential oil

imports and to improve their export markets to help pay for their oil imports.

Heavy oil, tar sands, and oil shales also are great potential energy sources. As drilling increases in the OIDCs, much natural gas may be found.

Except for China and India, very little exploration for coal has been done, perhaps because industrialisation in the OIDCs had not begun before oil displaced coal as the preferred fuel for industry. Many experts feel that the potential for coal in the OIDCs is great.

Nearly two-thirds of the world's conventional hydroelectric potential is in the Third World, but less than 10% of the conventional hydroelectric potential there has been exploited. A closely related and even less explored energy source is small-scale or mini-hydropower. The Chinese experience suggests that this may be an important source of energy.

Whether nuclear fission will prove to be an important energy source for developing countries depends on whether nuclear technology is successful in solving its cost, safety, and waste disposal problems in the North and, if so, whether it will come in units small enough to match the grids in most OIDCs.

Traditional energy is in jeopardy in the Third World, where it is the dominant and indispensible source of energy. The shortage of firewood is acute in most regions, and the price of firewood and charcoal is skyrocketing. The growing demand for charcoal is accelerating deforestation. Traditional methods of production are very inefficient, and the pressure on forests increases. In some areas, there has been a movement from wood to kerosene. With the rapid increase in oil prices, however, there has been a reverse trend from kerosene back to wood and charcoal. The firewood problem is serious everywhere.

The firewood shortage has led to far-reaching environmental problems. Forests are disappearing at an alarming rate. A sizeable percentage of the world's forests could disappear before the end of the century, with unknown conse-

quences on regional and global climatic changes and on food
production.   For most countries, there are virtually no
alternatives to wood except hydropower or agricultural wastes.
Given present rates of deforestation, Senegal will be bare of
trees in 30 years, Ethiopia in 20, Burundi in 7.   In nine
African countries surveyed by the World Bank, present annual
rates of afforestation would need to be increased by 8–50
times, in order to meet domestic fuel needs to the year 2000.

While the industrial countries have to move away from
oil to other more plentiful energy sources, the developing
countries have to make a double transition: i) they must make
the same transition for the modern sector of their economy and
ii) they must make the other transition from traditional
energy to more modern non-oil energy, even as they face the
transition to modern energy sources.   It makes little long-
term sense for a developing country to make a transition to
oil just at the time it must undertake a transition from oil
to successors.   The problem is that any decision to forego the
shift to oil-based technology is a decision that will immediately hurt development.   The dilemma of the OIDCs is this: if
they continue to shift to oil, they will be in great trouble
in a few decades; if they interrupt the shift, they will be in
trouble now.

An option that may be particularly open to the Third
World is to give much emphasis to modern decentralised renewable energy.   This is because i) people live in rural areas,
far from the reach of grids of modern energy, ii) modern
energy when available is highly priced, and iii) there is
relatively little investment in hard energy.

Solar energy is generally in more abundant supply in
the South in one or more of its four forms than in the North:
sunshine, falling water, wind, and biomass.   Most developing
countries have the potential for at least one or more of its
forms.   They are attractive to Third World countries because
i) they can be decentralised in the rural areas where most
Third World people live; ii) the costs of certain technologies
for the use of decentralised renewable energy are not expected
to rise as rapidly as the cost of oil; and iii) the future of
oil is increasingly uncertain.   But the technologies are still
being developed and are not yet sufficiently reliable or cheap
enough to compete with conventional energy sources.   In the

rural areas, more research and site testing is needed before its full promise becomes evident. There is not much prospect that renewable energy will soon become competitive in the modern sectors of developing countries.

The OIDCs have several energy needs: i) access to increasing supplies of oil, ii) increased production and improved management of non-commercial energy, iii) improved efficiency in energy use, iv) development of indigenous commercial energy, and v) a smooth transition to oil's successors. Finally, they need to strengthen existing institutions and in some cases establish new ones which can plan and manage energy services, and they need to expand the numbers of qualified energy personnel.

OIDCs have short-run energy and balance of payments problems. Oil import bills of OIDCs are estimated at about $67 billion in 1980 and in the World Bank's view could rise by 1990 to some $230 billion ($120 billion in 1980-85). The low-income countries face serious financing problems. Middle-income countries are unlikely to find bilateral official finance as freely available as in 1974-75. The ability of the private sector to maintain as predominant a role in financing the major borrowing countries stands in doubt.

Severe imbalances in the 1980s will impose great human costs. How great the costs will be depends on the adoption of suitable national economic policies and on the performance of the external world. There are three basic options: i) developing countries can cut oil imports, ii) they can seek external financing, and iii) they can improve their merchandise exports.

If the developing countries are to have the possibility of even substantially reduced rates of economic growth, they have to have increased, not reduced, access to oil. This points to private and official external financing as the chief means of adjusting to high oil costs. There are several current and potential new sources. In particular, there are grounds for optimism that OPEC will yet further increase its development assistance. OECD aid is not likely to increase much over the shortterm. There is need for increased assistance from IDA and the soft-loan windows of international financial institutions, and the IMF.

In the long-run, OIDCs' most constructive course of action is to increase merchandise exports. But the inability to increase exports is severely limited by external factors over which they have no control. Borrowing money is no more than a temporary solution, albeit highly essential for the immediate future. To get at the roots of the balance-of-payments problem will take much more heroic measures, involving international cooperation.

Industrialised countries' markets must be increasingly open to export from OIDCs. Prices of Northern exports to LDCs must not inflate too much. Oil must remain physically available to OIDCs, along with the means to finance it.

Proposals for reform of the international economic order include trade reforms (improved access of Southern exports to Northern markets), as well as improved treatment of commodities exported from the South (e.g., Common Fund proposals to finance buffer stock agreements). The South has found particularly burdensome the Northern practice of escalating tariff barriers on Southern goods, to the extent these goods are processed.

Regarding the transfer of resources, the Brandt Commission urged that a concerted effort be made to establish automatic sources of revenue for development finance. Other proposals have been made for debt relief for LDCs. Others are that LDCs should be granted a) preferential access to private capital markets in the North, and b) a greater voice in the decisions on the allocation and management of development aid.

Developing countries complain that multinational corporations have control over technology and effectively prevent or delay its transfer to the South; they seek a general code of conduct.

The World Food Conference in 1974 called for a number of reforms to ensure enough food for all. Among proposals under consideration is a buffer-stock of foodgrains, which would stabalise prices and offer supply security in times of shortfall.

A number of proposals have been heard for reform of the international monetary system. One is that LDCs be given a greater share of the benefits from SDRs. The conditions governing access to the IMF by developing countries are seen by many to be excessively onerous and inflexible; they also argue that IMF funds should be made available over longer periods of time. Proposals have been made for a new facility to help OIDCs adjust to the oil price rises of 1979; this may very well call for an expansion of funds available to the IMF. Others argue that pressure should be brought on countries in persistent balance-of-payments surplus to adjust, instead of putting the entire adjustment burden on the shoulders of the deficit countries. Some also argue that LDCs should be given a greater voice in managing the international monetary system. Finally, there is a need to consider international rules governing management of currency markets, which are now beyond the control of the monetary and banking authorities in any one country.

Inflation in industrialised countries has placed a burden on OXDCs and OIDCs and has damaged the industrialised countries themselves. Oil price increases have contributed to inflation, but have not necessarily caused most of the inflation. There are other factors at work. Many economists believe that in most industrialised countries inflation is now self-perpetuating, so that it will continue even in the absence of any further oil price rises, unless better economic management is forthcoming.

Virtually all the funding for research, development, and demonstration (RD&D) of new or improved forms of energy comes from industrialised countries. Small but important exceptions include Brazil's work on gasohol, India's on biomass, and significant work in China. The ability of the entire world to make the critical transition from oil to more abundant and eventually renewable sources, depends very largely on the success of these RD&D programs. But there is reason for OXDCs and OIDCs to question how far the allocation of RD&D funds is relevent to their needs.

2. The Oil-Exporting Developing Countries

Is there sufficient converging interest between OXDCs
and oil-importing countries to contribute towards the basis of
a global energy policy? The little progress during the last
seven years gives scant ground for optimism. But the problems
are becoming more acute, particularly regarding three central
issues: i) the OXDCs' desire to stretch out reserves,
ii) planning and managing an orderly transition in industrial
countries from dependence on imported oil to alternative
energy, and iii) the OIDCs' difficulties in earning foreign
exchange to finance oil imports.

There are about 28 OXDCs, of which 13 are OPEC
members. To some extent, OXDCs share the development problems
of other developing countries. But there are four areas which
would have to be the subject of accommodation within an overall global energy policy: i) exploration and development of
oil (particularly heavy oil and secondary and tertiary
recovery projects), ii) development and commercialisation of
natural gas resources, iii) conservation of oil and gas, and
iv) the treatment of financial assets held by capital-surplus
OXDCs in industrialised countries.

Any approach can only hope to be successful if
industrial countries fully comprehend the importance which
developing countries and in this instance OXDCs place on their
sovereignty. They view the old long-term concession agreements as unequal treaties, virtually imposed upon them by oil
companies with the backing of their home governments. Having
gained sovereignty in the 1970s over their petroleum
resources, the OXDCs view with great suspicion any attempt by
industrialised countries to draw them into political agreements which would once more limit their freedom of action on
supply and price. This is the real background to the hostility shown by OPEC to the IEA and to the difficulties inherent
in any accommodation with OXDCs.

The central problems for all the main OXDCs are the
depletion of their petroleum reserves and the economic transition to a diversified and developed economy, once the oil
revenues decline. The present unparalled prosperity of the
OXDCs obscures to other nations the fact that this transition
will ultimately be infinitely more difficult for them than for

industrialised nations.   It is unfortunate, through perhaps natural, that the North's attention has been largely focussed on oil prices rather than economic development issues of most OXDCs, a field which would provide much more room for future dialogue.

The implications for supply and price resulting from the depletion and transition problems of OXDCs reflect some-what different approaches on their part.   Some, producing close to physical capacity and without great hope of expan-sion, will emphasise maximum price.   Venezuela is in an inter-mediate position with its vast Orinoco heavy oil resources. Others still have an ample resource base (Saudi Arabia, Iraq, Kuwait, and UAE) and emphasize conservation, because the accumulation of financial surpluses is politically undesirable and economically unprofitable.

There are several interrelated issues affecting OXDCs' decisions on oil supply and price.   The most important is conservation, but others include investment policies, security of financial assets held abroad, and political factors.

By conservation is meant a policy of production restraints which are designed primarily not to maintain price but to prolong the economic life of the petroleum reserves. Several OXDCs (e.g., Kuwait and UAE) have taken the opportun-ity of reducing production when oil surpluses appear on the market, in order to reduce surplus financial revenues which cannot be spent profitably at home nor invested safely abroad.

Investment policies for exploration and development of capacity are a facet of long-run conservation policy. Policies vary from country to country.   The most important example of muted investment policies is Saudi Arabia, where plans to develop capacity have been successively scaled down. In Kuwait there has been no investment in development of new capacity for some years, and the present limited exploration activity is mostly for gas.   By and large, other OXDCs are pursuing active exploration policies, some quite vigorous.   In some of them, vigorous exploration is accompanied by produc-tion ceilings.

The financial assets held by OXDCs abroad are vulnerable to inflation and political action, i.e., blocking. The main countries are Saudi Arabia, Kuwait, and UAE. Clearly, if sufficient guaranties could be given to these countries, some of the constraints on their production would be greatly attenuated. Several schemes have been mooted, mostly centered on long-term bonds indexed to compensate for inflation. Producing countries fear that such bonds are more politically vulnerable to freezing and are less mobile in the short-run than other financial investments. There are several other obstacles inhibiting the investment abroad by capital-surplus countries. Removal of these obstacles would represent a positive step and could be an element in any rapprochement between some of the OXDCs and industrialised countries.

The Arab-Israeli conflict is without doubt one of the most important obstacles to any solution of energy problems between OXDCs and industrial countries. It is rarely discussed candidly. But no permanent solution on energy will be possible until solution is also found to the Palestinian problem which is acceptable enough to a majority of the oil-producing Arab states.

Essentially, OPEC pricing policies aim at shifting the price of oil upwards to the cost of alternative energy sources. This cost is not specified, although several OXDCs think in vague terms of the cost of coal gasification. There is now firm agreement within OPEC countries that the current price of oil should escalate to keep pace with inflation. They mostly believe that the deflator should be an OECD index of export prices. They generally agree that the speed at which the real oil price should move up towards the undefined cost of alternatives should be pari passu with the growth of real GNP in OECD countries. The rationale is that the growth in GNP is a measure of ability to pay as well as an indication of the time span within which the alternatives will be needed.

OPEC countries see their administration of prices as entirely manageable and a matter exclusive to the seller at the political (though not commercial) level. It is not a point open for negotiation with industrialised countries, unless the latter were surprisingly willing to regulate their own export prices for manufactured goods and food to OXDCs.

Of growing importance to OXDCs is the future development of their natural gas reserves. Twelve have excellent
prospects for natural gas in large exportable surpluses. In
view of the much greater difficulties in developing these
reserves for export, they must clearly be a further element in
any global energy strategy.

The policies of OXDCs towards OIDCs are now acquiring
some sharpness of definition. The recommendations of the OPEC
long-term strategy committee were unanimously adopted by full
Ministerial Conference in May 1980.*   They envisage that:
i) OIDCs be guaranteed oil supply at no more than official
government prices in priority over supply to industrialised
countries, ii) bridging loans be made to the higher-income
OIDCs at essentially commercial rates to cover oil-induced
balance of payments difficulties, and iii) soft loans and
grants be made to other OIDCs to help finance both short-term
balance of payments difficulties and longer-term development
of domestic energy sources and other projects.

OPEC policy has consistently rejected a generalised
system of two-tier oil pricing. It renders the aid element
invisible; there is fear of oil supply leakage into other
markets; and it ties the amount of aid to the volume of oil
imports regardless of the countries' actual needs. Nevertheless some oil has been sold on a two-tier price system.
Examples include the agreement between Mexico and Venezuela to
set up a system to supply Central American and Caribbean OIDCs
at prices effectively discounted by one-third.

OPEC countries have been giving about US$5 billion in
official development assistance to other developing countries
through national and international institutions, notably the
OPEC Fund for International Development. Current proposals
envisage a sharp escalation in their aid flow. An important
part would be earmarked for development of energy resources in
other LDCs, with emphasis on hydrocarbon exploration. This
proposal runs parallel with that of the World Bank to create a

---

*   Their consideration by OPEC heads of state is temporarily
    stalled by postponement of their summit meeting (previously
    scheduled for November 1980 in Baghdad).

separate affiliate, which would be financed partly by industrialised countries and partly by OPEC countries.   It is
presently an open question whether the two proposals will be
fused.   But indubitably this is one area where the interests
of OXDCs and industrial countries coincide.

3.   Industrialised Countries

        The strong growth of industrialised countries during
the 1950s and 1960s depended on cheap abundant energy.
Domestic coal production gave way to low-cost oil, domestic or
imported.   Reliable access to cheap imported oil was not
doubted. This complacency was upset in the 1970s.   Industrialised countries now face an era of high-cost oil.   Oil
policies in OXDCs are now determined by their own governments
and not by the major oil companies.

        Part and parcel of the concerns of industrialised
countries is that they have diverse interests.   Their energy
supplies range in source from complete self-sufficiency to
utter dependence on imports. This diversity itself can create
strains and even divisiveness among industrialised countries
themselves.

        However, they have made efforts to deal in a
concerted manner with energy policy.   Particular efforts have
been made within the framework of the European Community,
OECD, and the International Energy Agency.   The IEA has the
roles of i) promoting energy conservation and the enhanced
development of secure energy supplies and ii) ensuring the
adequate distribution of oil supplies in an emergency.   In
1974 the IEA's creation symbolised the confrontation inherent
in the energy crisis, though it was not intended by most
participants to be confrontational.

        A subsequent attempt to reconcile NorthSouth view-
points was made at the CIEC Conference of 1975-77; one cause
of its qualified failure was the reluctance of the North to
look at all the issues of North-South relations and instead to
prefer discussing only the energy issue.

        Since then, cooperation has begun to reduce confron-
tation, and industrialised countries have taken steps to ease
the energy crisis. They have agreed to principles on pricing,

conservation, and accelerated development of alternative
energy supplies. Some constructive steps were taken by the
IEA, including the setting of oil import targets.

Despite such steps, there has been continued strong
competition for oil. This competition doubled oil prices in
1979-80, which contributed to economic recession, inflation,
and unemployment but added no new oil to the market.

Today there is an overriding concern by all industrialised countries for secure and assured supplies of oil at
what they see as reasonable prices. This is part of the
current concern over high inflation and unemployment. The
energy problem is not the sole cause but is a key component,
especially with such large outward flows of money to pay for
oil imports.

General economic adjustment in the 1980s is generally
expected to prove more difficult than during 1974-78.
Compared with those years, capital surpluses of some OXDCs
could stay at a high level for longer than in recent years;
the prospects for capital flows between oil-importing
countries are less favourable; and the industrialised
countries face more serious economic difficulties. They will
have to accept a large but diminishing current account
deficit, corresponding to their share of the counterpart of
the OPEC surplus, for some time to come.

Conservation and accelerated development of new and
renewable energy sources are cures for the long-term transition. But in the short-term industrial countries also need to
deal with potential pre-transition crises through such steps
as demand restraint, stockpiling, and oil import targets.

Economic success of industrialised countries will
depend largely on how well they manage the energy problem.
The challenge will be to find effective strategies for main-
taining reliable access to oil imports which are at best
expected to remain constant and could even decline, as things
look at present. The structural changes needed in the
industrialised countries are very deep but are at last being
made.

4. Convergences and Conflicts

It is a basic requirement of most OIDCs that they have enough oil for their economies, to support their rapidly growing modern sector and in some cases their traditional sector. Oil imports should be made available on financial terms that will not leave OIDCs with crushing debt burdens. But they must also make a transition from oil to renewable and other more plentiful sources.

OXDCs also wish to make a transition to the post-oil era. Meanwhile they seek to maximise and protect the value of their oil export earnings. They intend to keep control over their oil resources, including control over prices, production rates, and allocation among consumers. Some wish to expand their internal oil-producing capacity.

Industrialised countries are concerned about having a reliable supply of oil. Some hope to do so by securing a political commitment from one or more producers, and others by expanding capacity at home or abroad. These countries prefer orderly increases rather than erratic jumps in oil prices. They also wish to make a nontraumatic transition from oil to renewable and other energy sources.

The first goal shared by all nations is to keep the world economy performing well. The second is to make the transition from oil to renewable and other more plentiful sources of energy. The third is to resolve common energy problems in ways that protect the world's ecosystems.

The least contentious approach to reliable oil supplies is to expand capacity. But even if oil supplies are adequate, some OIDCs may be threatened with shortage for want of financing. There is no great disagreement that OIDCs be helped to finance their oil imports. OPEC countries are also considering how to give OIDCs priority over industrialised countries in the allocation of oil.

A very controversial approach to supply reliability is that oil producers agree to an international covenant which would limit unilateral control over oil production and exports. OPEC countries are sensitive about any proposals which might reduce their unilateral control over their oil.

Some larger importers have sought supply reliability by making bilateral arrangements with individual oil exporters. A system of competing bilateral understandings may be good for individual importers but not necessarily for the world, as it ignores small importers and financially weak countries.

Industrialised countries which are IEA participants have sought short-term supply reliability through emergency-sharing arrangements. Some industrialised countries have programs of official stockpiling; this has prompted some OPEC nations to threaten retaliation.

It is not easy to correct this patchwork quilt of arrangements. But the dialogue between oil exporters and importers should search for acceptable formulae which might help.

Many experts believe that the level of oil prices is not as important as the sudden, unpredictable, and uneven pace of change. They believe that the inflationary impact could be substantially reduced if price changes occurred in small, predictable increments. However, there is another view that economies only adjust to price shock. There is also a strongly held view that prices are much determined by buyers' competition for available oil, and that "official" OPEC prices merely confirm what the market has already determined.

The most controversial proposal is that a price formula be multilaterally negotiated which would be binding upon oil exporters. They have reacted as negatively to this as to proposals for negotiated formulae for oil supply. They have been reviewing but not yet agreed on a plan of their own for orderly prices of oil, linking them to the rate of inflation and real GNP growth in the industrialised countries; the OPEC formula would constitute a floor price for oil rather than a ceiling or a target.

With oil-induced disturbances, some countries will impose further restrictions on merchandise imports. Trade barriers already exist, especially burdensome to developing countries that do not have economic power to protect themselves. Several proposals have been made to eliminate tariff escalations and to return tariff revenues collected from developing countries' imports.

A few oil exporters earn more than they can spend in the short run. Unless these surpluses are moved quickly into use, the result will be economically depressing on oil importers, like a tax suddenly imposed without matching expenditures. Over time, the surplus countries' demand for merchandise goods and services will reduce this surplus, but this does not help in the short run. Much of the surplus will be recycled routinely by the banks in loans to investors. But a large part of the current deficit is in the OIDCs, and banks may be reaching the limits of prudent lending to some developing countries.

A number of ideas have been evolving to deal with the recycling problem. The private banking system is likely to continue carrying the main burden. However, industrialised countries could greatly expand the movement of funds to creditworthy Third World nations. The World Bank could participate in a program to guarantee developing countries' bonds against default. Activities of the IMF in deficit countries could be expanded. But these general approaches would be of most use only to those countries that can afford to pay commercial rates and, except for the IMF, to countries that have established credit ratings in the international money markets. For other countries, one approach would be for international financial institutions to make loans with very low interest rates and long repayment periods. Another approach under consideration is expansion of the OPEC Special Fund into an international aid agency with increased capitalisation.

The entire world shares the goal of making a transition to renewable and other more plentiful sources of energy. Four actions can help in this transition:

i) Energy conservation. A barrel of oil conserved in any nation contributes to the energy security of all nations. Even more directly, it contributes to the financial strength of the conserving country.

ii) Discovery and development of oil and gas. OPEC and World Bank proposals for special facilities to help develop energy in developing countries suggest that this is a very promising approach.

iii) Accelerated development of energy alternatives. The sooner these are put in place, the more oil and gas there will be left in place to use for non-energy purposes over the centuries ahead. But vigorous action will be needed. Major obstacles include government budgetary restraints, lack of trust between private investors and public authorities, and imperfect understanding of the common stake in the success of such programs.

iv) Structural adjustment of OXDCs' economies. At the end of the oil era, they will lose the oil revenues and will need other economic activities in substitution.

There is also need for rational pricing during the transition. The right price is important to finding more oil, developing alternative energy sources, and conserving energy. Sound pricing policy for the domestic market is also important to OPEC countries' efforts to prepare for the economic transition when oil output begins to decline.

Certain of the world's ecosystems may be threatened by the energy choices made. Deforestation and devegetation may lead to soil erosion, reduced water tables, downstream siltation, flooding, and desertification. The construction of large dams destroys valleys and in some cases may bring water-borne diseases to a region. Nuclear accidents may make an area uninhabitable for long periods, and there is the problem of how and where to dispose permanently of spent fuels. Decisions to move to coal and synthetic fuels bring the likelihood of an increase in the CO_2 in the atmosphere, together with a possible dislocating warming trend. Energy planning must give careful regard to environmental conse-quences before investment decisions are made.

The OXDCs have a further strong interest, that of maximising their economic gain. One approach is to make it easy for them to invest surplus funds in industrialised countries. A second is to encourage them to invest in OIDCs; means must be found of sharing the risks with other countries whose dollar value increases with the decline in the dollar's purchasing power, or by paying them in SDRs. As stated above, OPEC countries have been giving thought to a floor formula for oil prices, which would escalate with inflation and real GNP growth.   If this were to happen, they might conceivably be willing also to prescribe a ceiling as well as a floor, within which the actual price would range, in return for concessions from oil importers.

III.   GLOBAL OPPORTUNITIES

Taking into account these convergences and divergences, there are global opportunities in managing the remaining decades of oil and gas, and in pressing ahead with the transition from oil to other energy sources and technologies.

1.   Managing the Remaining Decades of Oil

a.   Development of Oil and Gas in the OIDCs

The development of oil and gas resources in OIDCs is one of the few areas where there is a clear convergence of interest between industrialised countries, OXDCs, and OIDCs. Indigenous production of oil and gas in OIDCs benefits all countries.

Exploration in developing countries is far from having responded adequately to recent price rises.   Exploratory efforts in North America have reached record levels.   A relatively small amount has taken place in OIDCs.   The lion's share was in those of them which were oil producers.   Exploratory efforts were very small in OIDCs which do not produce oil.   It may be that exploratory interest will pick up after the 1979-80 price increases, though this is difficult to predict.   Unless great improvements can be made in discovery rates, import requirements will continue to grow, or else demand (and probably economic growth) will have to be severely constrained through lack of foreign exchange to pay for the imports.   It is possible that lead-times are so great that it is still too early to judge the response in the exploratory effort to the 1973-74 oil price increases.   However, on present evidence, the response to price increases is rather low in view of other constraints: a) geological prospects,

b) boundary disputes, c) monopolisation of acreage by a single company or consortium of companies, d) government policy and legal framework, e) political risk, and f) industry structure.

Historically, companies with an interest in exploring in the Third World have been first and foremost interested in access to oil supplies for their markets in the industrial countries, and they have essentially not been interested in exploring for oil for the local markets which have typically been too small to interest them. The smaller deposits which may satisfy local markets are of little interest to companies, because opportunities elsewhere are more attractive. It seems doubtful if many Third World countries will ever be in a position to attract companies prepared to amount more than a minor exploratory effort (one or two rigs) for fields whose potential production is unlikely to exceed (say) 2-3,000 b/d.

All this argues in favour of stimulating exploration through other means, whether out of official development assistance (ODA) or otherwise. Some programs are already under way through the World Bank and the OPEC fund for International Development, and proposals for larger programs are being considered. There are a number of bilateral assistance programs. These are encouraging signs that the importance of the problem is starting to be recognised. But a much greater effort must be made if OIDC production of oil and gas is to be significantly expanded in the next two decades.

b. Energy Efficiency

One of the largest potential source of energy supplies is the savings from improved efficiency in their use. There is an overwhelming necessity for a major structural readjustment to improve efficiencies and conservation in the use of energy in oil-importing countries, whether developed or developing, if energy supplies are to be sufficient.

The largest absolute savings can and must be made in the industrialised countries. But OIDCs must make similar efforts, if their economic prospects are not to be jeopardised. Even for the OXDCs, there are concerns to stretch out the life of oil reserves, not only by pacing their own production but also by curbing domestic oil consumption through conservation measures and substitution of other fuels such as gas.

The growth of energy consumption in oil-importing countries has been much reduced since 1973. In part, this has been due to slower economic growth or recession, augmented by milder winters in some years. But there are also perceptible improvements in efficiency of energy use. However, much more could be done to reduce energy demand without hampering economic growth. Strong action has typically not been adopted, in contrast to the emphasis on accelerated development of energy supplies.

The prerequisite to improved efficiency is an appropriate energy pricing policy. Energy forms should be priced at their long-run marginal cost, which for most countries is the cost of imported oil. If higher energy prices result in unwarranted prices to producers and inequities to low-income consumers, these problems can be met by solutions such as investment incentives, windfall profit taxes, and relief measures for particular consumer groups. Certain housekeeping incentives can be taken quickly. Others need time and capital investment. There is the burden of existing infrastructure, and the delay in installing new capital stock.

The long-term prospects for large improvements in energy efficiency could be very promising. Several studies have indeed suggested that energy supplies at today's level or even lower could support reasonable economic growth during the next two decades, if the right policies are taken.

2. Managing the Transition from Oil to Other Sources

Higher oil prices have created urgent challenges to shape new national energy policies in oil-importing countries, as has the problem of deforestation particularly in developing countries. The desire for relief from the insecurity of imported oil is a powerful motive for governments to promote domestic energy supplies even if they are more costly than imported oil, and most are not. Even more fundamental is that long-term prospects suggest increasing constraints on conventional depletable energy supplies, above all oil.

The next two decades will be faced with an era of transition towards the next generation of energy sources and technologies. There is need to keep energy supply options open wherever possible. There is the danger of being locked into short-term palliatives. Hence a wide range of RD&D is needed to retain flexibility of technical options. Some changes to the energy mix could be made today with little adjustment to the existing capital stock, but more radical changes will take time to make the necessary structural adjustments to the economy.

Developed and developing countries alike have limited financial, technical, and manpower resources to devote to energy. Not every energy process can or should be pursued; each must be economically, socially, and environmentally justifiable.

Much use can be made of existing technologies for energy conservation and supplies. But in the long-run new and better technology must be developed. This points to the fundamental importance of well-directed national programs for energy research, development, and demonstration (RD&D). Countries need to define priorities by technology areas. They should identify which of these technologies they would develop themselves and which they would import.

The ultimate goal of energy RD&D is to meet long-term needs for energy and to open technological solutions for incorporation into energy policy. Such policy should provide clear guidelines for RD&D.

Much of the work worldwide is being done in the industrialised countries both by governments and the private sector. The pace should be accelerated to develop and bring new energy technologies to commercial use. Virtually all energy technologies have environmental and social impacts, and this should be taken into account at all stages of technology development. There is need for rational pricing signals to assist the proper introduction of new technologies as well as conservation.

For the developing countries, alternative energy includes not only commercial energy for the modern sector but also small-scale, decentralised renewable energy in the rural areas, such as wind, flowing water in small streams, biomass, and sunshine. Despite these signs of promise especially for application in remote areas, renewable energy requires much more research and site testing before its full potential will become evident. A growing amount of RD&D of decentralised renewable energy is under way in laboratories of industrialised and developing countries. The concepts and technologies need to be tested in actual village sites. Offers by industrialised countries to conduct a major program of assistance to Third World countries in renewable technologies could be highly attractive. This might also be linked to initiatives now under consideration by OPEC and industrialised countries to help OIDCs find and develop indigenous energy resources.

3. Meeting the Energy Needs of Developing Countries

        Human material progress depends on use of energy. Without sufficient energy in useable forms and at affordable prices, there is little prospect for improving the conditions of the majority of people in the world. In many countries, the oil prices increases have most seriously affected the poorest segments of their societies.

        Agriculture has also suffered from higher fuel and fertiliser costs, which have made for shortages and higher prices of food which mainly affect the poor. To pay for oil imports at higher prices, many countries have had to reduce imports of other essential commodities and thereby lower economic growth. The consequences of relying on non-commercial fuels also affect the poor, as the expanding deforestation, devegetation, declining water tables, soil erosion, silting, and flooding harm agriculture.

        The energy problems of developing countries are so serious and complex that they cannot be tackled without massive help from the international community. Good energy planning begins with a comprehensive national energy assessment. The international community can help the recipient country to develop the institutional ability to make its own continuing assessment.

        One of the most promising methods of alleviating the energy problem is to help develop domestic energy resources in

OIDCs. Exploration and development of oil and gas offer excellent opportunities for external assistance. Yet only about 5% of world investment (excluding the centrally planned economies) in petroleum exploration now takes place in non-OPEC developing countries. Industrialised countries can therefore encourage the exploration and development of oil in OIDCs. Their governments can encourage their private and national oil companies to undertake such investment. International institutions can help OIDCs to take all or part of the risk of exploration. OPEC countries are also envisaged to help in the effort to develop oil reserves of OIDCs.

In the long-run, the development of energy alternatives to oil in developing countries will be more important than finding or conserving oil. To this end, a massive program of assistance is warranted from bilateral and multilateral agencies. This applies not only to large-scale commercial but also to decentralised renewable energy forms. The declining availability of energy fuels is critical; and assistance is needed for programs of afforestation, fuelwood plots, improved stoves, and better charcoal kilns. External assistance can also help in improving efficiency in energy use of developing countries. In the long-run these countries will have to make fundamental structural adjustments to the energy problem. Since such adjustments are difficult and costly, there is urgent need for massive international assistance.

4. Improved International Cooperation on Energy

Sectors other than energy are given careful attention by one or more international bodies. Some have urged that a similar international organisation be created for energy. It may be helpful to identify the energy problems which are not adequately manageable nationally and need attention internationally by existing or possibly new bodies.

a. Forum for Southern Views on Energy

The industrialised countries have consulting and cooperative arrangements on energy from which the South is mostly excluded. In a world-wide forum OIDCs could express their views on energy issues.

b. Oil Supply Security for the Third World

One of the IEA's functions is to maintain emergency-sharing arrangements for oil supplies. There are no such plans for OIDCs. An international agency could be established to create such arrangements or at least to monitor those of the IEA, to ensure that the interests of the OIDCs are taken into account.

c. World Energy Balance-sheet

Such a balance-sheet would be helpful, similar to that published by the FAO for food. It would assemble data on energy supply, demand, costs, investment levels, technologies, and national needs. It would prepare analyses on an international energy balances and emerging energy problems.

d. Finance for Renewable Energy Development in the Third World

Just as there is the IAEA to promote nuclear energy, so there might be a special assistance program for international solar (or renewable) energy.

e. Exchange of Information on RD&D for DRE Technologies

The existing worldwide network of researchers on international food issues might serve as a model for decentralised research energy (DRE) research. One task for international energy machinery may be to establish and monitor such an information exchange mechanism.

IV. FRAMEWORK FOR ENERGY POLICIES
     IN THE OIL-IMPORTING DEVELOPING COUNTRIES

Regarding the main energy supply options for OIDCs during the next 10-15 years, these countries will be competing with the rest of the world (and among themselves) for very limited additional global supplies of oil. Unless they can secure special treatment from suppliers on a government-to-government basis, the competition will be largely on a market-determined basis, and the stronger buyers will more likely be favoured. There is serious danger that OIDCs will get

relatively less and pay relatively more than the industrial
countries and the CPEs.

        OIDCs should therefore investigate and pursue other
less constrained sources of energy. In particular, gas and
electricity from neighbouring countries brought in by pipeline
and transmission lines may prove equally beneficial to the
importer and exporter. Nevertheless, development of domestic
supplies and efficient use of energy are the main options to
be pursued. Imported oil cannot be expected to support their
future energy needs.

        The pre-1973 availability of low-cost oil from
external sources provided little incentive for the exploration
and exploitation of domestic resources. Most countries
concentrated on hydroelectric generation. Coal development
outside India and South Korea has been limited. As for oil
and gas, efforts by the international oil industry were
concentrated in a few exceptionally promising areas with a
clear potential for exports. In the OIDCs the work was done
mostly by national oil companies. Foreign companies were, of
course, pursuing a global optimisation and moved to countries
which offered better geological prospects as well as financial
terms.

        The crisis of 1973 caught OIDCs generally weak and
unprepared to face the new situation in terms of organisation,
management, and technical skills, as well as knowledge of
their potential energy resources. Part of this gap could have
been covered by international development banks and other aid
organisations, but these also were initially unequipped in
terms of staff and policy to be very effective. The quick
response to the crisis was to turn to external sources for the
financial means to secure the necessary skills. In trying to
secure these skills OIDCs were competing i) with pressures in
industrial countries for increased domestic efforts, ii) with
claims and requests of OPEC countries, iii) with other
established exporters which had more negotiating strength and
leverage, and iv) among themselves.

        Even if most OIDCs adopt optimal policies i) in the
longterm to attain a national implementation capability, and
ii) in the short and mediumterm to accelerate energy exploration and development, they would still face very serious

obstacles because of their modest development and export prospects relative to OXDCs, their weak local infrastructure, and investors' concern with political instability and non-commercial risks. To overcome these obstacles, enlightened, pragmatic, and stable government policies are needed. Also required are de facto international guarantees which can be given by development banks as "third parties."

With very few exceptions (islands or very small countries), OIDCs are endowed with a variety of actual or potential energy sources. Most OIDCs, particularly the medium-size or larger, could become self-sufficient and in some cases, exporters of energy. To achieve these aims, massive increases in exploration and development are needed as well as a quantum jump in official technical assistance and financing. The type of assistance needed by different countries depends on i) their experience in energy development, ii) the strength of their existing economic institutions, and iii) the strength of their economies vis-a-vis the financing (particularly the risk capital) needed for an accelerated effort.

OIDCs' investments in commercial energy development are envisaged to grow by about 10% p.a., twice as fast as GNP. The World Bank estimates these investment needs at US$450-500 billion (in 1980-$) during the decade. Of these amounts, investment in electric power will continue to take up about three-quarters. Oil exploration and development are estimated to grow from about US$2.5 billion in 1980 to about $3.5 billion p.a. (in 1980-$) during 1981-85 and $4.7 billion p.a. during 1986-90. The financing of such a program will make heavy demands on domestic and foreign saving. But such a program could cut their oil import bills significantly (they were about $67 billion in 1980 alone).

Despite the significant dimension of the financing problem, the main obstacles to energy development, which might otherwise be achievable in purely physical terms, will not be financial. Those OIDCs which adopt realistic energy policies and the minimum managerial and institutional capabilities will have access to those official and private sources of know-how and finance which are necessary to improve their energy position.

External aid assistance can take several forms: i) technical and financial assistance from official institutions, ii) financial assistance from private banks, and iii) foreign investment.   Foreign   private   investment   is   especially important in areas such as oil development and LNG.   It is profit-oriented and concerned with political as well as commercial risks.

Foreign investment can play a leading role in the following types of country situations: i) countries with potential for oil exports, ii) countries with large potential for gas exports particularly in the form of LNG to industrial countries, iii) countries with medium to large potential for coal exports, iv) countries with lowcost energy resources which cannot be exported but can be used industrially to produce exportable goods, and v) countries with large domestic markets for energy, where government policies and overall economic outlook allow withdrawal of investment and net revenues in foreign currency.

Official development assistance (ODA) is needed to cover many other country situations.   Financial support is needed in almost all cases where domestic energy developments are unlikely to lead to exportable surplus.   This means most development projects for electric power, coal, geothermal, and gas, as well as oil in countries with modest prospects.   In middle- and high-income countries, ODA financial support should be complemented to the maximum extent by cofinancing with private banks.   A much larger share of ODA should be allocated to pre-development stages of energy investments, as little help can be expected from private sources.   Finally ODA is needed to overcome non-financial weaknesses, such as policy advice, strengthening of planning and management institutions, and training programs.

In principle, it would be possible from the above criteria to prescribe the mix of official and private assis- tance which would be individually feasible for each country, type of project, and particular timing.   In this manner, a program for global energy development could be designed, and the requisite human and financial resources could be quantified. Recent efforts by the World Bank seem to point in that direction and may provide the basis for a major new international initiative in this field.

energy
FOR DEVELOPMENT

INTRODUCTION

The North-South dialogue has a potentially endless agenda. Discussions have encompassed everything from legal regimes to economic forecasts, from social standards to food quality standards, and the agenda continues to grow. A new attempt is being made to revive the dialogue, this time within a United Nations framework of global negotiations, the corner-stone of a Third Development Decade. This is just the latest in a long series of international efforts to resolve the problems of North-South relations. It is essential to remember the context in which all these efforts fit.

Concerns of developing countries about the current international order have focussed on three inequities: i) the evident imbalance in the distribution of the world's wealth, ii) the unequal addition of value to goods made in the North and South, which favours the North, and iii) the merely pro-forma participation allowed to the South in the decision-making of the present international economic order. Even while the UN was working on the first two Development Decades, the gulf between rich and poor countries grew wider. The developing countries argue "that in the international order --just as much as within national orders--all distribution of benefits, credits, services and decision-making gets warped in favour of a privileged minority, and that this situation cannot be changed except through fundamental institutional reforms."[a]

It is easy to see the causes of conflict and misunder-standing. The North has viewed the problem in terms of votes in international fora. Indeed, the increasing number of independent developing countries do form a sizeable majority in such organisations as the UN, where the developing world can pass resolutions which reflect their view on the world economy. However, the North has for the most part achieved its economic dominance by the long and arduous process of the Industrial Revolution and is not about to give up the fruit of its labours. Subsequent to the colonial era, the North has offered economic assistance to the majority of developing countries. But it has typically seen the OPEC countries as a

1

special group which was successful in adjusting the
international economic order in their favour.

For their part, Southern countries feel that they have
not yet achieved their sovereign rights in managing the international economic order. Nor do they appreciate the arbitrary
division of history into eras which apparently absolve the
North of responsibility for past actions. Moreover, the OPEC
countries are an integral part of the Group of 77 (G-77, the
block which represents more than one hundred countries). The
G-77 has felt that it would have much less leverage in global
negotiations without the OPEC countries, which therefore have
enjoyed a position of leadership in the Third World.

At the time when independence was first being granted
to trusteeships, colonies, and territories, one of the first
actions taken by the UN was to pass a resolution in 1952 on
"Permanent Sovereignty over Natural Resources." But, as with
the "Charter on the Economic Rights and Duties of States,"
there was strong opposition from the North on key provisions.
The issue of natural resources has been at the forefront of
developing countries' efforts to improve the international
economic order. The reason is that the South supplies the
North with much of the raw materials needed to fuel its
industries, on which are based the North's economic success.

The key is relative bargaining strengths. Shifts in
economic power do take place, within a system in which there
is at least a minimum agreement on ground rules. The commercial exploitation of natural resources in developing countries
offers many examples of how shifts in power take place over
time. Indeed, some argue that the acquisition of economic
power by OPEC countries fits a pattern of inevitable
evolution.

For example, the original concession agreements were
made at a time when industrialised countries had most of the
necessary skills and capital. Thus Northern investors had a
legal and financial advantage in the concession agreements,
which consequently yielded a low return to the developing
countries. In due course, developing countries acquired the
requisite skills and knowledge, which gave them increased
bargaining strength and has led to today's revised generation
of agreements. The wrangle over the sanctity of contracts

versus the right to renegotiation is still not completely
finished. Nonetheless, there have been enormous changes in
the legal arrangements regarding petroleum between OPEC and
industrialised countries. The fears which had been expressed
by some Northerners that OPEC countries would be unable to run
their own petroleum affairs have proven unfounded.

Similar examples can be found for other natural
resources, but not yet of the same magnitude. No other
natural resource has turned out to be as strategic to the
world as oil.

This evolution in petroleum relationships during the
1970s did not go unnoticed in the Third World. Oil became a
catalyst for the movement towards an improved international
order. In 1974 at the UN's Sixth Special Session, the
Algerian proposal for a New International Economic Order
(NIEO) was embodied in a resolution for a Program of Action.
As has been well discussed elsewhere, there has been little
progress since then towards establishing the NIEO.[b] For its
part, UNCTAD went so far as to blame the "shortsighted nature
of the priorities in the policies of major industrialised
countries."[c]

At the Conference on International Economic Cooperation (CIEC) held during 1975-77 the North preferred to discuss
energy separately from other development issues. The
Conference ended in qualified failure for numerous reasons.[d]
Since then, there have been several successful discussions on
more limited, technical issues in an atmosphere devoid of
politics. The latest private initiative is that of the Brandt
Commission, which has led to its report of 1980 on "North-
South: A Program for Survival."[e]

After many setbacks, the North-South dialogue is
officially again under way, this time within the UN framework.
Once again, the catalyst is concern about the world's natural
resources, in particular oil. While many of the old obstacles
still remain, there is some growing awareness of the mutual
benefits of a more equitable world.

This basic framework report is predicated on the
existence of a new consensus between the parties involved,

ties.   Three themes run through the report: i) that the
world's problems are not insurmountable, ii) that as nations
go through the process of development, it becomes harder to
categorise them into neat groups, and iii) that a basic
consensus on some substantative issues is evolving.   One of
the failures of the past has been the rhetoric of the parties
involved, leading to a "dialogue of the deaf."   Today's
efforts must rest on a more complete understanding of the con-
texts and constraints affecting each country in formulating
its positions, policies, and goals.   What will help is a
clearer exposition of perspectives and a fuller understanding
of each party's objectives and options.

CHAPTER I: THE GLOBAL ENERGY SCENE

1.   ENERGY AND DEVELOPMENT

Human material progress and the use of non-human energy have gone hand in hand.   Man the hunter-gatherer used very little of such energy and consequently had to live a very frugal, primitive, and even precarious life.   Fire to cook and warm with came early in the human ascent and remains to this day a major user of energy.   The domestication of animals and plants which occurred in the misty past were early energy breakthroughs (each a special form of stored solar energy), which represented quantum leaps in human progress.

Wind was harnessed first for sea transport and later for grinding grain.   Originally primitive but increasingly complex irrigation systems used the gravitational energy of flowing water to extend cropland and intensify its productivity.   The discovery of coal and the invention of steam power allowed a great deal of inanimate energy to be employed and opened the way for the industrial revolution. Electricity, internal combustion engines, oil, nuclear fission, electronics, and the computer are all words which connote great bursts of human material progress based on new sources and new forms of using inanimate energy.   As the electric motor has contributed to saving human physical energy, the computer is saving mental energy.

Energy is one of the most important inputs in the process of development.   Thus any speculation about the future of energy should be viewed in human terms, i.e., the mix of man, nature and technology.

The importance of energy differs for different regions and different countries.   In a country such as Ethiopia, imported energy is essential for the country's survival.   For North America, imported energy may mean the difference between economic growth or recession, and possibly a massive change in lifestyles.   Many developing countries are first concerned with food security, even before economic growth becomes an option; and energy may be a factor in food security.   Oil-exporting developing countries (OXDCs) depend on hydrocarbons to build their economies.   The industrial

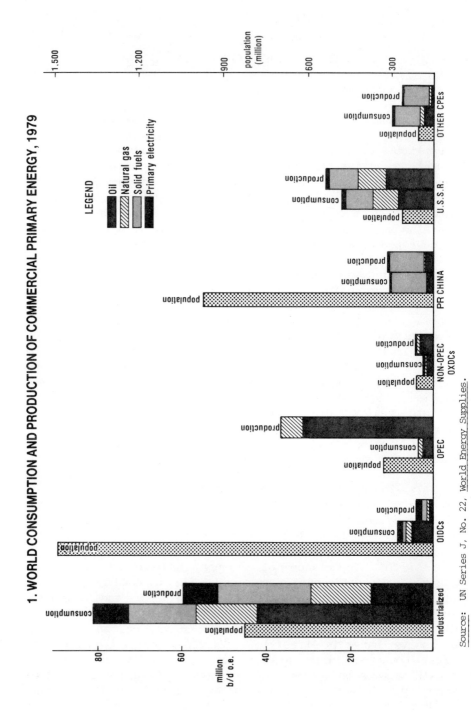

1. WORLD CONSUMPTION AND PRODUCTION OF COMMERCIAL PRIMARY ENERGY, 1979

LEGEND
- Oil
- Natural gas
- Solid fuels
- Primary electricity

population (million)
- 1.500
- 1.200
- 900
- 600
- 300

million b/d o.e.
- 80
- 60
- 40
- 20

Industrialized — consumption, production, population

OIDCs — population, consumption, production

OPEC — population, consumption, production

NON-OPEC OXDCs — population, consumption, production

PR CHINA — population, consumption, production

U.S.S.R. — population, consumption, production

OTHER CPEs — population, consumption, production

Source: UN Series J, No. 22, World Energy Supplies.

countries see energy as a vital input for their economic growth.

The Brandt Commission Report made the point that one American uses as much commercial energy as two Germans or Australians, three Swiss or Japanese, six Yugoslavs, nine Mexicans or Cubans, 16 Chinese, 19 Malaysians, 53 Indians or Indonesians, 109 Sri Lankans, 438 Malians, or 1072 Nepalese. All the fuel used by the Third World for all purposes is only slightly more than the amount of gasoline which the North burns to move its motor vehicles.

This is only one part of the picture. Another is the difference in the way in which energy is used, even between industrialised countries. This can be illustrated by primary electricity. Two-thirds of the electricity generated in the developing countries is used in industry, while only two-fifths goes to that sector in the industrialised countries. There is also the concept of embodied energy. For example, in growing rice the land may be tilled by tractors or animals. The oil input for tractors is a known cost; is the same true of the energy input represented by feedgrains fed to buffalos?

Because of the close connection between economic progress and the use of non-human energy, those interested in human progress today--particularly in those parts of the world that have enjoyed the least material progress--are properly concerned about whether energy (especially oil, gas, and wood-fuels) will be adequate in supply and available at prices which will permit progress to continue. This is a recent concern. Experts have warned for many decades that the most convenient energy forms would one day begin to run short. But it was not until the oil embargo and price rises of 1973-74 that the world awakened to the fact that at last that day was just over the horizon.

In many countries the reaction has been one of great concern or even near panic. For the most part, countries have sought to achieve energy security either by reducing their dependence upon outside sources or by bilateral arrangements with suppliers. There was one unsuccessful effort in the latter part of the 1970s to resolve the problem through global cooperation. Since that time, collectively, the oil-importing

2. SECONDARY ENERGY CONSUMPTION BY END-USE, 1976

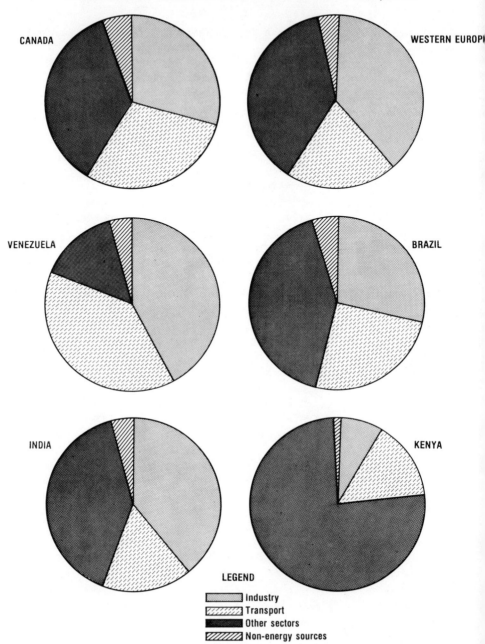

CANADA

WESTERN EUROPE

VENEZUELA

BRAZIL

INDIA

KENYA

LEGEND

Industry
Transport
Other sectors
Non-energy sources

Note: Other sectors include: agriculture, commercial, residential, and public service.
Source: IEA Workshop on Energy Data of Developing Countries, December 1978.
         Paris: OECD, 1979.

countries have spent many billions of dollars to resolve the problem, almost all of it as a part of national programs.

This project begins with a hypothesis that nations can make greater progress toward achieving energy security and do so at less cost if they treat the problem as a global one and attempt to resolve it through cooperative international action rather than attacking it solely through unilateral or bilateral action.

World energy problems are not confined to oil, though oil is a preoccupation because of a) its finite nature and the need to conserve its use and develop alternative energy sources, b) its impact on balance-of-payments, international financial flows, inflation, and economic growth, c) the dangers of supply disruption, and d) its importance as the prime form of commercial energy used in developed and developing countries alike. It is by far the largest single primary commodity by value entering into world trade.

Nor are world energy problems confined to commercial forms of energy. These are the ones mainly used in industrialised countries and in the modern and urban sectors of developing countries. But equally crucial are the problems of societies based on traditional energy. It is a fundamental fact that some 70% of the world's population--developing countries and PR China--use only 13% of the world's commercially traded energy.

The fuelwood crisis and other constraints on living standards are a fact of life for the majority of the world's population. Of the world's population of 4 billion today, some 60% or 2.5 billion live in rural areas and mostly rely on traditional energy fuels. These fuels are typically not statistically measured nor necessarily traded; they include firewood, crop residues, and animal dung. Nor is this number of rural dwellers likely to fall despite rapid urbanisation. Of the world's population estimated at some 6 billion by the year 2000, some 50% or 3 billion could still be living in rural areas. Moreover, those who live in urban slums will continue to rely in part on traditional fuels.

Thus much of the world's population is faced with a threefold energy problem: i) obtaining enough traditional energy, ii) shifting to better-quality fuels, and iii) making the transition to more plentiful energy sources than oil. Rapid urbanisation and industrialisation in developing countries will result in substantial growth in their use of world commercial energy. In the World Bank's view, it might grow by some 6% p.a. during the 1980s, thus expanding its share of the world's commercial energy consumption from 13% in 1980 to perhaps 17% by 1990.[a] Liquid hydrocarbons would continue to dominate their commercial energy mix, retaining a two-thirds share. They will remain of paramount concern to the developing countries, because they will fuel their energy needs in the course of industrialisation and urbanisation.

The industrialised countries are basically reliant on commercial fuels. During the 1950s and 1960s economic growth in those countries was very high compared with its performance since the industrial revolution. It was fuelled by a yet greater expansion in energy consumption. It was provoked by an unforeseen abundance of extremely low-cost oil supplies. The huge oil discoveries in the Middle East led to a wholesale swing from coal to oil supplies and to an era of steady decline in the real price of energy.

This era came to an abrupt end in 1973-74. During the 1973 Arab oil embargo, panic oil purchases made possible the fivefold price increase by OPEC countries. Oil prices rose sharply again in 1979-80. The earlier appetite for oil in industrialised countries has been dampened by the most difficult economic situation since World War II, with its peculiar combination of economic recession, faltering recovery, inflation, unemployment, higher oil prices, shifts in commodity prices, balance of payments disequilibrium, and exchange rate fluctuations.

For the developing countries, the 1970s were a period of mixed fortunes. As a group, their economic growth was a little lower than in the 1960s. But individual economies are very diverse in nature. Almost thirty are net oil exporters (OXDCs), including the 13 OPEC nations of which some six are in major capital surplus. At least 120 are net oil importers (OIDCs), including at most 14 which produce oil. A relatively few OIDCs import most of the oil, but most OIDCs each import relatively little.

3. SECONDARY ENERGY CONSUMPTION BY TYPE, 1977

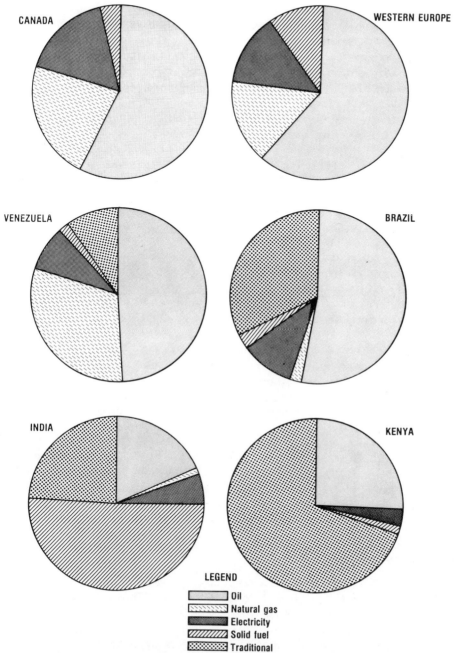

LEGEND

- Oil
- Natural gas
- Electricity
- Solid fuel
- Traditional

Source: IEA Workshop on Energy Data of Developing Countries, December 1978. Paris: OECD, 1979.

11

The economic performance of OXDCs improved in the 1970s compared with the 1960s. It was also striking in some middle-income OIDCs of East Asia but it deteriorated in low-income African countries. During the two decades, consumption of commercial energy grew faster than GNP, and energy-intensity also rose. Many of the OIDCs now face severe foreign exchange constraints in seeking to maintain their present energy patterns.

The difficult economic events since the mid-1970s have reinforced the call of the South for a new international economic order. They have also triggered efforts to help finance a) development of energy resources and b) balance-of-payments deficits for some developing countries.

The focus of this report is on the developed and developing countries (North-South). But a global view has to include consideration of China, the Soviet Union, and Eastern Europe. Their economic and energy prospects are basic to an understanding of their impact on North-South prospects.

While there are a number of energy studies which have a national or regional perspective, just a few attempt a global approach and they are typically concerned with the implications for industrialised nations. Moreover, renewable and non-commercial energy sources have typically received insufficient attention. Recent landmark reports of the long-term global scene include the 1977 report by WAES[b] which looks to 2000 (as does Exxon's World Energy Outlook of 1980[c]), the 1977 study by the Conservation Commission of the World Energy Conference which looks to 2020,[d] and IIASA's study[e] which looks to 2030. Reports in 1980 on medium-term global energy prospects (to 1985 or 1990) include those of IEA,[f] World Bank,[a] and the US Congressional Budget Office,[g] among others.

The pre-1978 studies mostly saw world oil supplies becoming tight by the mid to late 1980s. Those of 1978 tended to wish the constraints into the 1990s, heartened by some evidence of further dampening in energy growth and increased oil supplies from the North Sea, Alaska, and Mexico.

Perceptions have changed again. Since 1978, world economic performance has slowed down and in 1980 has stalled or even declined in a number of industrialised countries. This is reflected in consumption of commercial energy, above all oil.

World economic growth is generally expected to be sluggish during the next few years as oil-importing countries reduce their current account deficits and adapt to higher energy costs. In today's atmosphere of uncertainty, it seems unlikely that the high growth of the 1960s (5% p.a. worldwide) could be resumed. Were it to do so, much stronger constraints on world energy supplies would emerge with even greater upward pressure on international oil prices. But the ensuing financial and economic adjustments could gravely disrupt economic growth itself.

Moreover, the prospects for energy supplies are sharply reduced from previous expectations. Although uncertainty inevitably surrounds the prospects for new energy discoveries, the supply of energy could well remain tight during the 1980s.[a] Hence, the need is to decouple growth of energy consumption from economic growth as much as possible. This necessitates a major structural readjustment to improve efficiency in energy use, as well as to accelerate development of new energy sources. Otherwise, economic growth, at a rate modest by standards established since World War II, could be constrained by energy input.

2. GLOBAL ENERGY PROSPECTS

In the developed countries the Industrial Revolution was powered by coal and steam. It was essentially after World War II that these countries shifted the predominance in their energy mix from coal to oil. This is discussed further in Chapter II.

In the developing countries, industrialisation has begun much more recently and has been powered mostly by oil. In most of them the rural areas still rely on animal traction and traditional fuels (Chapters II and IV).

The present world energy prospect can be viewed as virtual stagnation in the overall trade of oil, and little growth in non-commercial energy sources. These constraints point to a future transition to the accelerated development of

4. WORLD: CONSUMPTION OF COMMERCIAL PRIMARY ENERGY, 1960-1979
(million b/d o.e.)

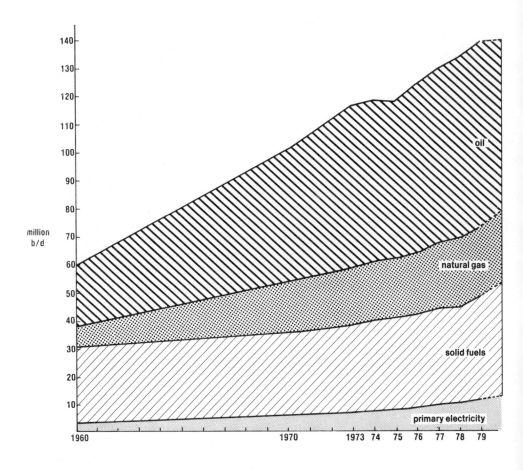

Source: UN Series J, No. 22, World Energy Supplies.

14

alternative energy sources and, equally important, to increased efficiency in energy use.

At their present rate of development, supplies of commercial primary energy in developed and developing countries as a whole are now generally expected to grow at moderate rates during the next two decades. This prospect is in stark contrast with that of 5.5% p.a. experienced during the years 1960–73. Indicative is that, after a decline of 1% p.a. in the recession years 1974–75, energy supplies resumed growth at only 2.7% p.a. during the five years to 1980. Studies published in 1980 have stressed the implications of reduced economic growth, improved energy conservation and lagging expansion in energy supplies (WDR III,[a] Exxon,[c] IEA,[f] IMF,[h] and UNCTAD[i]).

The OIDCs are generally perceived[j,k,l] to remain highly dependent on oil imports for their supplies of commercial energy. However, accelerated efforts are needed and are expected to be made to develop domestic energy sources, including traditional as well as conventional and non-conventional new energy forms. Their domestic supplies of energy are envisaged to grow at a higher rate than in industrialised countries.

A basic issue in industrialised countries is the acceleration of development of energy sources to compensate for the constraint on conventional oil availability. Strong initiatives will be needed to accelerate their development. The Venice summit of Seven industrialised countries in June 1980 put forth a pledge that by 1990 oil will comprise only 40% of total primary energy consumption, with a doubling in coal use and production, and an increase in nuclear energy. However, expansion of energy supplies in industrialised countries is subject to a variety of constraints (discussed later in this chapter).

Heretofore PR China has been virtually energy self-sufficient. Its industrial and urban economy is mostly fuelled by coal, though oil and gas consumption is increasing rapidly. There is also very large consumption of traditional fuels, particularly in the rural areas. China is seeking to expand exports of oil and coal to help finance its imports of technology and capital goods. But it is highly probable that the amount of exportable oil will be constrained as China modernises its economy.

The Soviet Union's energy consumption has grown fast over the last two decades, fuelled by a rapid expansion in all energy supplies. It is a substantial exporter of gas and oil, basically to Eastern and Western Europe. Gas exports will continue rising. But a number of observers believe that oil exports may have hit a ceiling and could shortly start declining.

The Eastern European countries produce much low-grade and some high-grade coal but relatively little hydrocarbons. On balance, they are a net energy-importing region, heavily reliant on the Soviet Union. Their gas imports continue to grow. But they are diversifying their sources of oil imports to other regions, particularly the Middle East. This makes it conceivable that the Soviet bloc could phase out its net oil exports and become a net oil importer.

3.   OIL

The remarkable growth of world oil consumption during the 1950s and 1960s was facilitated above all by the extra-ordinary increase in production and exports from OPEC countries, particularly in the Middle East. World production in the 1960s grew at 8% p.a. While the greatest expansion in absolute terms came from the OPEC countries, other developing countries also moved up at a rapid pace but from a rather small base.

The story for the 1970s is quite different. Oil production increased by only 3% p.a. during the decade. It is true that this has been due to a slowdown in the growth of demand in volume terms, which has not been constrained directly by available supply except in moments of political crisis. But it can be argued that the price increases which have occurred since 1971 foreshadow constraints in supply and have themselves contributed in large measure to the slowdown in the growth of demand.

5. WORLD: OIL CONSUMPTION, 1979
(Including Bunkers) (million b/d)

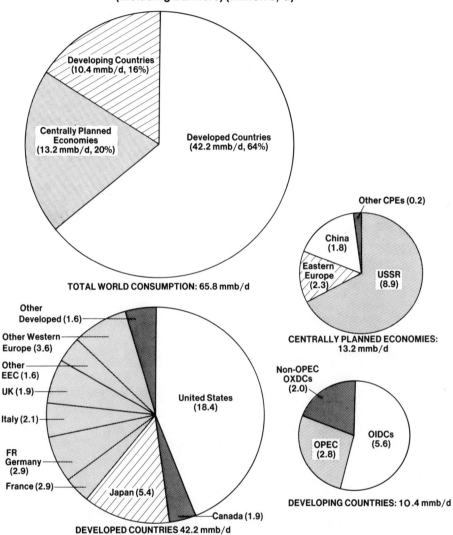

Developing Countries
(10.4 mmb/d, 16%)

Centrally Planned
Economies
(13.2 mmb/d, 20%)

Developed Countries
(42.2 mmb/d, 64%)

TOTAL WORLD CONSUMPTION: 65.8 mmb/d

Other CPEs (0.2)

China
(1.8)

Eastern
Europe
(2.3)

USSR
(8.9)

CENTRALLY PLANNED ECONOMIES:
13.2 mmb/d

Other
Developed (1.6)

Other Western
Europe (3.6)

Other
EEC (1.6)

UK (1.9)

Italy (2.1)

FR
Germany
(2.9)

France (2.9)

United States
(18.4)

Japan (5.4)

Canada (1.9)

DEVELOPED COUNTRIES 42.2 mmb/d
of which I.E.A. is 38.9 mmb/d

Non-OPEC
OXDCs
(2.0)

OPEC
(2.8)

OIDCs
(5.6)

DEVELOPING COUNTRIES: 10.4 mmb/d

Source: BP Statistical Review, 1980.

17

A. Consumption

World oil consumption grew by 7.5% p.a. from 1960 to
1973. Growth was vigorous in all groups of countries: industrialised, developing, and centrally planned. Having fallen
during the years of recession and mild winters 1973-74, it
resumed again at 4% p.a. to reach 66 mm b/d in 1979.

In 1980 oil consumption may have been a little lower
(about 65 mm b/d), as it has declined since 1979 in industrial
countries. In part this reflects the downturn in economic
activity in industrialised countries, substitution of other
forms of energy for oil, and a mild 1979-80 winter. But
expectations are also raised that measures to improve energy
efficiency are at last taking effect.

Of this amount, the developed countries consume about
65%, the developing countries about 15%, and the centrally
planned economies (CPEs) 20%.

As already discussed, there is general consensus that
world oil consumption will be constrained in growth by supply
limitations over the next two decades. Of course, within
these overall confines there could be wide regional divergences. Nations which are relatively rich in oil resources or
have the economic strength to buy imported oil could take more
of the available oil supplies than less favoured nations.

Oil   consumption   in   the   developed   countries
(42 mm b/d in 1979) represents an overwhelming share of the
world total. The world's single largest market is the US, 28%
of the world total. As a group, Western European countries
constitute the second largest market, 23% of the total.
However, the second largest single consuming country is the
Soviet Union. The third is Japan.

Oil has been a key input to economic growth in developing countries. (See Chapters II and IV.) Oil consumption
there grew very strongly during the last two decades, by 6.5%
p.a. in the 1960s and again in the 1970s to reach about
10 mm b/d in 1979 or 15% of the world total. Oil is mostly
used in the fast expanding urban areas rather than in the
countryside. The inland market pattern is by and large
different from developed countries, in that consumption is

preponderantly LPG and kerosene for cooking and lighting, diesel oil for commercial transport, and fuel oil for electricity generation, rather than gasoline for private motoring.

It is helpful to distinguish developing countries into oil-importing and oil-exporting categories, in order to analyse oil's contribution to their foreign exchange burden or earnings. This does not mean simplistically that developing countries which import oil are in trouble and those which export are in good shape. Economic performance is the result of many different factors. But oil trade is a highly significant one.

There are more than 120 OIDCs. Their oil consumption grew rapidly during 1960-73, by 8% p.a. It stagnated in the next two years to 1975 but then resumed growth at an estimated 5.5% p.a. to 1979, when it averaged some 5.6 mm b/d.[*] There have been increasing efforts to conserve the use of oil in these countries without at the same time harming economic growth. It is still too early to know how successful these efforts have been, This issue is discussed further in subsequent chapters.

Oil consumption in OIDCs is highly skewed in distribution. Most consume very little oil, and a relatively few countries account for most of the trade. (See E. below.) This does not mean that the relatively small oil consumption in smaller countries is not important to their economies. On the contrary, these countries are among the most severely disadvantaged by high costs and potential scarcities of imported oil. But it indicates the order of magnitude of steps which may need to be taken in the transition to a broader diversity of energy sources.

---

[*] This list excludes the following middle-income countries: Greece, Israel, Portugal, South Africa, Spain, Turkey, US territories, and Yugoslavia which are defined as developing countries in the World Bank's report WDR III. In 1980 these countries could have consumed about 2.5 mm b/d of oil (including bunkers). These countries (except for Spain) are also defined by the IMF as developing, consuming 1.5 mm b/d.

Since 1973, oil consumption in OXDCs (OPEC and others) has continued to grow at over 7% p.a., similar to the years 1960-73. A significant part of the oil consumption volume goes to bunkers and refinery fuel. There is a strong concentration of oil consumption in a relatively few countries. Among the OPEC countries, four account for three-quarters of consumption: Indonesia, Iran, Saudi Arabia, and Venezuela. Among other oil exporters, Mexico accounts for half their oil consumption.

Oil consumption in OXDCs is generally expected to continue growing strongly.* In some of these countries, this has given rise to concern that the strong growth of inland demand should not eat into future export earnings, their engine of economic growth. A number of OXDCs are accelerating the substitution of gas for oil in the inland market and petroleum industry, in order to free up oil for export and to reduce gas flaring.^{m}

B. Supply Prospects

There are now only a few countries where production is large and still clearly expanding. These are Argentina, PR China, Egypt, Iraq, Mexico, Norway, and the United Kingdom. Between them, in 1980 they will account for about 17% of world oil production. In none of them is future production thought likely to exceed by much that required to support their national objectives. There are a small number of other countries which are expanding and which could perhaps reach a level of 500,000 b/d each before the end of the century: Brazil, India, Malaysia, and Oman.

Chinese output expanded very rapidly in the last two decades to reach just over 2 mm b/d in 1980. PR China is gearing up for an intensive exploration effort in onshore and offshore areas. The program offshore is taking place in rank wildcat areas, and the outcome is just not known. If the geological prospects in these areas prove favourable and if exploration efforts meet with luck, production could rise

*   For example, this is analysed in studies by OPEC
    Secretariat, OPEC Fund, UNCTAD and World Bank.

rapidly to reach conceivably 5 mm b/d by 2000. This is way below earlier official aspirations to develop ten fields like Daqing (Ta-ch'ing), i.e., a total of about 10 mm b/d. But it would still be a quantum jump from the present and would represent a great achievement.

Mexico's output depends on government policies regarding a) the speed of developing new discoveries and b) export ceilings. It is installing enough capacity to supply the growing domestic market as well as exports sufficient to finance the nation's foreign exchange needs for economic development. Production of crude and natural gas liquefied (NGL) was close to 2.15 mm b/d in 1980, and exports were 827,000 b/d. Mexico's export ceiling (1.1 mm b/d) is reported to be 1.45 mm b/d in 1981. Policy after 1982 has not been determined. It is conceivable that output could be in the range of 4 mm b/d by 1990.

North Sea oil production is likely to rise during the next few years but could decline during the 1990s, unless new virgin exploration in the more difficult and unknown northern areas meet with success. Prospects for expanded output in other industrialised countries do not look bright for expanded output, although there could be surprises from the vast areas offshore north-western Australia.

Several producing regions of the world have reached maturity. US production, despite the large contribution of Alaska, has continued to decline slightly. This trend presently looks very difficult to reverse. The huge increase in exploratory drilling has only stabilised the rate of additions to reserves in the lower 48 states. Most studies now envisage a decline in output during the 1980s.[n-q]

Production of conventional light and medium crude oils from existing fields in western Canada appears to have levelled and is expected to decline. But this decline is likely to be more than offset towards the end of the 1980s by new discoveries in the western provinces and frontier areas, as well as development of tar-sands and heavy oil.

Other important countries where production of crude oil appears to be approaching a plateau are Algeria, Indonesia, Libya, Nigeria, Qatar, and Venezuela (see Chapter

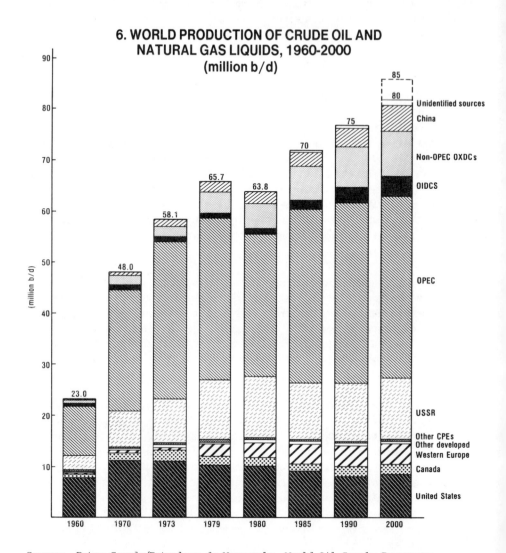

6. WORLD PRODUCTION OF CRUDE OIL AND NATURAL GAS LIQUIDS, 1960-2000
(million b/d)

Source: Petro–Canada/Petroleos de Venezuela, <u>World Oil Supply Prospects</u>, February 1980.

22

II).   All of these happen to be OPEC members.   In 1980, together with the US and Canada, they will account for an estimated 15% of world production.

OPEC countries can be distinguished between those with mature provinces from which little extra production can be expected, and those with substantial potential for expansion but which, with the possible exception of Iraq, no longer are interested in developing capacity rapidly.

Four of the most important OPEC countries are dedicated conservers.   They do not all wish to produce at capacity and are reluctant to undertake further large scale expansion.   These are Iran, Kuwait, Saudi Arabia, and the United Arab Emirates.   Their production is 1980 is expected to average less than some 15 mm b/d, accounting for 24% of world production.

OPEC countries at present contribute about 45% of the world's oil supply.   These 13 countries' production of crude oil and natural gas liquids was 27 mm b/d in 1980, and is estimated at about 25 mm b/d for 1981.[*]   As things presently stand, they are unlikely to expand output of crude oil beyond 33 mm b/d by 1985, hardly rising thereafter.[r]

Undoubtedly the most contentious issue between developed consuming nations and OPEC countries will be the rate of development and production in the few countries where there is a large potential for expansion.   (See Chapter II.2.)   These are Iran, Iraq, Kuwait, Saudi Arabia, the UAE, and Venezuela.

In 1979 there were about 15 non-OPEC OXDCs.[**] Together they produced almost 4 mm b/d in 1980.   This could

[*]   The 13 OPEC countries are: Algeria, Ecuador, Gabon, Indonesia, Iran, Iraq, Kuwait, Libya, Nigeria, Qatar, Saudi Arabia, United Arab Emirates, and Venezuela.

[**]   The 15 non-OPEC developing countries which were net oil exporters in 1979 are: Angola, Bahrein, Bolivia, Brunei, Cameroon (since 1979), Congo, Egypt, Malaysia, Mexico, Oman, Peru, Syria, Trinidad & Tobago, Tunisia, and Zaire. Burma had been a marginal exporter in 1978.

double to 8 mm b/d in 1990 but may be only a little higher by
the year 2000.   Mexico alone accounts for about half of
production during the whole period.

        Exploration in the OIDCs has been picking up in
recent years.   Drilling intensities, however, are unlikely
ever to come anywhere near US levels.   Nevertheless, a large
number of countries can reasonably expect to become medium to
small producers.   Their combined output is estimated at
1.25 mm b/d in 1980 and is expected to triple during the next
two decades.   Most of the increment would be in the dozen or
so countries which produced oil in 1979.[*] But a substantial
increment (perhaps 400,000 b/d by 1990) is also envisaged from
numerous countries which now produce no oil at all.   (See
Chapters III and IV.)

        The Soviet Union's production expanded quite rapidly
during the 1970s.   Prospects for future production are an
enigma.   It is generally expected to have reached its peak of
some 12 mm b/d by 1980.   The more pessimistic view is that
published in 1980 by the US CIA; it believes that output will
then decline throughout the 1980s, and that, even with
successful exploration and continued access to Western
equipment and technology, output would slide to 10 mm b/d or
less by 1985.[s] In contrast, a study by Swedish consultants
PetroStudies sees potential for further growth in output.[t]
On balance, it might be prudent to plan as if output may have
levelled out and could perhaps decline somewhat less than
foreseen in the CIA report, perhaps to 11 mm b/d by 1985,
before reviving again in later years, once the large resources
in remote areas of the nation are developed.

        Throughout most of the 1980s and during the 1990s oil
demand is likely to be constrained by supply availability,
although this must be understood in the context of production
limits for political and economic reasons in some major
oil-exporting countries.

   *   The 14 OIDCs which produced oil in 1979 are: Argentina,
       Brazil, Burma, Chile, Colombia, Ghana, Guatemala, India,
       Ivory Coast, Pakistan, Philippines, and marginally
       Afghanistan, Barbados, and Rep. of China (Taiwan).

C. Oil Resources

Is the world's oil resource base large enough to support these expectations for future oil production?

There have been many estimates of ultimate recoverable reserves of conventional oil. They are no more than academic, as they are guesses at the unknown. But they do give some indication of the constraint on the rate at which additions may be made to presently known reserves of conventional oil.

Past production of oil amounts to about 400 billion barrels (BB). Remaining known reserves are estimated in the order of 660 BB, enough to last 35 years at the present level of output. Additional potential resources could be in the order of 1,200 BB in the average estimate of a range of experts, published in the Desprairies report to the Conservation Commission of the World Energy Conference in 1977.[d] Thus it estimated total resources at roughly 2,250 BB; the pessimistic end centred around 1,700 BB, and the optimistic around 2,900 BB.

The world's known reserves are highly concentrated in a relatively few countries. The ten largest with 20 BB or more each contain 80% of the total: in order, Saudi Arabia, Soviet Union, Kuwait, Iran, US, Iraq, UAE, Mexico, Libya, and China. Alternatively put, OPEC countries contain 68% of the total, the Middle Eastern member countries 55% and Saudi Arabia alone 25%.

The world's oil reserves are concentrated in a relatively few sedimentary basins. There are roughly 600 worldwide, depending on how they are defined. There are producible hydrocarbons in nearly 240. But just 30 contain 90% of the world's recoverable oil, and two of these (Arabian-Iranian and West Siberian) have over half.

Additions to world oil reserves have depended heavily on the discovery of giant oilfields, and this is likely to remain true for the future. World reserves are concentrated in just a small number of large fields. Of about 30,000 fields worldwide, there are less than 1,900 (or 6%) which each

7. WORLD ULTIMATE RECOVERABLE RESOURCES
(billion barrels)

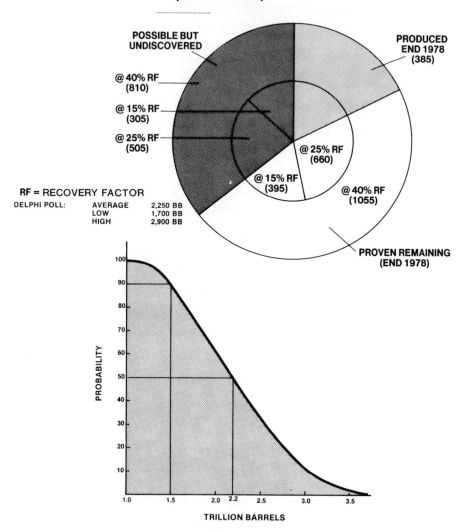

POSSIBLE BUT
UNDISCOVERED

@ 40% RF
(810)

@ 15% RF
(305)

@ 25% RF
(505)

RF = RECOVERY FACTOR

DELPHI POLL: AVERAGE   2,250 BB
             LOW   1,700 BB
             HIGH   2,900 BB

PRODUCED
END 1978
(385)

@ 25% RF
(660)

@ 15% RF
(395)

@ 40% RF
(1055)

PROVEN REMAINING
(END 1978)

PROBABILITY

TRILLION BARRELS

Source: World Energy Conference, 1977.

Source: P.J. Wood, World Oil, June 1979.

contain the equivalent of 50 million barrels or more of hydrocarbons (oil and gas). But they contain 93% of the world's known recoverable reserves.

Unfortunately, estimates of world oil resources and reserves typically exclude so-called unconventional oil, such as deposits of very heavy oil, tar-sands, and oil-shales as well as oil in polar regions and beneath deep water. This begs a large question, as these deposits are potentially huge. In the past, they have been little touched, because their development costs are much higher than those of conventional oil. At today's prices, however, they become increasingly economic to exploit. This is clearly the direction for the future, i.e., increasingly from conventional to non-conventional oil.

D. Exploration and Development Efforts

Higher oil prices have improved the economic viability of exploitation of small fields, enhanced recovery, exploration in high-cost areas such as polar and deep water, heavy oil, tar-sand, and oil-shale deposits, and fields with poor reservoir characteristics.

Even though exploration efforts in new provinces are likely to find the larger fields in the earlier stages of exploration program, there could still be smaller fields which would be well worth looking for thereafter. In many countries small fields will continue to be found well into the next century. Their cumulative impact could be great, and their support to economies including those of the oil-importing developing countries will be significant. (See also Chapters III and IV.)

Some of the future increase in world oil reserves will come from enhanced recovery from existing fields rather than from discovery of new fields. Prospects are strengthened by secondphase discoveries in older established basins, encouraged by improved economic viability of smaller fields at today's oil prices, better technology and exploration concepts, offshore extensions, and deeper drilling.

Exploration techniques have improved significantly in recent years. Drilling techniques have greatly advanced,

8. WORLD: OIL TRADE, 1960-1979
(million b/d)

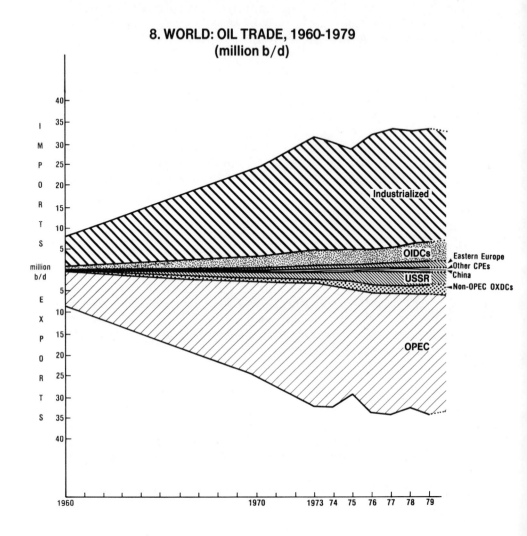

Source: BP Statistical Review, 1980.

particularly in polar and deep water regions such as the
Canadian Arctic and offshore Labrador. But good judgement is
still fundamental to successful exploration. It still remains
true that the evaluation of geological provinces is very
dependent on the degree to which high grade prospects are
tested by the drill. Relatively small areas of sedimentary
basins can contain significant volumes of oil.

Of the world's ultimate recoverable resources of oil,
a substantial part could lie offshore. Attention has thus far
been focussed on the continental shelf. Little is known about
the deep water basins in the adjacent continental margin.
Uncertainties are political, economic, geological, and technological. The problem is development, not exploration. Oil
cannot yet technically be produced from potential fields in
deep water. Provided this problem is solved, the next will be
the cost of producing any oil found.

Heavy oils and--even more so--the bitumen in tar-sand
deposits have been the Cinderella of the crude oil market.
Their economic feasibility has brightened considerably at
today's oil prices. Future expansion will involve enormous
capital investment with long lead-times a) in extraction,
including enhanced recovery and b) in upgrading. The pace of
development will be set not only by technological and environmental constraints but also by government policy. Increasing
volumes will come on stream during the next two decades but at
a relatively slow pace.

Shale oil production is small, though resources are
huge. At present oil prices, projects may at last be
approaching threshold of economic viability, though very
little development has begun. There are huge environmental
and technological problems in their exploitation on a
commercial scale.

E. International Oil Market

World oil trade is mostly supplied from OPEC
countries. The balance comes from other OXDCs, the Soviet
Union, and PR China.

TABLE I-1:   WORLD OIL TRADE, 1979-80
(million b/d)

Exporters	1979	1980	Importers	1979	1980
OPEC countries	28.7	25.0	Industrialised	27.2	24.8
Other OXDCs	2.0	3.0	OIDCs	4.5	4.5
Soviet Union	2.8	2.8	Eastern Europe	1.9	2.0
PR China	0.3	0.2	Other CPEs	0.2	0.2
				33.8	31.5
			Stock rundown afloat	...	0.5
	33.8	31.0		33.8	31.0

International oil supplies in 1979 were tight, because of the disruption to Iranian exports. During the first quarter, the constraint resulted in a strong rundown of stocks ashore and afloat above the usual seasonal rate. Oil-importers quickly rebuilt stocks in subsequent months of 1979 to a safe working level, plus an additional stock cushion to provide some measure of protection against increased insecurity of supply. They were accordingly willing to buy for stockpiling at prevailing spot prices much higher than official export prices, in the expectation that they could pass on the higher procurement costs to customers. This oil balance for 1979 was initially dismaying and certainly strained. It finally resolved itself, helped in part by the slowdown in oil consumption in industrialised countries (particularly the US).

The oil balance during 1980 was less strained, because of the economic downturn in industrialised countries, and the extraordinary stockbuild which continued during the year. Oil imports were more than 2 mm b/d lower than in 1979. The decline reflects lower consumption in the US and Western Europe. On the supply side, exports from non-OPEC OXDCs (above all Mexico) were 1 mm b/d more than in 1979, but OPEC countries' exports were almost 4 mm b/d less.

In 1980, the Iraqi-Iranian conflict did not significantly disrupt world supplies, and any short-term deficiencies were compensated from stocks and increased output from other OXDCs. But the balance was very fragile and could

easily have been shattered, for example if oil exports from
the Middle East or elsewhere were further disrupted or were
insufficiently available.

In 1981, the market has eased greatly, reflecting a
decline in oil consumption in industrialised countries.

The prospects for the next two decades presently
appear to be at best a continuance of international oil trade
at its 1979 level, on grounds of constraints in exports from
OPEC countries and the Soviet Union, together with imports
stagnant in industrialised countries but rising in OIDCs.

i. Net Exports

As things stand at present, exports from OPEC
countries are generally envisaged to be less than 30 mm b/d
during the next two decades, in view of a) constraints on
expansion in capacity and allowable production and b) growth
of their domestic oil markets.[m]

A large increase in production is foreseen for non-
OPEC oil exporters during the next two decades. But consumption of energy and particularly oil in OXDCs (including OPEC
countries) continues to increase rapidly, fuelled by strong
economic and population growth. Pricing and other policies to
make for more efficient energy use are often weak.   Thus it
does not follow that oil exports from non-OPEC OXDCs will
continue their previous rapid expansion.   Even were this
technically feasible, these countries may impose policy
policy ceilings on production or exports, as Mexico does now.
For these reasons, it is felt that exports from these
countries are unlikely to exceed 4 mm b/d through the 1990s.

Chinese policy has shifted significantly since 1977
towards an accelerated development of its oil resources, to
fuel its modernisation program. Projections of oil exports
from PR China remain speculative. There is a general feeling
that most production in the several years ahead may be
absorbed by the burgeoning domestic market, leaving a
relatively small share for export. Even this assumption could
prove optimistic, unless the new exploration efforts in
untested frontier areas on and offshore are successful.

9. WORLD: ESTIMATED OIL IMPORTS, 1980
(Including Bunkers) (millions b/d)

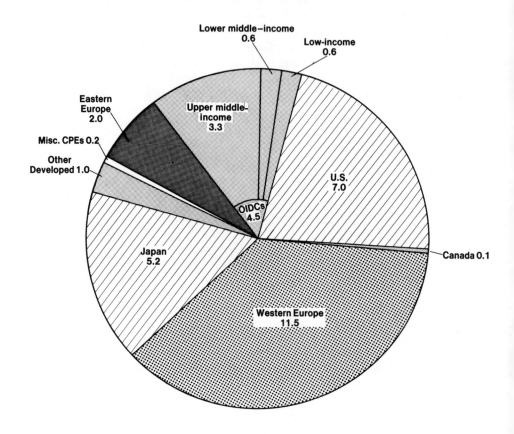

Total : 31.5 million b/d

<u>Source</u>: John Foster, estimate, October 1980.

A particular area of uncertainty is the extent to which the Soviet Union/Eastern European bloc may move from being a net exporter (1 mm b/d in 1980) to becoming a net importer (see page 24). Eastern European countries' demand for imported oil is likely to expand from its present level (2 mm b/d), given the limited scope for expansion of domestic energy supplies. Hence they will probably turn increasingly to the Middle East for incremental oil imports.

This leads to a widely held view that the Soviet bloc may become a net oil importer during the 1980s. The CIA's view published in 1980 envisaged net imports of at least 1 mm b/d by 1985, and some others are beginning to move towards it. If they are right, pressures on international oil trade could become acute. The problem is largely logistical; the Soviet Union has huge unexploited energy sources but they are mainly in remote, physically inhospitable areas and will take great efforts and time to exploit. If successful achievements lead to a brighter outcome for oil production than is generally supposed, this would be global good fortune. There are many unknown variables which could ameliorate their prospects for oil trade. They include improved energy efficiency (for which there is huge potential), accelerated development of energy resources, and substitution of other energy forms for oil. However, even if oil consumption in the Soviet Union were to grow only slightly and output were to hold level, the bloc still might have to phase out its net exports and could become a net importer during the second half of the 1980s.

ii. Net Imports

Earlier we had discussed aspects of oil consumption and production in the more than 120 OIDCs. The volume of their oil imports grew by just under 7% p.a. during the decade, similar to that of the 1960s. OIDC imports in 1980 are estimated at about 4.5 mm b/d, after taking into account

10. OIL-IMPORTING DEVELOPING COUNTRIES: ESTIMATED OIL IMPORTS, 1980
(Including Bunkers) (thousand b/d)

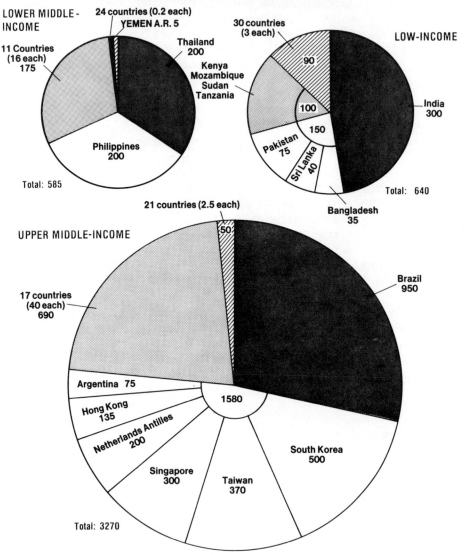

Note: Definition of OIDCs excludes the middle-income countries of Southern Europe.
Source: John Foster, estimate, October, 1980.

34

total production of 1.25 mm b/d from some 14 countries.[*] The cost of these oil imports and the implication for current account deficits are discussed in Chapter II.

We find a great concentration of oil imports into a relatively few OIDCs. This is hardly surprising, as it reflects the strong skew in distribution of oil consumption between OIDCs, offset for only about 14 countries by domestic oil production.

First, let it be said that the 14 which produced oil in 1979 account for almost half or 2.2 mm b/d of net imports by OIDCs.[**] Most of these countries are in Latin America and the others basically in Asia. Despite their oil production, the oil imports of those 14 OIDCs accelerated in growth from 7% p.a. in the 1960s to 9% p.a. in the 1970s, reflecting their strong economic growth and the slower growth in oil output.

Significantly, several of these producing countries are the largest oil consumers. The three largest producers and largest consumers are: Brazil, Argentina, and India. This may not be entirely coincidental, as they have had the greatest incentives to look for and develop oil fields to supply their large domestic markets.

It is instructive to look at the oil imports of OIDCs from the viewpoint of per capita GNP. The upper-middle income countries will import the lion's share of all OIDCs' imports in 1980, some 3.3 mm b/d. Brazil is the giant of them all, importing 900-950,000 b/d (approximately 20% of OIDC imports).

[*] OIDC imports are estimated by the World Bank at 6.2 mm b/d in 1980 (president's address to Board of Governors, September 1980). Imports include those of Portugal, Spain, Greece, Israel, South Africa, Turkey, US territories, and Yugoslavia (2.2 mm b/d) and exclude bunkers (0.5 mm b/d).

[**] The 14 OIDCs which produced oil in 1979 are: Argentina, Brazil, Burma, Chile, Rep. of China, Colombia, Ghana, Guatemala, India, Ivory Coast, Pakistan, Philippines, and marginally Afghanistan and Barbados.

Another six countries import 1.6 mm b/d together. Two of them are the other main net importers in Latin America, Argentina and Netherlands Antilles, as others such as Chile and Colombia are closer to self-sufficiency. The other four are the newly industrialised countries of East Asia: South Korea, Hong Kong, Singapore, and Rep. of China (Taiwan). The remaining 740,000 b/d of oil imports into upper middle-income OIDCs is spread over some 38 countries. Almost all goes to the 17 which each import in a range of 10-100,000 b/d (40,000 b/d average). The balance goes to 21 countries (2,500 b/d each), mostly island-states.

In contrast, the lower middle-income countries import just 600,000 b/d. Of this amount, Thailand and the Philippines import 200,000 b/d each. Another 11 countries import more than 10,000 b/d each (16,000 b/d each) and one (Yemen AR) 5,000 b/d. The balance of 24 countries import an average of 200 b/d each.

Similarly the low-income OIDCs import just 600,000 b/d. India accounts for one half, Bangladesh, Pakistan, and Sri Lanka for one-quarter together, and the remaining quarter is spread over 35 countries, mostly African south of the Sahara. Twenty of them each import volumes in a range of 1-10,000 b/d, and ten of them less than 1,000 b/d each. Thus for many countries, the oil import volume is minuscule in relation to world oil trade. But to each of them their oil imports could be a heavy burden.

If the prospects for the next two decades are truly for increasing constraint on international oil supplies and for just a modest increase in access to these supplies by oil-importing developing countries, the implication is inescapable that developed countries will import no more oil than at present, and quite likely less. This was recognised by industrialised countries within the IEA, EEC, and the Seven in the formulation of oil import targets. (See Chapter II.3.) Except for the few industrialised countries with prospects of expanding their production of hydrocarbons, this raises the key issue of demand restraint. Their oil consumption could be supply-constrained during the next two decades to levels lower than in 1979-80.

F. Crude Oil Prices

The international oil scene has turned around since 1978. This is in large part due to the recent turmoil of political events in the Middle East.

International oil prices surged during 1979 due in part to panic buying by consumers in the wake of the Iranian oil disruption. The "spot" market became overheated and crude oil was bought at prices several dollars higher than official export prices. Transactions at spot price grew rapidly to become 25-30% of international oil trade, as opposed to the 3-5% previously characteristic of the spot market. However, today the differentiation between long-term and spot deals is becoming increasingly blurred.

During 1980, international oil was basically traded at different tiers of official prices. Saudi Arabia increased its prices in December 1979 and May 1980 with the announced intention of moving towards price unification. But other prices advanced in step.

In early 1981, the marker price (Saudi Arabian Light) was US$32 per barrel fob. Official prices for most Middle Eastern crude oils were on the order of US$35-36, to which differing premia were added. It remains to be seen whether international oil prices will finally realign themselves during the next year. The odds on this happening have increased, with lower demand for OPEC oil and continued high Saudi output.

The balance between world energy demand and supply is fragile. The one certainty is continous surprise and uncertainty. The prudent conclusion for policy decisions is that constraints on international oil supplies could remain with us for the foreseeable future. The outcome could, of course, prove quite different. The international oil market could tighten or weaken for a variety of combining factors. It could make real oil prices jump again. It could conversely put them under downward pressure, e.g., if demand for imported oil were by chance to fall below a critical (but unknown and so far untested) level, to which OXDCs might find it hard to adjust output. But this takes no account of supply disruptions for political, military, or other reasons.

On present evidence, we believe it prudent to plan on a
continuously tight oil market with modest increases in real
prices (say, 2-3% p.a.).

4. ENERGY OTHER THAN OIL

During the 1960s and indeed until 1973-74 when international oil prices quadrupled, there was a strong worldwide
substitution of oil and gas--and increasingly nuclear power--
for coal. By 1973 oil had increased its share of the energy
mix in developed and developing countries to 54%, and natural
gas to 19%.

Since then, there has been much concern expressed in
oil-importing countries to reduce dependence on imported oil
and to promote the development of indigenous energy supplies.
In particular, coal consumption is gradually picking up
momentum, growing by 5% p.a. from the recession year of 1975
to 1979, compared with (about) 1% p.a. during the 1960s.

But the slow pace of economic recovery has dampened
energy demand particularly in the industrial and electricity
generation sectors. This has adversely affected conversion
back to coal consumption, as have requisite environmental
measures. Similar factors plus that of public acceptability
have slowed the completion of nuclear power stations. Natural
gas is a preferred fuel, but domestic supplies have been
constrained in the US and the Netherlands, and liquefied
natural gas (LNG) projects have been set back by technical,
financial, and regulatory difficulties.

There seems to be a consensus that future non-oil
supplies will grow but slowly during the 1980s and into the
1990s. If economic growth were more ebullient, there could be
a faster expansion of non-oil supplies. For example, more
coal might be used in electricity generation. The expansion
of non-oil supplies will nevertheless require a huge effort.
It could represent virtually a doubling during the next two
decades. Coal may provide about one-third of the increment,
and gas and nuclear power about one-quarter each.

In view of growing public concern over environmental
issues, rapid expansion of coal and nuclear power in a number
of industrialised countries (post-Three Mile Island) is diffi-

cult, though planned. A major constraint in the development
of nuclear power in developing countries has been the concern
of supplier countries about the non-proliferation of nuclear
weapons, matched by the concern of recipient countries to
retain the principle of sovereignty over national policies.

Hydroelectric power and other forms of renewable
energy are seen to provide only a small share of the increment
for most countries during the 1980s. But the expectations of
strong research and development programs in renewable energy
forms such as solar, wind, tides, and biomass should lead to
accelerated growth in their use during the 1990s.

5. NATURAL GAS

Natural gas is likely to make an increasing major
contribution to world energy supplies. It will be an important transitional fuel. Gas expansion in the past has been
held back by technological and economic constraints. These
have recently been greatly reduced. As gas is relatively
expensive to transport compared with oil or coal, its production has basically been developed in countries close to large
energy markets, particularly the developed and socialist
countries. It has been relatively little exploited in developing countries. Unlike oil, gas cannot be widely marketed
until a costly pipeline network for local distribution is
built. Natural gas now looks likely to be the fastest growing
energy source in the developing countries as well as elsewhere
worldwide. Moreover, international trade in gas is likely to
grow even faster than its consumption.

The development of gas resources has been
inadequately pursued in the developing countries. But a
substantial part of the growth of conventional natural gas
production during the next two decades is expected to take
place in these countries. Expansion of local gas usage should
be considered the main policy aim. But where the domestic
market is limited, exports by pipeline or LNG tanker may be
advantageous. Where the export market is very distant, it may
be worth converting the gas into methanol prior to shipment
rather than liquefying it.

LNG technology is highly advanced but readily available. The main markets are the US, Western Europe, and Japan.

Existing LNG exporters are OPEC countries (Algeria, Indonesia, Libya, and UAE), Brunei, and the US (Alaska), while gas is exported by pipeline from the Soviet Union. Other LNG projects are under construction or at the planning stage.

In recent years pricing, financial, economic, technical, and environmental reasons have led to the delay or cancellation of many projects. In particular, the high cost of moving gas compared with liquid and solid fuels has made for a relatively low price netback for gas at the wellhead. Hence petroleum-producing countries have typically pursued other uses for their natural gas. These include reinjection for oil field pressure maintenance, other field applications, extraction of natural gas liquids for domestic and export markets, and commercial applications for the gas in local markets, particularly energy-intensive industries such as petrochemicals and aluminium-smelting. The balance of the gas is being flared when it is produced in association with crude oil, or is being shut in when it is non-associated.

Today's international oil prices have greatly improved the economic viability of LNG projects. By the same token, they have also improved those of other high-cost sources of energy and gas in countries which are now energy-deficient, and investment decisions for LNG projects will have to be justified in relation to the possibilities for alternative energy supplies.

Deep conventional gas refers to accumulations found at depths greater than 4,000 metres. The potential for such gas accumulations may be much greater than has been assumed in the past. They could well be one of the world's major fossil fuel sources when oil begins to be depleted in the next century.

A major deterrent may be the increased cost of seismic surveys and drilling. In some countries where oil reserves are plentiful, there is little incentive to drill where the sources rocks go deeper, especially if there is no ready market for large gas discoveries. The Middle East could have giant deep gas deposits, but it is doubtful if these horizons will be tested until oil reserves will have to be more drastically depleted.

Considerable attention has recently been given to the possibilities of finding and producing unconventional natural gas with today's higher energy prices and improved technology. Much of this gas is not yet explored. Hence any estimates of gas in place are highly speculative. Even if the gas does exist, we cannot now predict that it can be produced economically in significant amounts. Nevertheless, a comprehensive survey of energy resources must include these unconventional gases. They include gas dissolved in water (including geo-pressured gas), natural gas from coal-beds, gas from Devonian shales, gas from tight sands, and gas hydrates.

6. COAL

The world's resources and reserves of solid fuels (coal, brown coal, lignite, and peat) are huge, much larger than those of oil and gas. They are unevenly distributed geo-graphically. Most of the known reserves are concentrated in three countries: the Soviet Union, PR China, and the United States. The balance is mostly in a relatively few other countries, including: Australia, Canada, Britain, FR Germany, South Africa, Poland, DR Germany, Czechoslovakia, and some developing countries, in particular India and Republic of Korea as well as Botswana, Colombia, Mozambique, Vietnam, and Zimbabwe. Much of the world's production is also in these countries.

The geographical concentration of known coal reserves may also reflect large differences in intensity of exploration effort. The world's ultimate recoverable resources of solid fuels are still poorly known. There are many countries which are believed to have untapped and unassessed coal reserves. Africa and South America have only sporadically been examined for coal. Worldwide, a large production base exists which could be expanded, if markets were developed.

The international oil price increases since 1973 have made coal competitive in many end-uses where previously it was not. There are now great new opportunities for expansion. No entirely new technologies would need to be developed, as coal was at one time the dominant commercial fuel worldwide. But improved technology is desirable, to reduce costs and adverse environmental impacts. The single largest end-use for coal in recent years is in electric power generation, where the technology for coal burning has significantly improved, including the introduction of fluidised bed combustion. New opportunities for coal usage, particularly in developed countries, could include the development of plants to produce synthetic oil and gas in future decades.

In early 1980 the World Coal Study (WOCOL)[u] said that "coal will have to supply between one-half and two-thirds of the additional energy needed by the world during the next 20 years, even under moderate energy growth... To achieve this goal, world coal production will have to increase 2.5-3 times, and the world trade in steam coal will have to grow 10-15 times above 1979 levels."

Industrialised countries are likely to move strongly back to the use of coal. Among them, the US is the single largest coal consumer and producer. Developing countries have new opportunities to exploit smaller coalfields, which may be large enough to contribute to their domestic energy needs. For these countries, the key to resource development lies with government policies to encourage such exploitation, which UN agencies should increasingly be willing to assist (See Chapter IV).

A critical issue for the expansion of coal demand is its acceptability to end-users. Other problems include relia-bility of supply from an industry which has not enjoyed the best management/labour relations. Particularly in developed countries, unresolved questions on environmental issues have typically not been adequately covered, for example, air-pollution, acid rain, and the accumulation of CO_2 in the atmosphere. It is not known whether there is serious risk of climatic change from the rapid expansion of fossil fuel use. There is a lack of consensus on the seriousness of future accumulations of CO_2 and its implication for energy policies. The problem needs continuous monitoring, but it is not yet generally envisaged to constitute a serious limitation on coal development.

Meanwhile, there are serious constraints on the expansion of coal supplies which need governments' attention. These include the environmental impact of strip-mining, recruitment of miners and engineers, the lead-times and considerable investments needed to establish and expand mines, transport, storage, handling, and port facilities. Despite these constraints, there is likely to be a substantial increase in coal demand and output.[v]

At present, most exports are from the US, Australia, South Africa, FR Germany, and Poland; Canada is a growing net exporter. Major importers include France, Italy, and Japan. Most trade is in coking-coal for steel-making, though some steam coal is also traded. There could be a very sharp increase in international trade of coal, in particular steam coal. Australia is likely to expand dramatically its coal exports during the next two decades. South Africa could also do the same. Poland will continue to export but may not be able to expand significantly. Of the developing countries, Botswana, Colombia, Venezuela, India, and Mozambique may become exporters in the future.

Underground coal gasification offers a relatively low-cost, environmentally sound method to produce clean fuels from coal. This opens up the opportunity to exploit coal which is unmineable by present-day techniques. It could thereby enable vast and widely distributed resources to be reclassified as recoverable reserves. The Soviet Union has developed a commercial technology which US interests have purchased. Field tests in the US to date have confirmed the potential economic and environmental advantages of this technique. Critical technical environmental issues are being resolved, and the process is being scaled-up. Interest could lead to commercial direction in the US by late 1980s.

Often neglected in earlier years, solid fuels of low calorific value have recently seen an upsurge in their development. In descending order of heating value, they include sub-bituminous coal, brown coal, lignite, and peat.

World reserves of brown coal and lignite are large, some 10% by heating value of all solid fuels. Production in 1978 amounted to more than 900 million tons of hard coal equivalent and represented about 14% of all solid fuel production. Some countries have exploited brown coal, lignite, and peat for many decades. The supply of brown coal comes mainly from the Soviet Union as well as Czechoslovakia, DR Germany, FR Germany and—to a lesser extent—some other European countries, Australia and some Asian countries. Recently there have been large-scale plans to expand the use of lignite in the Gulf states of the US. The environmental impact of strip-mining brown coal and lignite is great, and well-designed laws are a pre-requisite.

The cost of transporting solid fuels of low heating value is high. Consequently, it makes economic sense to burn these fuels in applications close to the mine. For example, they can be used as fuel in minemouth electric power stations. The technology of power generation from large peat-fuel boilers has reached an advanced stage of development in several countries including the Soviet Union, Finland, and Ireland.

7. NUCLEAR POWER

Most governments have pinned great hopes on nuclear power. But these aspirations have been frustrated to a considerable degree by a barrage of serious obstacles. The present outlook for nuclear power is consequently uncertain in all respects.

A. Industrialised Countries

The outlook for nuclear power is very mixed. The Soviet Union and France are implementing programs which will greatly increase their nuclear capacities, while in the US and some other countries, development of nuclear power continues to be retarded by public concern with safety and economic issues.

In the United States, public confidence in safety was badly shaken by the accident in March 1979 at Three Mile Island, Pennsylvania, where the Kemeny Commission's report found great inadequacies in operational competence and in government and public utility safety procedures.[W] There are concerns about reactor safety, radioactive emissions, thermal effects, disposal of wastes, and siting. The treatment of spent fuel elements, radioactive wastes and decommissioned reactors is not solved.

Furthermore, in some countries such as the US, nuclear power is not demonstrating the clear economic advan-tages which had earlier been expected. There have been rising capital costs, longer lead-times, high repair cost, longer down-time for repairs and maintenance, and financing difficulties. There are also strong doubts voiced whether economic comparisons of nuclear versus other forms of generating electricity have fully taken into account such costs as decommissioning nuclear power stations, disposing of radioactive wastes, and retrofitting plants with equipment to satisfy improved safety and environmental standards. Long lead-times and the burden of interest–during–construction at today's money costs have compounded the present lack of enthusiasm among most electricity corporations to install new nuclear plants unless they are already advanced in construction.

Meanwhile, the slowdown in economic growth since 1973 has sharply reduced the growth of electricity demand. This has fallen disproportionately on nuclear power which had been expected to account for much of electric incremental capacity.

All these factors have led to the deferral or cancellation of a large number of orders for new plants in a number of industrialised countries.

Despite these radically lowered expectations, nuclear energy is still expected to account for a gradually rising share of electricity generation in a number of industrial countries. A few (particularly France and the Soviet Union) are also moving ahead towards introducing breeders. Plans in Britain, FR Germany, and Japan for breeders have been delayed, and those in the US suspended.

B.   Developing Countries

Technical complexity and proliferation have not per se ruled out consideration of nuclear energy for developing countries. However, the number of such countries which can handle the technology and have a large enough electricity sector to accommodate major increments of base-load generating capacity is relatively limited. For example, Argentina, Brazil, India, Mexico, Pakistan, and South Korea have active programs. Elsewhere, most developing countries are going slow in their approach towards nuclear power at this time. (See also Chapter IV.)

C. Non-Proliferation

The issue of nuclear energy in the context of international relations raises concerns of weapons proliferation in
developed and developing countries alike. No matter how
dangerous these concerns are, nuclear power is still an
enticing means of solving the energy problem. Yet because of
the nature of nuclear power, it raises all kinds of internal
and external political and social problems within all kinds of
societies.

If a developing country wants the nuclear option,
either for peaceful or other uses, it must inevitably obtain
assistance from a nuclear supplier country, typically one of
the industrialised countries. The issue as perceived by
nuclear supplier countries is therefore how they can export
nuclear power equipment and technology on a basis which would
ensure that nuclear materials would not be directed by governments for weapons or by terrorist groups for non-peaceful
ends. This raises questions whether existing international
agencies can adequately apply nuclear safeguards, and whether
supplier countries should weigh up the political and strategic
risks in relations with recipient countries.

The International Consultative Group on Nuclear
Energy,[x] which included members from both developed and
developing countries, felt that "if nuclear power is to be
available to meet an increasing fraction of the world's future
energy needs, at least five conditions will have to be
satisfied": i) nuclear power, despite the difficulty of the
short-term climate, will have to be systematically developed,
without interruption or undue delay, ii) nuclear power must
earn and retain public acceptance, iii) technologies for using
uranium more efficiently must be developed and tested as soon
as possible, with both the coming decades and the 21st century
in mind, iv) the fear of nuclear weapons proliferation
resulting from an expansion of nuclear power must be further
reduced, and v) countries depending on nuclear technology,
services or materials to ensure their energy supply must be
convinced of continued international access to them, under
safeguards, on acceptable terms.

The Nuclear Non-Proliferation Treaty had already a decade ago incorporated a provision that nations without nuclear weapons would agree not to acquire them and would accept international safeguards on their nuclear facilities, including IAEA inspection. In return, nations with nuclear weapons would help make the benefits of the "peaceful atom" available to signatories of the treaty and would make progress on nuclear arms control and disarmament. Thereupon, numerous countries introduced large nuclear power programs.

With a view to reducing the risks of nuclear weapons' proliferation, the Nuclear Suppliers Club was formed in 1975 and has issued guidelines for tightened fuel cycle safeguards in nuclear exports.

The US enacted the Nuclear Non-Proliferation Act in 1978, under which the US would supply nuclear fuel, services, and technology only if recipients would accept a US veto over certain fuel cycle activities. Canada and Australia also made acceptance of full safeguards on all nuclear facilities the condition for further nuclear cooperation. But governments of most European countries, Japan and developing countries took exception to the US restrictions and were unwilling to defer reprocessing spent fuel, recycling plutonium in existing reactors, and introducing breeder reactors.

In response to other countries' adverse reaction to US non-proliferation measures, the US initiated in 1977 the International Nuclear Fuel Cycle Evaluation (INFCE) as a 50-country study which might identify fuel cycles with a minimum danger of weapons proliferation.^{y} It completed its report in early 1980. It did not find a technical fix to restricting nations' access to weapons-grade material, though it did indicate fuel cycle modifications which could make plutonium less easy to steal.

With prospects diminished for nuclear power, and improved for uranium reserves, the early needs for breeder reactors and large-scale reprocessing of spent fuel have also lessened. Nevertheless, some nations' interests continue as ever in access to uranium and in breeder reactor programs. Nor are some countries willing to desist from reprocessing of spent fuel. Many countries continue to believe that the US unduly stresses the possibility of nations acquiring nuclear

weapons through misuse of nuclear power programs rather than
through plants operating in weapons production.

8. HYDROELECTRICITY

The use of hydroelectricity is expected to continue
growing during the next two decades. New sites are becoming
harder to come by in most developed countries other than
Canada and Norway. But there are still huge opportunities in
developing countries for hydroelectric projects.

Hydroelectricity has many evident advantages. It is
a continously renewable and widely distributed resource. It
is nonpolluting, in that it does not produce by-products similar to thermal effluents. It can be integrated into multi-use
developments. It is one of the more efficient energy-
conversion technologies. Projects have a long life, low
operating costs and no fuel costs, and the technology is well-
known. Generating plants can be expanded with relative ease.
Energy is storable as water in the reservoirs.

Hydroelectricity does have certain disadvantages. It
is highly capital-intensive. Most promising sites are far
from markets. Projects can have undesirable environmental
impacts. There are geo-political constraints associated with
flooding.

The use of small-scale hydro plants had generally
been declining in number for years. This trend may now be
changing, particularly in developing countries. A striking
example is PR China.

9. GEOTHERMAL ENERGY

Geothermal energy is the energy contained in the
natural heat under the earth's surface. There are six kinds
of geothermal systems: three of these are fully developed
(dry steam fields, hot-water fields, and low-enthalpy fields)
and three are at the stage of research and development (magma
energy, geopressurised zones, and hot dry rocks). Hot water
fields are the most commonly exploited form of geothermal
energy. But dry-steam fields have the advantage that steam
can be directly used in generating electric power. Geothermal

energy can also be used in space-heating, horticulture, and pisciculture.[z]

Geothermal resources are very common and commercial nearly everywhere. The technology is mature, and expertise is available. But commercial development has until recently been slow. Development efforts of geothermal energy in recent years are impressive. Iceland is by far the leading country in the use of geothermal energy for space and greenhouse heating.

Other countries now exploiting geothermal energy include China, El Salvador, France, Hungary, Indonesia, Italy, Japan, Mexico, New Zealand, Philippines, Soviet Union, and the US. The UN has made a key contribution in technical assistance towards this development. Worldwide, geothermal electric plants now amount to about 1,800 MW of installed capacity, compared with 680 MW in 1969. By 1985 perhaps 10,000 MW could be in operation based on known exploration work and projects.

10. OTHER RENEWABLE FORMS OF ENERGY

Interest in renewable energy has been increasing with the continued rise in international oil prices. In developed countries attention has been particularly focussed on concentrated and large-scale application of renewable energy. In developing countries it is focussed on decentralised and small-scale applications in rural areas.[z]

Renewable energy covers a range of energy sources. They include biomass, biogas, wind power, solar energy, tidal power, and others more at the research and development stage such as wave energy, salinity energy, ocean thermal energy conversion, electrostatic energy and magnetic electricity, and solar power satellites.

In the developing countries, only about half of the need for useful energy is met from commercial sources. Of the balance (mostly in rural areas), perhaps two-thirds are met from inanimate sources such as wood and one-third by muscular efforts of people and animals.

One single phenomenon which developing countries are experiencing is a high rate of urbanisation. This implies a

radical change in the supply base.   Rural dwellers consume
mostly non-commercial, locally produced energy forms, and they
produce much of their own food.   The basic needs of urban
dwellers must be met from commercial and frequently imported
supplies. Hence urbanisation will lead to a vast expansion in
the demand for commercially traded energy.   But even by the
end of the century, most Third World people will still live in
rural areas, despite the migration to cities.   And if energy-
based amenities were more available in the countryside, some
experts believe the migration might be slowed.

The limited availability of energy infrastructure in
many developing countries justifies the development of small
resources near to markets.   Small deposits will have an
increasingly vital role, and they can supply small decentralised systems in rural areas.   Small production units are
needed and are available: geothermal, hydro, coal-mines,
oil-shale, oil, and gas fields.

The key problem for OIDCs, particularly low-income
countries, is the need for energy in food production and
household use.   This requires more efforts to develop new
technologies for use of biomass, particularly fuelwood and
charcoal.   This resource base is fast being depleted or
mismanaged. Most developing countries' population live in the
tropical and sub-tropical zones which receive the most solar
radiation. This in principle gives much promise for prospects
for solar energy and other renewable energy technologies
applicable to rural areas. But much more will have to be done
before these prospects can be realised on a large scale.
These technologies were well assessed in the OECD's report on
Renewable Energy Technologies for Developing Countries,[aa]
which suggested the following criteria:

    a. reliability,
    b. ease of maintenance,
    c. feasible and optimum unit size,
    d. environmental impact,
    e. social and cultural suitability,
    f. feasibility of local manufacture of components,
    g. expected   course   of   future   technological
       development.

The use of these technologies will depend on financing, transfer of technology, and expertise. The key to their adoption is a better understanding and quantification of the resource base.

A. Biomass

Biomass refers to a variety of plant materials which can be used as feedstocks for conversion to useful fuels and products. The plant materials with the greatest potential are trees, forestry, and agricultural residues (such as sugarcane, cassava, and sorghum).

i. Plant Biomass

Wood and charcoal meet about 80% of rural requirements for lighting and cooking in the developing countries. The fuelwood crisis is the result of deforestation for those energy needs, and the opening of arable land for agricultural uses. Due to deforestation, the populations of some developing countries are forced to travel large distances to acquire their fuelwood needs, thus taking time out from other valuable activities. (See also Chapters II and IV.)

The decreasing amount of available fuelwood has meant that manure has had to replace fuelwood as an energy source, thus depleting a valuable source of fertiliser. Therefore the two-edged sword of the fuelwood crisis reduces both the fertility and exploitation of agricultural lands.

The ratio of forest use for fuel purposes to industrial uses is 5:1 in industrialised countries as opposed to 1:6 in developing countries. This would indicate that industrialisation will decrease even more the availability of forest uses in the future.

According to recent studies, the capital cost of reforestation required is quite high. The World Bank estimates that roughly 50 million hectares of forest will be needed to be planted by the year 2000; the present rate of reforestation is estimated at only one-tenth that required.

ii.   Ethanol

There has been significant development of processes
for large-scale production of ethanol by fermentation from
carbohydrate raw materials.   This ethanol could replace a
significant proportion of gasoline in motor engines.   It is
often described as power alcohol or colloquially as gasohol.
All starch crops can be fermented to alcohol.   But the most
important ones are sugar (raw sugar and molasses) and starchy
roots (such as cassava).   One or more are grown in Europe,
North America, and many developing countries.   These crops are
expensive and subsidised in Europe and North America and
cannot serve as cheap raw materials for ethanol fermentation.
In contrast, they are usually cheap in developing countries.

There are a number of Latin American and Caribbean
countries as well as the Philippines, India, Thailand, Sudan,
and Ivory Coast which have the potential to grow sugar-cane
and molasses for ethanol fermentation.   The major producers of
starchy roots such as cassava (Brazil, Nigeria, Indonesia,
India, Thailand, and Zaire) also have this potential.   The
total ethanol potential from these producers is nearly 7
million tons (135,000 b/d) by 1985.   Brazil and Thailand
account for some 40% of this potential, Cuba and India another
20%, then the Philippines, Nigeria, and Zaire.   In particular
Brazil's National Alcohol Program aims at producing
11 million m^3 (185,000 b/d) of ethanol by 1985.

iii.   Biogas

Among various renewable energies, biogas is now
receiving much interest.   It is produced from anaerobic diges-
tion of animal and vegetable wastes.   A household-sized plant
can produce gas for cooking and lighting.   The effluent and
sludge from the digester can be used as fertiliser.   The
process is generally referred to as "biogas technology" (BGT).
It has been promoted extensively in some countries, particularly China and India.   The degree of its success in some
countries is controversial.   In Thailand the adoption of BGT
has been relatively slow in rural areas due to high capital
cost, the availability of firewood and charcoal, and corrosion
of digester covers.   The feasibility of large-scale biogas
plants needs investigation.

iv. Methanol

Methanol can be synthesised from biomass, low calorific coals, natural gas, or any material with enough carbon. It has value as a fuel, solvent, petrochemical, and gasoline feedstock. It can easily be transported by pipeline or tanker. If natural gas is produced more than a few thousand miles from market, it will be cheaper to ship it as methanol than to transport the gas by pipeline or LNG tanker. To be economically viable, methanol conversion would have to be done in very large high-cost plants.

B. Wind Power

Wind energy has been used since time immemorial for ships and windmills. But during this century the use of wind energy has become restricted to remote areas.

In recent years there has been a revival of interest in wind power based on modern technology. Wind energy can be used to generate electricity or direct heat, to drive pumps, and to propel ships of increasingly large size. Prototype and experimental wind energy converters have been built in a number of countries as part of research or demonstration programs by private and government institutions. These programs include study of wind data, the performance and reliability of wind turbine generators, their environmental acceptability, and their integration into electric supply systems. Similar units are available commercially.

The best sites are along ocean shorelines or offshore where the wind's velocity is unimpeded; sites may exist onshore at greater heights or special locations. Some national energy programs envisage that wind energy could be used to generate significant amounts of electricity by the mid-1980s. There is also a significant market for smaller converters to supply farms and isolated houses.

C. Solar Energy

The economic aspects of solar water and space-heating have been studied in many countries, with conflicting conclusions.   Cost comparisons can only be made on a country-by-country basis, taking into account local conditions, including the price of alternative energy forms.

For example, in developed countries solar energy systems normally cost more initially than conventional alternatives.   The economic merits of solar systems are longer-term.   Consumers might be willing to trade off higher initial costs for future energy savings.

In developing countries, the actual cost of every resource in remote areas should be considered.   Some countries are conducting research into and developing renewable energy systems including solar box cookers, water-heating, and distillation systems.   Efforts are concentrating on finding energy technologies applicable in rural areas, which are much more affected by the firewood crisis than the oil-import burden.

Solar ponds are a potential source of low-temperature heat in large quantities, unlike solar collectors which are typically small-area devices.

There are two methods of generating electric power from sunlight.   One is the sequential conversion of sunlight to heat, mechanical energy, and ultimately electic energy. The other uses solar (photovoltaic) cells which directly convert sunlight to electricity.   The technology of solar cells is well proven for use in satellites and space vehicles, but solar cells have been of relatively high cost. Large-scale programs of research and development are being carried out with a view to reducing the cost of solar cells, and commercial companies are now showing great interest in investing in solar cell technology.

Photovoltaic energy is also beginning to be introduced for rural applications in developing countries, typically through international or bilateral programs of technical assistance.   Indications are that it is becoming economically viable, particularly in remote areas.

11. CONCLUSION

This chapter has outlined some future difficulties confronting the world energy scene. Perhaps the greatest danger is a continued perspective that the world is faced with a zero-sum game, where any change in one party's position is seen to be another party's loss. What is needed is more flexibility, both technically and diplomatically. Confrontation between parties is self-defeating when it clouds points of convergence and agreement. The following chapters discuss the world energy scene in more detail, in terms of the parties involved and future global opportunities.

CHAPTER II: THE PARTIES INVOLVED

1.   OIL-IMPORTING DEVELOPING COUNTRIES

A.   Introduction

The oil-importing developing countries (OIDCs) have over half the world's population. Although the life expectancy of the people is low and infant mortality rates are high, the population in these countries is growing rapidly. The majority of the people are poor, and a substantial number of them suffer from hunger and malnutrition. In many of the OIDCs, food production grows more slowly than population, and the basic needs of life for many are not met. A sizeable proportion of the people live at subsistence level, and many are barely surviving.

These countries are basically agrarian; and industrial development, generally, is in its infancy. The agricultural sector provides employment to the majority of the people, and its contribution to GDP is very high. Agricultural products also account for a high percentage of export earnings. Basically, the OIDCs get their export earnings from a limited number of primary commodities. For imports of capital and technology, the OIDCs depend mostly on the industrialised countries with an increasing flow of capital coming from OPEC countries. Unstable markets, fluctuating prices, falling real prices for their exports, as well as tariff and non-tariff barriers to their exports have cut their export earnings and thereby slowed their development efforts. For many of them the international terms of trade have been unfavourable.

In most of the OIDCs, the level of unemployment and underemployment is very high. When work is available, the pay is always very low, and the working conditions are frequently intolerable. The per capita income of the people is very small, and most of the countries have very low GNP. Furthermore, the economies of these countries are characterised by highly unequal distribution of income and wealth. The poorest people, who are usually in the majority, have a very small share of the national income. Despite decades of development efforts, the strategy of development which assumed that the fruits of growth will "trickle down" to the poorest segments

of society has been a failure in many countries. In fact, in
many nations the gap between the privileged few and the
majority has been widening. Therefore, many countries have
been inclined towards a deliberate intervention to
redistribute income and wealth in their societies.

Although the spread of education is an important
element in development, the number of school-age children that
are enrolled in schools is relatively low. A very large
percentage of the population is illiterate, and in many cases
there is a serious shortage of skilled and trained manpower.
Frequently, too, the skills supplied in the schools may not
match the skills that are required by employers.

In many developing countries, the provision of health
services is biased towards the urban areas and is basically
tailored to meet the requirements of the rich. People living
in poverty normally do not have access to health facilities.
Although preventive medicine is widely believed to serve the
people better, the health care system in many of these
countries gives emphasis to curative medicine, which can reach
only the richer few.

Urbanisation has been an important phenomenon in
developing countries. Although there is a difference in
characteristics of urbanisation in the different regions, the
rate of population growth in most of these countries has been
very high. The shift in the balance between rural and urban
sectors has been leading to rapid changes in social, cultural,
political, and economic conditions in these countries. Urban
services and facilities, in many cases, have been unable to
keep up with the increasing population. Many people come to
the cities in search of jobs and better living conditions.
However, few of them are absorbed into the labour force at
rates of pay which are sufficient to meet minimum needs.

The OIDCs have many economic, political, social,
cultural, and environmental differences and similarities. The
difference between a huge and nucleared India and a small,
underdeveloped Nepal, an industrialised Korea and a poor
Somalia, a highly urbanised Argentina and a basically rural
Ethiopia is self-evident. There is a great disparity in their
resource potential, economic structure, development approach,
level of education, quality of health, and income

distribution. They also differ in their political systems,
ideological orientations, and social philosophies.

But whatever their differences, they have also many
things in common. Their common heritage as colonies, their
present status as producers of primary commodities, and their
future interests, hopes, and aspirations bind them together.
Their historical, cultural, religious, linguistic, and other
affinities give them a degree of unity in diversity.

B. The Energy Characteristics of the OIDCs

In considerable measure, what is said in this section
about the energy characteristics of the OIDCs applies to oil-
exporting developing countries (OXDCs) as well. This is true
of each of the characteristics identified below, except that
OXDCs are not dependent upon oil imports.

i. Low Consumption of Commercial Energy

OIDCs consume much less commercial energy (oil, gas,
coal, and electricity) than industrialised countries. For
example, the average North American uses about 1,000 times as
much commercial energy as the average Nepalese, 800 times the
average Upper Voltan, and 25 times the average Indian. The
average Dutchman also consumes 266 times as much as the average Ethiopian, 31 times as the average Pakistani, and 14 times
as the average Bolivian. The average American uses more in a
day than the average Third World person uses in a year.

ii. Increasing Consumption of Commercial Energy

Between 1950 and 1976, world use of commercial energy
increased more than three times. But in the Third World it
increased more than seven times, doubling every eleven years.
Since the oil crisis of 1973, consumption in the industrialised countries fell to 0.5% p.a., but in the developing
countries it continued strong growth at 5.7% p.a. By the year
2000 the Third World's commercial energy (including China)
will be nearly 2.5 times higher than today and will account
for about 30% of the world's total, compared with 20%
today.[a]

iii. Unequally Distributed Use of Energy

There is, of course, great variation among the OIDCs in their use of energy. For example, on a per capita basis India uses 16 times as much commercial energy as neighbouring Nepal, and Argentina 26 times as much as Zaire. Moreover, only ten countries account for 74% of the net oil imports of all OIDCs, while 58 others import only 12%. There is also great inequality within countries. For example, in India commercial energy used per capita in the city is nearly 20 times and electricity 28 times as great as in the countryside, even though rural electrification programs have been pushed by the Indian Government for 30 years. Even within cities great disparity exists, with the modern sector getting the lion's share and the informal sector (e.g., backyard industries, domestic employees, street vendors, and service providers) and urban slums getting very much less. For example, modern industry alone consumes about 40% in Mexico and more than 80% in China.[b]

iv. Substantial Reliance on Non-Commercial Energy

Rural people, urban slums and, to a lesser extent, the informal economies of the Third World rely upon traditional energy. Among other forms, this includes wood, crop residues, charcoal, and animal power. In urban areas, this kind of energy often may be bought and sold; in rural areas it is more often used by the gatherer.

In the cities, most low-income people (and some middle-income people) cook with charcoal. Charcoal may also fire the backlot furnaces or blacksmithies used to heat metals for hand fabrication of such items as kerosene lanterns. A host of domestic servants perform tasks that in the industrialised countries are increasingly assigned to machines. Goods and people are transported as much by pushcarts, pedicabs, porters, horse-drawn vehicles, and bicycles, as by truck and car.

In the rural areas most people live out their lives largely untouched by modern energy. Instead they rely on traditional energy. About 60 to 80% of rural energy goes to the growing and cooking of food. Crops are planted, tended, harvested, and processed by human and animal labour. A typical rural scene in Africa features the picturesque but onerous process of women pounding grain. Another in Asia or Africa is the long lines of women and children bearing firewood on their heads or backs for long distances, that become longer over the years as available woodlands recede. There is increasing evidence of deforestation and devegetation, and a consequent decline in water tables and an increase in soil erosion and downstream silting and flooding.

Prices of wood and charcoal (usually in cities) are climbing. A poor family during some parts of the year spends up to 30% of its income on fuel for cooking. As the price of kerosene has gone up, a bad situation is made worse by increasing demand for scarce wood. It is common for a large fraction of rural wood supplies to be harvested for use in cities, where people have been forced to buy charcoal for cooking because of the high price of kerosene. This leaves less wood for use by rural people. They also suffer from the higher prices of modern energy such as electricity or gasoline in the countryside, compared with the cities. For example, in West Africa gasoline in 1977 cost about $1.60 in the port cities but $2.00 only a few miles inland, while electricity soared from $0.24 per kilowatt-hour in Dakar to between $0.40 and $0.90 in inland towns.[c] In the rural areas, this not only limits personal amenities and essential educational and health services but also cuts agricultural production and hence income and jobs. One of the consequences is the continuing flow of rural people to already overcrowded and overburdened cities.

v. Inefficient Use of Energy

When one thinks of energy waste, a host of luxuriously wasteful practices commonly observed in the North come to mind such as buildings overheated in winter and overcooled in summer, large single-passenger commuter vehicles, and recreational driving. Energy waste also abounds in the South but for reasons quite different from those described above. Typically, energy waste is due to inefficient practices and equipment. The cure for this problem is not to exhort people to restrain consumption or to raise the price of energy but to provide the funds and expertise required to improve efficiency.

In rural areas, there are two outstanding examples of waste:

a. in the use of fuel for cooking and
b. in the making of charcoal.

In the use of fuel for cooking, about two-thirds of all rural household energy is used for cooking. A frequent method is over an open fire using three stones to define the fire area. With this method only 5% or so of the energy in the fuel (typically wood or crop residues) is transferred to the cooking pot. It is generally believed that the use of inexpensive stoves could increase this rate of efficiency dramatically.

In the making of charcoal, a typical method is to dig a pit, put in wood or other fibrous material, light it and reduce the oxygen available to the fire by covering over the wood with earth. This pyrolysis process may yield charcoal containing no more than 15% of the energy in the wood or other raw material. The rest is charcoal or chargas which is lost, or heat which escapes. The use of small continuous combustion kilns could greatly increase the efficiency of making charcoal.

For urban areas, a few examples will illustrate the problem. In industries, management practices are wasteful of energy; fuel-to-air mixtures on boilers are often badly out of adjustment; steam pipes leak or are clogged; pipes and hot water storage are not insulated; machines are scheduled to start up at peak energy times; energy equipment is not properly maintained; compressed air leaks are tolerated; and furnaces are not loaded to efficient capacity levels. These problems would not take major capital inputs to correct.

Even greater savings would be possible by investing in more efficient equipment. Another example of urban energy waste is in transportation. In the long run, dramatic savings would be possible through better urban layout so that people would live closer to jobs, schools, and shopping, and through improving the spatial organisation of production so that there is less unnecessary movement of materials and goods (e.g., hauling logs from Northern to Southern Brazil to fabricate doors that are used in Northern Brazil). In the shorter run, improved traffic management would reduce gasoline-wasting traffic delays, and a program of engine maintenance could increase miles per gallon.

vi. Energy Dependence upon Outsiders

The average OIDC is somewhat less dependent on oil imports than Europe but more dependent than the US. Most of the non-oil commercial energy consumed by the OIDCs is consumed by a few larger OIDCs (India, Pakistan, Zimbabwe, South Korea, and Zambia).[c] On the other hand, at least 73 OIDCs (excluding some small island-states) depend on imports for 100% of their oil needs.[d]

Moreover, most OIDCs are dependent on outside technology to reduce their dependence on oil imports, whether by finding and producing their own fossil fuels or by improving their energy use efficiency or by adopting new and more plentiful--including renewable--substitutes for oil. In addition, scores of OIDCs will need outside help a) to pay for their essential oil import needs and b) to improve their exports so that they can increasingly pay for their oil imports.

vii. Great Potential for Conventional Energy

Most OIDCs have large potential for conventional energy. To begin with, there is thought to be a great deal of oil in the OIDCs. Some geologists believe that a substantial fraction of the oil yet to be discovered in the world may be on or offshore the OIDCs.[e] There are about 30 million square miles of promising sedimentary basins, of which OPEC countries have only 4 million, the US only 3 million, and the OIDCs 13 million. Yet the drilling rates in the OIDCs are low in relation to the oil-producing industrialised countries. For example, the drilling intensity (ratio of number of wells to area of potentially oil-bearing terrain) in the US is 50 times greater than in Latin America and nearly 1,000 times than in Africa. Heavy oils, tar sands, and oil shales also are great potential energy sources, which may be exploited one day when the price of conventional oil is high enough and the cost of extraction and refining these potential sources is low enough relative to one another.

Natural gas is often found in prospective oil-bearing terrain. Hence it is likely that as drilling increases in the OIDCs, a great deal of gas will be found. Coal reserves in the OIDCs are officially not counted as great; these countries have only about one-sixth of the (world's) known recoverable reserves, and more than 90% of the OIDCs' reserves are in just two countries: PR China and India. However, very little exploration for coal has been done, perhaps because the industrialisation of the OIDCs had not begun before oil had displaced coal as the preferred fuel for industry. Many experts believe that when a search for coal in the OIDCs takes place, a great deal will be found.

Major hydroelectric conventional projects offer great potential energy. Nearly two-thirds of the world's conventional hydroelectric potential is in the Third World. However, less than 10% of the Third World's conventional hydroelectric potential has been exploited.[f] A closely related and even less explored energy source is small-scale or mini-hydropower. Units are available that will generate as little as a few hundred watts and can be operated from very small streams. It is widely observed that a significant fraction of rural people live near a year 'round stream and that there are many sites where electricity might be produced for nearby villages. The experience of the Chinese with more than 60,000 of these units suggests that this may be an important source of energy.

Whether nuclear fission will prove to be an important energy source for developing countries depends on whether nuclear technology is successful in solving its cost, safety, and waste disposal problems in the North, and if so, whether it will come in units small enough to match the grids in most OIDCs.

viii. Great Potential for Renewable Energy

Solar energy is generally in abundant supply in the OIDCs. The amount of energy coming to the Earth each day from the sun is about 10,000 times as much as is used each day from all conventional sources. It comes in four forms:

a. direct sunshine;
b. falling water (powered by the sun and gravity);
c. wind (driven by the sun's energy); and
d. biomass, the basis of all life on earth.

In general, the OIDCs, most of which are in the tropics or semi-tropics, have more energy from each of these systems (except for wind) than countries in the temperate zones. Although not all OIDCs have all four solar energy forms in abundance, most of them have much potential of energy from one or more of them. The problem is not in most cases one of limited supply. Indeed, the more that is used, the cheaper it becomes as experience is gained in gathering it and converting it to useful form. The problem, rather, is that the technologies for doing so are--with several exceptions-- still being developed and are not yet sufficiently reliable or cheap enough to compete with conventional energy sources. Already several decentralised renewable technologies are cost competitive with oil and the electrical grid in areas that are remote from the cities. If the price of oil continues to rise faster than the cost of such technologies, the area of cost competitiveness will increase.

These energy sources have characteristics that make them especially interesting for Third World countries. First, they are inherently decentralised to the rural areas where most Third World people live (except for Latin America where slightly less than half are rural). This is important because distributing centrally produced energy (e.g., electricity and diesel fuel) to rural areas has proved to be a problem in many countries. A World Bank report of 1975 estimated that only 4% of the rural people of Africa lived in areas served by electricity, and the pace of extension seems very slow.[g] Second, the costs of certain technologies to collect and use decentralised renewable energy (DRE) are not expected to rise as rapidly as oil, and the costs of at least one (photovol- taics) is expected to decline. Third, the long term future of oil does not seem bright and even the short and medium term outlook is uncertain, adding to the interest in technologies that can collect and convert into useable form the generally very ample renewable supply of locally available energy.

However, despite these evidences of promise, there is
not much prospect that (except for conventional hydroelectricity) renewable energy will soon become competitive in the
modern sectors of the OIDCs. Even with respect to rural
areas, renewable energy needs a great deal more research and
site testing before its full promise becomes evident.

ix. Traditional Energy is in Jeopardy

Most of the people in the world rely upon traditional
energy such as wood, crop or animal residues, animal power, or
sunshine (for drying) as their principal energy source. The
vast bulk of such energy is the fourth kind of solar energy
discussed in Section viii above, i.e., biomass. Although it
is abundant on earth, there are many areas where, due chiefly
to the pressure of population on the available land, this kind
of energy is in jeopardy.

The majority of the people in developing countries,
particularly the poor, depend on firewood as their main source
of fuel. While the contribution of traditional energy sources
is minimal in the industrialised nations, firewood is the
dominant and indispensable source of energy throughout the
Third World. In many countries in Africa, for example, it
accounts for more than four-fifths of the total energy used.

In many regions demand exceeds supply. The shortage
of firewood is acute in most regions, and the prices of firewood and charcoal are skyrocketing everywhere. Many families,
especially the poorer ones, spend a sizeable fraction of their
meagre income on firewood. Others walk long distances to
procure wood, frequently taking an entire day which can add up
to many man-days per year.

Although the pattern and amount of consumption vary
from place to place, most firewood and charcoal is consumed in
the home. This is mainly for cooking and heating, both in
rural and urban areas. A sizeable amount is also used for
agricultural and industrial purposes. For example, countries
like the Philippines and Tanzania consume hundreds of thousands of tons of wood for curing tobacco, while countries like
Mali use large quantities of wood for smoking fish. Partly
because it can be made relatively easily, charcoal has become
increasingly popular in developing countries, especially in

urban areas.   In many countries a considerable amount of
charcoal is used for brick-making, and in other places it is
an places it is an important fuel for railways.   Countries
like Brazil are highly dependent on charcoal for their steel
production.[h]   Furthermore, some nations in Africa and Asia
export charcoal to the oil-exporting countries, industrialised
nations and some developing countries.[h]   Consequently, in
many areas where its use is uncontrolled, the growing demand
for charcoal is accelerating deforestation.   As traditional
methods of charcoal production are very inefficient (often
yielding a product having only 25% or less of the heat value
of the original wood), the pressure on forests is great.

TABLE II-1:   ENERGY IMPORTS AND DWINDLING FIREWOOD: AFRICA'S
              DOUBLE BIND

COUNTRY	ENERGY IMPORT DEPENDENCE			FUELWOOD DEPENDENCE		
	The squeeze on					
	Export Earnings			Forest & Firewood		
	Merch. Exports	Energy Imports as % of:		Energy Consumption: 1976		
		Merch. Exports	Comm'l Energy	Comm'l Energy	Wood-fuel	Woodfuel as % of Energy
	1976	1976	1975			
	(US$ mm)	(%)	(%)	(per cap.in kg of coal eq.)		(%)
Ethiopia	278	27	95	27	352	93
Ghana	804	18	78	157	452	74
Kenya	656	54	97	152	430	74
Mali	97	25	97	27	956	97
Niger	86	NA	100	35	239	87
Senegal	426	15	96	156	265	63
Tanzania	459	22	100	66	1,021	94
U. Volta	53	19	100	18	274	94
Zaire	930	16	76	62	200	76

Sources: World Bank Report 1978 and 1979, Cols. 1,2; UNCTAD
           Compilation, Col. 3; ODC (J.   Tarrant) compilation
           for Cols. 4-6: from UN World Energy Supplies, Series
           J, for Col. 4; from FAO Forestry Statistics Series,
           energy value calculated on basis 2.3 cubic metres of
           wood to 1 metric ton of coal equivalent.

In some places the demand for wood for cooking is so intense that all the trees are cut for many miles around population centres. In some areas there had been a movement from wood to kerosene for cooking. With the rapid increase in oil prices, however, there has been a reverse trend from kerosene back to wood and charcoal thus putting additional pressure on the forests. The firewood problem is serious in most parts of the developing world. Whether it be in the tropical regions of Africa, the Indian subcontinent, or the Andean valleys in Latin America, wood is fast becoming scarce and expensive.

In such diverse countries as South Korea, Pakistan, Mali, Ethiopia, Bolivia, and Peru, for instance, massive use of firewood is creating acute problems. The problem is not confined to the supply and price of fuel; there are also far-reaching and in the long-run more damaging environmental problems associated with it. Forests, which are the richest ecosystems, are disappearing at an alarming rate. And if the present trends continue, many studies indicate that a sizeable percentage of world forests is likely to disappear before the end of the century. This has unknown consequences on regional and/or global climatic changes and on food production. Furthermore, the alternative use of animal dung and crop residues for cooking is depriving the soil of much needed agricultural nutrients and is damaging the soil structure, fertility, and quality. Some of the consequences are falling food production and the expansion of deserts in many regions.

Awareness of the critical importance of energy to the development of LDCs has grown rapidly in the past few years. LDCs and donor countries alike have watched with increasing unease as sharply rising commercial outlays for oil imports eat into scarce export earnings and development resources, while growing urban and rural demand for firewood strip many countries of trees and erode their watersheds. Long overlooked, the dominating role of firewood in the developing countries' overall national energy balances is beginning to be recognised as its longer-term availability has come into doubt. And for most countries there are virtually no alternatives to wood except hydropower--still largely untapped--or agricultural wastes.

Despite the dire consequences of excessive burning of wood for fuel, the world continues to consume more and more of it. As population grows and consumption increases, forests continue to be depleted. According to one source, the amount of wood that the people in the developing countries (excluding China and other centrally planned economies of Asia) burn in a year "would stand at least 20 feet high and 20 feet wide and extend completely around the equator" or 1.3 billion cubic metres[h], which many think is a rather conservative estimate.

A brief look at the problem on the continent of Africa will illustrate the point.[i]

Given present rates of deforestation, Senegal will be bare of trees in 30 years, Ethiopia in 20, Burundi in seven. Outside of Ouagadougou, the land has been stripped of trees for 45 miles in all directions. In Accra and Lagos, people in search of fuel tear the scaffolding from construction sites.[j] According to a 1978 energy experts' report, much of the eight nation region of the Sahel will have become desert by the year 2000 unless massive reforestation and fuelwood planting--"50 times" the present plans--is undertaken soon.[k]

In nine African countries surveyed by the World Bank, present annual rates of afforestation would need to be increased by 8-50 times in order to meet domestic fuelwood needs to the year 2000. Even this assumes that a third to one-half of total rural energy requirements could be met by other forms of energy than wood, or through increased end-use efficiency. (See Table II-2.)

For Africa as a whole, Reidar Persson[l] estimates that annual new plantations will be needed to meet rural and urban fuelwood needs over the next 20 years at about one million hectares a year. Of this total, 700,000 ha. are in the savannah and steppe zones, about 100,000 ha. in rural areas of North Africa (excluding Egypt), about 50,000 ha. around large urban centres in rain-forest zones, and another 100-150,000 ha. in highland and dry areas. Additional plantations would be required for domestic timber and pulpwood needs, but these are quite modest compared with the plantations needed for fuelwood: 150-200,000 ha. for domestic

TABLE II-2: COMPARISON OF CURRENT ANNUAL RURAL AFFORESTATION
PROGRAMS IN SELECTED DEVELOPING COUNTRIES WITH
THE APPROXIMATE SIZE OF PROGRAM NEEDED TO MEET
DOMESTIC FUELWOOD REQUIREMENTS TO THE YEAR 2000

COUNTRY	Current Annual Afforest- ation Program	Approximate Annual Program To Meet Domestic Fuelwood Needs to 2000	Total Planting Target Required by 2000 To Meet Domestic Needs	Factor Indicating How Much the Present Annual Rate of Planting Must Be Increased to Meet Domestic Needs to 2000
	(000's ha.)	(000's ha.)[a]	(mm ha.)	
Ethiopia	1.0	50.0	1.00	50.0
Burundi	1.5	5.4	0.11	3.6
Malawi	2.5	13.0	0.26	5.2
Mali	0.5	4.0	0.08	8.0
Niger	0.5	3.5	0.07	7.0
Nigeria	10.0	100.0	2.00	10.0
Rwanda	1.5	13.0	0.26	8.6
Sierra Leone	0.5	2.5	0.05	5.0
Tanzania	2.5	20.0	0.40	8.0

Note: [a]Assumes that one-third to one-half of total rural
energy requirements could be met by other forms of
energy than wood, such as biogas plants or solar
cookers and by introducing greater end-use efficiency.

Source: World Bank Data. Table by John S. Speare, Forestry
Advisor, World Bank, Washington, D.C., in paper
presented at the 103rd Annual Meeting of the
American Forestry Association, October 8, 1978,
entitled "Wood as an Energy Source: The Situtation
in the Developing World."

timber and about 30–40,000 ha. for pulpwood, outside of South Africa.

Current annual planting rates for all of Africa appear to be under 10% of this targeted need.

Estimates of the costs of an adequate planting pro- gram vary widely. For the Sahel, an illustrative average for village woodlots is $725 per hectare (CILSS estimate, based on recent field experience). This covers the first year's major capital cost of planting, plus the next four years of mainten- ance to get the lot established. It also includes payment for labour and fencing, with labour accounting for 59% of the costs.[m]

World Bank estimates range between $300 and $1,000 or more per hectare, in specific projects which are considered pilot trials before large-scale plantation efforts are under- taken. An Algerian program reportedly has averaged $290 per ha., with much of the local labour being paid in kind with World Food Program assistance. One Ethiopian village claims costs of only $66 per ha., excluding village labour which was volunteered. Comparable costs for commercial plantations operated by the Ethiopian Forestry and Wildlife Authority (FAWDA) were cited at $400 to $1,250 per ha.[n]

Reasons for these variations need to be examined very closely. Whether financed from meagre African national budget resources or from already stretched and inadequate official development assistance funds, afforestation on the scale needed to meet fuelwood demand from sustained yield will require significantly larger outlays of public funds.

We do not have cost estimates for an adequate response to the deforestation problem in the entire Third World but it would likely be at least twice the size of the African task. Using the Sahelian figure of $750 per ha., this would suggest costs in the order of $1.5 billion per year. This is probably a minimum figure.

An offer by the countries with capital and technical knowledge (including perhaps both oil exporters as well as importers) to undertake a program of these dimensions could be a significant part of a negotiating package on energy. The

problem is one that all nations share an interest in
resolving. An adequate response to deforestation would help
in the medium-term to save oil, it would slow the process of
soil erosion and, according to some authorities, it would help
to resolve the problem of increasing CO_2 in the atmosphere.

x. OIDCs Face a Double Transition

The industrialised countries must make a transition
from oil to other more plentiful energy sources including,
eventually, inexhaustible sources. It is a painful process
that has unsettled people and governments in the North. The
acute problems of the US in setting a sensible oil pricing
policy illustrate the difficulties of this transition. The
problems of many OIDCs in making the transition will be
equally or more traumatic, because most of them depend even
more than the US on imported oil for their modern sector, and
many of them lack the capital and the technical and entrepren-
eurial know-how to make the changes. Yet most of them have an
even greater problem in making another transition: from
traditional energy to more modern energy. Why must they make
this transition? Why not continue to rely on traditional
energy? There are two reasons.

First, the transition from traditional energy
(notably wood and animal power) is necessary because that
source of energy, although renewable, is falling behind
demand. As we saw in item I above, there is simply not enough
wood to keep up with demand in many areas, and land formerly
used to pasture draft animals is needed to raise crops to feed
the expanding population. Whether the absolute quantity of
traditional energy is diminishing is not certain; but in many
areas the per capita availability of much energy is declining.
There is therefore a shift from traditional to modern energy,
and unless there is astonishingly good management of the
problem, the shift will continue.

Second, even if traditional energy were everywhere
abundant, the transition to modern energy is still necessary,
because the quality of traditional energy is not good enough
to help developing countries meet their development goals. It
does an adequate job of cooking and heating, and an acceptable
but not fully adequate job of transport and pulling farm
implements. But it does not meet the needs for lighting,

electronic communications, refrigeration (e.g., medicines), or shaft power.

For these two reasons, developing countries must make this second, more important, and more difficult transition from traditional to modern energy, even as they face the transition from oil to successor energy sources.

xi. OIDCs Must Make a Difficult Choice

Unfortunately, the transition from traditional to modern energy, which is already under way, is taking an ominous turn. With few exceptions, it is a shift to oil. To what extent the oil price rises of recent years have arrested the trend is not clear. But a series of case studies and much anecdotal evidence and personal observations strongly suggest that the trend continues toward oil in the traditional energy-using areas of the Third World.[o]

If, as most experts believe, the world is in the last few decades of the petroleum era and will see oil production peak at or before the end of the century, it makes little sense for a developing country to make a transition to oil just at the time it must undertake a transition from oil to successors. Why not make the transition directly to those successors? The problem is that those successors are not yet fully proven and available. Oil-based machines and equipment are highly perfected, they are on-the-shelf and easy to purchase, a cadre of people are at hand who can maintain and repair them, and--with some exceptions--they perform better and cost less than alternatives. Any decision to forego the shift to oil-based technology is a decision that will hurt development. In short, the dilemma of the OIDCs is this: if they continue the shift to oil, they will be in great trouble in a few decades; if they interrupt the shift, they will be in trouble now.

This discussion reveals an option that may be more open to the Third World than to the industrialised countries: i.e., to give much greater emphasis to modern decentralised renewable energy. Advocates of "soft energy" paths tout small decentralised renewable energy. But they have made little headway in the industrialised countries, because:

a. most people live in urban areas,
b. modern large-scale energy does a good job of meeting those people's needs,
c. it is cheaper than soft energy, given present market conditions—many of which reflect government decisions rather than the free play of competitive forces, and
d. there is a gigantic capital investment in "hard energy" systems (large, centralised, and depletable) that would be lost, along with many personal fortunes if those systems were replaced; hence some opposition to change may be expected.

By contrast, in most of the Third World:

a. people live in rural areas, far from the reach of grids of modern energy,
b. modern energy (i.e., oil and electricity), when available to those remote people, is very highly priced —often higher than soft energy is expected to be (though concrete evidence to prove this is lacking), and
c. there is relatively little investment in hard energy; the expansion of soft energy to the majority of people could proceed for many years before it threatened to displace hard energy. To this date, no government has made a decision to give priority to soft energy (though PR China and a few others are giving it extended trials). But the option is relatively more open to OIDCs than to industrialised countries.

xii. Energy in OIDCs Is Little Studied and
      Poorly Understood

There is relatively less quantitative information on commercial energy use and availability in the OIDCs than in the industrialised countries. But in the area of traditional energy, the lack of reliable information is almost absolute. Indeed, energy experts have come to use the term "energy" as synonymous with "commercial energy," even though the great majority of the world's people rely on traditional, and have little contact with commercial, energy. The reason for this seemingly gross oversight is simple: there is virtually no reliable quantitative information about non-commercial energy. A few surveys have been made of energy use in villages on a given day and the results multiplied to approximate annual energy use; but these fragmentary reports contain great errors. To obtain reliable data, reports would be needed by reliable observers who live in a sample of villages over a period of time.

xiii. Energy Institutions Are Young and Inexperienced

With some important exceptions (e.g., India, Korea, Egypt, and Brazil), OIDC governments have not had much experience in dealing with the kinds of energy problems described above. So long as commercial energy (mostly oil) was considered to be inexhaustible and was sold at prices so low that the cost of energy was not a constraining factor in government or business planning, few OIDCs paid very much attention to the subject, except for the work of electrical utilities in providing electricity to existing grids, and that of oil companies in distributing petroleum products. Thus there is little experience in collecting the information needed for sound planning, in designing plans, in designing RD&D programs, or in implementing energy plans. There are few private companies that can build energy technologies or service and supply them, perform energy audits, or do the wide range of activities needed in the 1980s. Skilled and experienced personnel are lacking in most energy specialties at all levels.

C. The Needs of the OIDCs

The above summary of the energy characteristics of the OIDCs suggests several needs (these will be discussed further in Chapter III). First, the OIDCs need to have access to increasing supplies of oil. Second, they need to increase the production and improve the management of non-commercial energy, specifically to reverse the process of deforestation and to exploit solar energy sources. Third, they need to improve the efficiency of energy use, both commercial and non-commercial. Fourth, they need to discover and develop their indigenous commercial energy. Fifth, they need to make progress in the transition to oil's successors. Sixth, they must decide whether to permit the continuation of the transition toward oil or to interrupt it. Seventh, they need to learn a great deal more about energy regimes of their economies, particularly in the rural areas. Finally, they need

to strengthen existing institutions and in some cases
establish new ones which can plan and manage energy services,
and they need to expand the numbers of qualified energy
personnel.

D. Short-Run Energy and Balance of Payments Problems

i. Dimension of the Problem

        It is normal for some countries' external accounts to
be in surplus and others' to be in deficit at any given time.
Beginning in the 1970s, these imbalances became larger than
normal, triggered by sudden and steep oil price rises, and
aggravated by the struggle within and among countries over
which groups of people would bear the cost of those price
rises.   Throughout the decade, the major OXDCs have run
surpluses on current account (including private transfers)
each year, which the IMF estimates to have grown from
$6 billion in 1973 to $68 billion in 1979 and $115 billion in
1980 (Table II-3).   It estimates that non-oil developing
countries (including some minor OXDCs) as a group have had
current account deficits each year, growing from $11 billion
in 1973 to $55 billion in 1979 and $68 billion in 1980,
although several advanced developing countries have managed
surpluses during several years of the decade. The industrialised countries as a group basically stayed in surplus throughout the decade (except for 1974 and minor deficits in 1976-77)
but moved into deficit in 1979 which reached an estimated
$52 billion in 1980.   However, some of these countries have
incurred very large deficits throughout most of the decade.

        The second and third waves of oil price rises which
occurred in 1979-80 are expected to result in a somewhat
similar pattern, in which OXDCs may generate surpluses in 1980
exceeding $100 billion and OIDCs may incur much of the corre-
sponding deficit.   Even in the 1970s which had relatively
manageable imbalances, there were serious human costs.   The
annual growth in production (GDP) fell sharply during most of
the decade for a large group of OIDCs, hurting both agricultural and manufacturing output. For many countries there was
little or no growth on a per capita basis, and for some there
were declines in some years. Buried in these aggregates are
many human tragedies: cases where, because the cost of
kerosene skyrocketed, wood was used which accelerated the

11. PAYMENTS BALANCE ON CURRENT ACCOUNT, 1973-1980
(US $ billion)

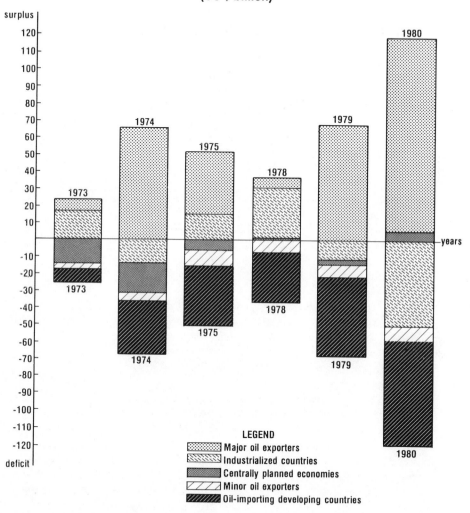

LEGEND
- ▨ Major oil exporters
- ▨ Industrialized countries
- ▨ Centrally planned economies
- ▨ Minor oil exporters
- ▨ Oil-importing developing countries

Source: IMF, World Economic Outlook, 1980.

process of deforestation; cases where, because diesel fuel was
unavailable or too costly, crops were not irrigated; and cases
where, because industrial growth slowed, people did not find
jobs and their children suffered from malnutrition.

TABLE II-3:   PAYMENTS BALANCE ON CURRENT ACCOUNT, 1973-1980[a]

	1973	1974	1975	1978	1979	1980 est.
(US$ billion)						
Indust. Countries	18.1	-13.2	16.2	30.8	-10.6	-51.5
Dev'ing Countries						
a. Major OXDCs	6.6	67.8	35.0	5.0	68.4	115.0
of which:						
six surplus	6.7	43.3	30.8	19.8	55.7	n.a.
b. Non-oil	-11.3	-36.9	-45.8	-36.2	-54.9	-68
of which:						
minor OXDCs	-2.6	-5.1	-9.8	-7.1	-8.2	-6
OIDCs	-8.7	-31.8	-36.0	-29.1	-46.7	-62
Other[b]	13.4	17.7	5.4	-0.4	2.9	-4

Notes: [a]Payments exclude official transfers.
         [b]PR China, Soviet Untion and Eastern Europe, plus
         errors, omissions and asymmetries in data.

Source: IMF, World Economic Outlook, 1980.

        In the 1980s there is concern that severe imbalances
will impose much greater human costs. A number of the more
advanced developing countries may be able to continue to
borrow from private financial markets.   Even this is not
assured, because banks may consider some of those countries to
be too indebted already. But there is little chance that the
low-income countries will be able to borrow in the private
market, and in any event most observers do not consider the
terms of that market suitable for these countries. How great
the human costs will be depends upon how vigorous these
countries are in adopting suitable economic policies and, to
an important degree, upon the performance of the external
world.   These external factors are discussed in section E

below. Judging from past experience, the problem will strike with different force in different countries. (See Table II-1).

In the 1970s, the average annual growth in GNP of East Asian countries continued at 8% and that of the Middle East and North Africa at more than 7% (both up from the previous decade), giving per capita GNP increases of 5.7% and 4.4% respectively. But in South Asia the rate of increase in GNP dropped from 4.3% to 3.5% and in Southern Europe from 7.1% to 5.1%, and the corresponding per capita figures dropped from 1.8% to 1.3% and from 5.6% to 3.5%.[p]

Out of more than 120 OIDCs, just over 100 do not produce any oil at all. Another 13 must import at least 45% of their oil, and more than three-quarters of them are more dependent on oil imports than the US. The World Bank estimates OIDCs' oil imports in 1980 at 6.2 million b/d of oil, increasing to 8 million b/d by 1990 (Table II-4). Indeed, if present trends hold, import volume could double from today's level by the end of the century. It estimates the cost of OIDCs' oil imports in 1973 at about $7 billion, or 8% of their total imports of goods. This rocketed to $25 billion (20% of imports) in 1975 and to about $30 billion in 1978 (a decline to 17% of imports). With the price rises of 1979-80 this is expected to rise in 1980 to about $67 billion, or about 23% of their total imports. It estimates the OIDCs' oil imports to rise by 1990 to some $230 billion ($120 billion in 1980-$), as shown in Table II-4.

Meanwhile, the sluggish economic performance in industrialised countries will pose some additional problems for OIDCs. The World Bank estimates that their deficit on current account (including private transfers) rose sharply from US$ 9 billion (in 1977-$) in 1973 to $44 billion in 1975[q]; the deficit declined in the next few years but hit the same level again in 1980 (Table IV-4). It is expected to stay in the order of $40 billion (in 1980-$) during the decade. Expressed as a percentage of GNP, the deficit jumped from 1% in 1973 to 5% in 1975; it declined in the next three years but rose to 4% in 1980.

12. OIDC CURRENT ACCOUNT DEFICITS, 1973-1990
(US $ billion)

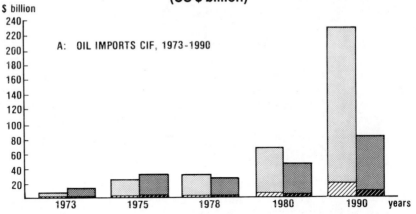

A: OIL IMPORTS CIF, 1973-1990

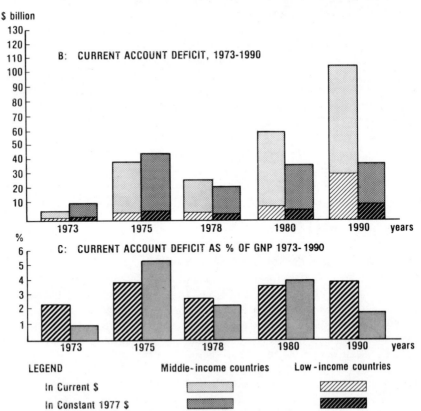

B: CURRENT ACCOUNT DEFICIT, 1973-1990

C: CURRENT ACCOUNT DEFICIT AS % OF GNP 1973-1990

LEGEND   Middle-income countries   Low-income countries

In Current $

In Constant 1977 $

Source: World Bank, World Development Report, 1980.

TABLE II-4:   OIDC CURRENT ACCOUNT DEFICITS, 1973-90[a]

	1973	1975	1978	1980	1985	1990
	(US$ billion, current prices)					
a. Oil Imports c.i.f.						
Total OIDCs	7	25	32	67	124	229
Low-income	1	n.a.	2	6	13	23
Middle-income	6	n.a.	30	61	111	206
	(million b/d)					
Total OIDCs	4.6	n.a.	6.4	6.2	6.8	8.0
b. Current Account Deficit						
Total OIDCs	6.7	39.6	27.1	61.0	78.4	104.2
Low-income	2.3	5.4	5.7	10.0	18.6	32.0
Middle-income	4.4	34.2	21.4	51.0	59.7	72.2
	(US$ billion, 1977 prices)					
Total OIDCs	9.2	44.4	23.5	43.2	38.7	38.5
	(% of GNP)					
Total OIDCs	1.1	5.1	2.3	3.9	2.8	2.1
Low-income	2.2	3.8	2.7	3.6	3.8	3.9
Middle-income	0.9	5.3	2.2	4.0	2.6	1.8

Notes: [a]Deficits exclude official transfers. High-case
projections, which assume successful economic
adjustment and better economic growth than in their
low-case.

Source: World Bank president's address to Board of Governors,
September 1980 (updating WDR III).

The low-income countries face serious financing problems. In the World Bank's analysis[q] (illustrated in Table IV-4), the deficits can only be financed if a) aid from industrialised (DAC) and OPEC countries were to treble in current prices during the next decade, b) support from multilateral institutions were increased, and c) the share of low-income countries in bilateral aid from industrialised countries were to rise to about 50% from the present 40%.

For middle-income countries, bilateral official finance is unlikely to be as freely available as in 1974-75. Lending by multilateral institutions at near-market terms will depend on increases in the capital which backs their own borrowing. As for private finance, some OIDCs which have borrowed heavily and have high debt service obligations will have to be cautious about further borrowing. Debt service payments of middle-income OIDCs could peak in 1985 at almost 30% of exports of goods and services.

The ability of the private sector to maintain as predominant a role in financing the major borrowing countries stands in doubt. In Morgan Guarantee's view[r], the IMF is still groping towards a meaningful capability to address those recycling needs which the private sector may be unable to meet. It points out the need to balance responsibilities among official and private lenders and governments, to achieve orderly financing and adjustment. The unpredictable growth of oil prices and balance-of-payments disequilibria makes highly uncertain the size of recycling needs and the ability of industrial countries to restore healthy economic growth. Unless developing countries can be assured of adequate finance, many will have no alternative but to curtail severely their economic growth. Continued growth in the developing countries is also vital to the economic prosperity of industrial countries, which exported $180 billion to non-OPEC LDCs in 1979.

ii.   Options Open to OIDCs

Two basic options are available to developing countries to deal with this problem, which do not involve basic international reforms. First, they may cut oil imports by reducing oil waste, substituting other energy sources for oil or cutting back development. Second, they may seek exter-

nal finance. A third option is that of undertaking to improve
their exports, but it is as much dependent upon reform of the
international economic order as upon internal actions (See
Section E below.)

a. Cut Back on Imports

There is a significant waste of oil in the OIDCs,
albeit not so large relative to that in the North. It is the
result of energy inefficiency more than that of luxurious use.
Over the next few years, a program of improving efficiency
could significantly save on oil costs.

Opportunities in the Third World to substitute more
plentiful forms of energy for oil also are significant. For
example, oil is frequently used to generate electricity. Yet,
only a small fraction (an estimated 4%)[s] of the hydroelectric potential in the Third World has been exploited. In
a number of countries, there may be coal that could be used to
generate electricity.

Another course of action that OIDCs may take is to
follow a policy of economic restraint. This would reduce the
pace of development. Thus, for example, the Managing Director
of the International Monetary Fund, J. de Larosière, recently
urged Africans to avoid dealing with their partly oil-induced
economic problems by borrowing too much or by increasing
taxes. Rather, they should do so by cutting back on demand,
by such steps as cutting their budgets, tightening money
supply, and keeping the costs of imports high through exchange
rate policies. He admitted candidly that "this will no doubt
involve difficult choices regarding education, housing,
health, and even public employment. But these choices have to
be made."[t]

b. Seek External Help

The second option for oil-importing Third World
countries is to seek more external financial support. The
deficit of the non-oil developing countries (including minor
exporters) is estimated by the IMF to reach about $68 billion
in 1980, which will leave a number of them in need of external
assistance.[u]

TABLE II-5: NET OIL IMPORTS AND THEIR RELATIONSHIP TO EXPORT
EARNINGS FOR EIGHT DEVELOPING COUNTRIES, 1973-1979

	Net Oil Imports				Imports in Relation to Export Earnings			
	1973	1974	1977	1979	1973	1974	1977	1979
	(US$ million)				(%)			
Kenya	47	191	252	280	9.0	28.9	20.2	25.2
Zambia	32	89	108	NA	2.8	6.4	11.6	NA
Thailand	175	510	806	1147	11.1	20.9	23.1	21.6
Korea	278	810	1926	3103	8.6	21.7	19.2	20.6
Philippines	167	548	863	1109	9.2	21.0	27.7	24.6
Brazil	986	3233	4201	6898	15.9	40.7	34.7	45.3
Argentina	83	328	338	351	2.5	8.3	6.0	4.5
Jamaica	71	193	242	NA	18.1	27.3	32.4	NA

Sources: IMF, International Financial Statistics, Vol. 33 No.
10, October 1980, lines 70 and 71 aa. Note also
data for 1973 and 1974 in UN ECOSOC, Committe on
Natural Resources, "Recent Energy Trends and Future
Prospects," Report of the Secretary-General, April
1977, Tables 8 and 9, pp 31-2.

c. Reviewing the Options

Reviewing these options, it seems evident that energy
efficiency and substitution of other energy sources for oil
offer important opportunities for cutting the oil deficit, but
not in the immediate future. To achieve these savings will
take substantial amounts of capital. Nevertheless, investments in efficiency and in substitution are frequently good
investments that should be made as soon as possible. The
returns on many such investments will be very high in a few
years, though they do not help with the immediate crisis.

With respect to the option of cutting back on development, we do not think that is in the interests of oil
exporters, industrialised countries, or OIDCs. Arguments as

TABLE II-6:
WORLD OIL CONSUMPTION: ANNUAL RATE OF CHANGE,1970-78[a]

	1970-73	1973-75	1976	1977	1978
		(percent p.a. change)			
World	7.1	-1.8	7.1	3.7	3.4
Dev'd Market Economies	6.2	-4.4	6.5	2.3	2.2
Dev'ing Countries[b]	10.8	2.3	10.7	7.7	5.2
a. OXDCs	9.2	3.0	11.8	13.7	4.4
b. OIDCs	9.3	0.3	9.4	4.1	4.7
Sub-total	9.2	1.4	10.5	8.3	5.2
c. Asian CPEs	21.5	6.6	11.4	5.1	8.6

Note: [a]Oil consumption includes inland demand for refined products, bunkers, refinery fuel and loss.
[b]This definition of developing countries includes Asian centrally planned economies (CPEs): PR China, Cambodia, Laos, Mongolia, North Korea, and Vietnam.

Source: UN World Energy Supplies, Series J, No. 22.

to why it is in the global interest to keep growth rates high in the Third World are made elsewhere.[v]

The Third World increased its consumption of oil at almost 11% p.a. during 1970-73 (see Table II-6). This growth rate fell dramatically to just over 2% p.a. during the two years of oil shock 1974-75, before resuming at its earlier rate of 11% p.a. in 1976. But it fell off sharply in 1977 and again in 1978 to 5% p.a., the latest year for which the UN has published data. This Third World definition comprises not only OIDCs but also OXDCs and Asian centrally planned economies, where the growth in oil consumption has typically been higher than the average.

To cut these rates in OIDCs much further would take a toll on development. There are few non-oil based machines ready to be put to use for certain modern industrial processes or for transport of goods and people. Even in rural areas, diesel or gasoline generators or pumps and kerosene lamps and stoves are the easiest to order, the simplest to maintain and operate, and frequently the cheapest to buy. A policy decision to cut back on oil, before substitutes are available, would inevitably slow the pace of development in the countries that can least afford such a turn of affairs. Because the oil-importing Third World uses only 8.5% of the world oil consumption, belt-tightening (not to be confused with improving the efficiency with which oil is used) in this part of the world at such a high cost in human well-being can hardly be justified. Moreover, if the developing countries are to have the possibility of even substantially reduced rates of growth (as compared to recent years), they have to have increased, not reduced, access to oil.

Leaving aside exports of goods and services which are discussed in Section E below, this leaves the option of increased reliance on foreign financing as the chief means of adjusting to high oil costs. This is discussed below.

d.   Sources of External Finance

Broadly, such foreign sources may be classified under two headings: private and official. On the assumption that industrialised countries make every effort to adjust and continue a foreign trade policy relatively free of import restraints, one might expect the middle-income countries to be able to borrow to cover a part of their deficit, say $10 billion p.a. on foreign capital markets (against bonds or from foreign international banks). As mentioned above, some of the poorest developing countries cannot borrow on commercial markets nor can they adjust their economies except at unacceptable cost in human and other terms. Accordingly, highly concessionary aid needs to be secured for these countries for an appreciable period ahead. Fortunately, the total financing required on a grant basis for these countries is relatively small and can be taken care of by increases of aid to them by OECD and OPEC countries.

Since the total OIDC deficit in 1980 is expected to be about $20 billion higher than in 1979, $10 billion will be left to be financed by public sources over and above current flows. There are several current and potentially new sources for such funds. First, there is OPEC aid. OPEC official development assistance to the OIDCs now runs at about $5.0 billion. At a meeting of the OPEC Ministerial Committee

on Long-Term Strategy in London on 21-22 February 1980, a
recommendation was approved that i) the OPEC Special Fund be
made into a development agency with an initial authorised
capital of $20.0 billion and ii) OPEC assist OIDCs with loans
and grants to meet the cost of their oil imports.[W] Although
this is not yet a final decision, there are grounds for some
optimism that OPEC may increase its contribution.

OECD aid to OIDCs is not likely to increase much in
the short term. There might be hope for another $1-2 billion,
including aid from IDA, the soft-loan windows of the regional
banks as well as the regular windows of the several international banks, additional aid in the form of postponements of
payments on past debts due to donors, and increases in food
aid.

This leaves some $8-10 billion to be financed each
year by the IMF for 1980 and 1981 at least. In the three
years 1979-81 the IMF has or will distribute each January 1
four billion SDRs to its members, of which about 700 million
SDRs accrue to OIDCs. Moreover, there are still resources
available in the Trust Fund which are to be lent on highly
concessionary terms (ten years repayment period at half
percent and repayment starting at the end of the fifth year of
the loan outstanding). Besides this, the terms of the loan at
the end of the ten-year period can be reviewed and may be
extended by the Executive Board of the Fund.

Furthermore, the Fund is in general reasonably liquid
to provide resources to the higher-income developing countries
to meet their urgent balance-of-payment needs on suitable
terms. Its ability to provide necessary finance would be
considerably enhanced, if the member governments were to agree
to increase their quotas as provided for in the seventh
General Review of Fund quotas. Moreover, the Supplementary
Financing Facility under which the Fund borrowed from member
countries has not been sub- stantially utilised, and the
Managing Director has been encouraged to start discussion with
potential lenders on the terms and conditions under which the
Fund could borrow funds to increase its resources.

Considering the nature of the adjustment problems
faced by member countries, the Fund has been encouraged by its
interim committee to review its policies both in regard to the

length of adjustment by member countries and also to explore
the possibility of obtaining other resources to subsidise its
lending to low-income developing countries. It was felt that
the Fund should study the possibility of using a part of the
Trust Fund repayments for ameliorating the conditions of loans
to low-income developing countries.[x]

E.   Long-Run Energy and Balance of Payments Problems and
     Reforms in the International Economic Order

   i.   Introduction

        In Section D above, we dealt with two courses of
action a country can take to improve its external account:
cutting imports and seeking outside help. This left out of
account the most constructive course of action, i.e.,
increasing exports. To an important extent, good management
of the internal economy will lead to increased exports. But
the ability of many countries to increase exports is severely
limited by external factors over which they have no control.
Borrowing money (discussed in Section D) is no more than a
temporary solution, albeit highly essential for the immediate
future. To get at the roots of the balance-of-payments
problem will take much more heroic measures, involving international cooperation.

        Industrialised countries' markets must be increas-
ingly open to exports from OIDCs. Industrialised countries'
demand for those products must remain buoyant and grow even
stronger. Prices of Northern exports to the OIDCs must not
inflate too much. Oil must remain physically available to
OIDCs, along with the means to finance it. Given these conditions, the external accounts of most OIDCs can be kept manageable, and consequently the human costs of the transition from
oil to its successors can be minimised. Indeed great progress
can be achieved during the transition. But if trade barriers
are erected, inflation remains unchecked, recession occurs,
physical shortages of oil take place, and credit is not available on suitable terms, then the transition will exact high
costs in human suffering in the nations of the South, and its
consequences will take a toll in the North as well.

ii. Structural Reform of the International Economic Order

Below we describe briefly several of the more familiar and a few newer proposals for reforms of the international economic order, which link logically with the efforts of the OIDCs to resolve their long-run energy and balance-of-payments problems.

a. Trade

The term "trade" is used in this context to include processed and manufactured goods. Raw materials are discussed below under the heading "commodities." The key trade reform needed is that the South's exports be given improved access and preferential treatment in Northern markets. A Generalised System of Preferences (GSP) for LDC exports was agreed to in the early 1970s, which eliminated import duties on a broad range of Southern exports. But during the same period tariff reductions were being negotiated that applied to other Northern countries as well, thus reducing the margin of preference accorded to Southern exports. Moreover, a number of Northern countries have erected non-tariff barriers to discourage imports of labour-intensive manufactured goods, as their own domestic labourers complained of being displaced by "cheap labour" imports from the South. These non-tariff barriers included, for example, actual quotas or maximum limits on imports of a given kind from a given developing country, or export restraints exercised "voluntarily" by LDCs (under threat of a quota). Developing countries have sought the progressive elimination of all non-tariff barriers and the reduction of tariffs, and have asked that revenues which are collected as a result of tariffs on imports from LDCs be rebated to the South as development aid.

b. Commodities

Closely related to trade is improved treatment of commodities exported from the South. A common fund has been proposed to finance buffer stocks agreements to support and stabilise the prices of such exports. The initial goal was a Common Fund of $6.0 billion (both to operate buffer stocks and to help LDCs diversify and develop new products, and process raw materials). In March 1979 agreement was reached on a

small piece of this goal, including a fund totalling
$750 million.

The South has found particularly burdensome the
Northern practice of escalating tariff barriers on goods from
the South to the extent these goods are processed. Thus a raw
material may enter free of barriers; but if it is semi-
processed, barriers are imposed. If it is further processed,
barriers escalate accordingly. The elimination of escalating
tariffs is sought especially by those countries which export
raw materials and aspire to improve their earnings by
exporting finished or semi-finished goods.

c. Transfer of Resources

In the UN strategy of the Second Development Decade,
donor countries promised their best efforts to provide 0.7% of
their GNP in Official Development Assistance. Currently the
average is 0.35%, although several DAC countries have reached
the target and a number of OPEC countries exceed it by a
considerable margin. Recently the Brandt Commission, recognising the difficulties some DAC countries have in meeting the
target through annual appropriations, urged that a concerted
effort be made to establish automatic sources of revenue for
development finance. Such sources might include a tax on
internationally traded oil, profits from exploiting the
resources of the oceans (or space or the Antarctic), an "SDR
link" rebate of taxes collected on imports from LDCs, rebates
of income taxes collected from skilled migrants to the North
(the "brain drain"), rebates of taxes collected by the North
on income earned in the South by multi-national corporations
(MNCs), and other sources.[y]

Another proposal has been made for debt relief for
LDCs. Since the reverse flows from some LDCs to the North in
payment for past aid loans have become large, cancelling or
softening these debts further would be the equivalent of new
aid to those countries. Not all developing countries are
enthusiastic about a generalised kind of debt relief, because
its benefits would be distributed unevenly and not always to
the poorest countries; and moreover, it might damage the
credit standing of countries which have been able to borrow in
private capital markets.

A related plan is that LDCs should be granted preferential (subsidised) access to private capital markets in the North. Finally, it is often urged that the South be given a greater voice in the decisions on the allocation and management of development aid.

d. Multi-National Corporations

Developing countries complain that MNCs which have control over technology effectively prevent or delay its transfer to the South. They have demanded that a code of conduct be established, which would guide MNCs in their relations with LDCs not only as regards transfer of technology but also spelling out rules on interference in domestic affairs of LDCs, corrupt practices, and other subjects. A general code of conduct is being prepared by the Centre for Transnational Corporations under ECOSOC.

e. Foodgrains

The World Food Conference at Rome in 1974 called for a number of reforms to ensure enough food for all. One of the proposals under active consideration is a buffer stock of foodgrains, which would stabilise prices and offer poor countries security of supply in times of shortfall. Until recently, negotiations have been active in the case of wheat; the issues involve technical mechanisms for the operation of a wheat buffer stock and a guarantee of exports of concessional food aid to LDCs. These negotiations, unfortunately, are at an impasse.

f. Reform of the International Monetary System

Since well before the US Government decision to abandon the gold standard, it was becoming apparent that the monetary system established at Bretton Woods was in need of reform. In recent years a number of proposals have been heard.

One was that LDCs be given a greater share of the benefits from the SDRs that for several years were created by the IMF. The conditions governing the access to the Fund by developing countries are seen by many to be excessively onerous and inflexible. These critics argue that IMF funds

should be made available over longer periods of time, because
the adjustments which funds are intended to facilitate in many
cases (e.g., the adjustments to higher oil prices) are
adjustments that take a number of years to complete.

Proposals have been made for a new facility to help
OIDCs adjust to the oil price rises of 1979. This may very
well call for an expansion of funds available to the IMF.
Some reform plans argue that pressure should be brought on
countries in persistent balance-of-payments surplus to adjust
also, instead of putting the entire adjustment burden on the
shoulders of the deficit countries. In addition, reformers
argue that LDCs should be given a greater voice in managing
the international monetary system. Finally there is a need to
consider international rules governing the management of
currency markets (i.e., the Eurocurrency Market), which are
now beyond the control of the monetary and banking authorities
in any one country. Until now, the discussions on this
subject have involved only the OECD countries; and little has
been heard on the subject of any special interest from OPEC
countries or OIDCs. As the issue comes to the fore, it may be
that these two parties will have particular points of view
that need to be heard.

g. The Management of the Economies of the
    Industrialised North

Oil price increases have been a triggering mechanism
which in many countries has led to inflation. These increases
have not caused most of the inflation. The major cause has
undoubtedly been the struggle within each country (and to some
extent among countries) over how to share the burden of these
oil price increases. One economist calculates the direct
effect of oil price increases on inflation to be only about 1%
in 1979. The rest of the 13% was due to wage-price escalation, government budgetary deficits, and other factors.[Z]
Others have thought that the direct effects were 3% or 4%.

Many economists believe that in most OECD countries
the inflation is now self-perpetuating, so that it will
continue even in the absence of any further oil price rises,
unless better economic management is forthcoming. It is also
clear that the oil price rises need not have triggered inflation. Evidence for this is that in three countries dependent

on oil (FR Germany, Japan, and Switzerland) general inflation was controlled for extended periods of time, although control was made more difficult by the continuation of uncontrolled inflation in other countries.

The inflation in the OECD countries has placed a burden on OPEC countries and OIDCs. It has also damaged the OECD countries themselves. It may be argued that it is just as important that there be a general system of surveillance of the management of these economies as it is that oil price and volume be the subject of such a system.

h.   The Allocation of RD&D Energy

Virtually all the funding for research, development, and demonstration (RD&D) of new or improved forms of energy comes from the industrialised countries of the North. Small but important exceptions include Brazil's work on gasohol, India's on biomass, and significant work in China. The ability of the entire world to make the critical transition from oil to more abundant and eventually renewable sources depends very largely on the success of these RD&D programs. At present there are no technologies ready to take over all of the jobs oil is doing. How soon there will be depends in part on the wisdom with which the RD&D funds are allocated, and on the quality of work in laboratories and in test projects. The whole world depends on RD&D decisions being made in a handful of countries.

There is reason for OXDCs and OIDCs to question whether the allocation of RD&D funds is very relevant to their needs. Most energy RD&D fund go to centralised electric systems of very large size, often too large for the grids in the Third World. The OECD countries are making those RD&D decisions because they control the funds, just as OPEC countries make oil volume and price decisions because they control the oil. Yet the future of the entire world will be affected by both sets of decisions. A case can be made that the allocation of energy RD&D funds is a topic which should go on the negotiating table along with oil price and volume.

F.   The Immediate and Long-Term Interests of OIDCs

The enduring energy-related interests of the OIDCs may be grouped under three headings:

i.   to have enough oil to meet their needs over the years immediately ahead,

ii.   to make a smooth transition from oil to more plentiful energy sources, and

iii. to develop the improved internal management to make these two goals possible.

Each of these will be described briefly in turn.

i.   Access to Oil

OIDCs need a reasonable assurance of supply of oil. They also need the means to pay for it. As stated in Section D above, some can get financing from private sources; others will need public sources. These latter need assurance of aid of the kind which would be provided if major automatic sources of aid were available. They also need to improve their export earnings, so they can pay for oil (and other) imports themselves.   This, in turn, logically calls for a variety of improvements in the international economic order, including (as stated in Section E above) reforms in trade, commodities, the monetary system, and improvements in management of the economies of the industrialised nations to avoid inflation and recession.   Finally, they need to find and develop any oil sources that may exist on or offshore their own territories. This process would be supported by NIEO reforms that would make advanced technology available to OIDCs.

ii.   Smooth Transition to Oil's Successors

To make a transition from oil to more plentiful sources of energy requires at least three things.

First, the transition will be smoother if there is enough time. Discovering and producing indigenous oil (see Section i above) will provide more time. Using available oil as efficiently as possible will stretch out the available time.   Improving energy efficiency will be facilitated by reforms in the international economic order which would provide more aid, make technology available to OIDCs, and improve the allocation of RD&D funds to develop energy efficiency technologies applicable to the Third World.

Second, discovering, producing, and employing more plentiful but depletable energy forms such as coal will make the transition from oil more reliable and smoother.

Third, the transition will be accelerated by more RD&D, testing, and installation of technologies which can capture and convert to useable forms the very large amounts of renewable energy available in most developing countries. Reforms which ensure that more RD&D funds are available for work on renewable—including notably decentralised renewable—energy will speed the transition. Beyond RD&D on decentralised renewable energy technologies, the transition will be improved if such technologies are tested in Third World rural sites to determine whether they perform village tasks well and inexpensively and are acceptable to villagers.

Fourth, if woodfuels and other traditional fuels are more plentiful, the transition will be supported by slowing the shift now underway from traditional energy to oil.

All of these efforts to smooth the transition would be improved by reforms in the international economic order, which would ensure more development assistance, more RD&D on relevant systems, and a reduction in impediments to the transfer of technology to the OIDCs.

iii.   Effective Internal Energy Management

In addition to reforms in the international system, achievement of both the above goals (access to oil and a smooth energy transition) depends upon the internal energy actions taken by individual OIDCs. The design and implementation of sound energy strategies require institutions and experts with experience and skills. But even with good institutions, sound planning must begin with a good grasp of the facts which currently prevail. Surveys of energy regimes (particularly rural and urban slum areas) and sites of energy technologies for those areas will help to supply those facts. In turn, these needs can be facilitated by a strong reliable flow of development assistance.

2. OIL-EXPORTING DEVELOPING COUNTRIES

    A. Introduction

        The present section examines the objectives and
policies of the oil-exporting developing countries (OXDCs),
with a view to determine whether there is a sufficient area of
converging interest with the oil-importing countries (both
developed and developing) to contribute towards the bases for
a global energy policy. The fact that there has been little
progress during the past seven years towards an accommodation
between the two groups of countries gives scant ground for
optimism. However, as time goes by, the problems are becoming
more rather than less acute, particularly with respect to
three of the central issues:

    i.   the desire in the exporting countries to stretch out
         reserves over as long a period as possible
    ii. the planning for and management of an orderly transi-
         tion in industrial countries from heavy reliance on
         imported oil to alternative sources of energy, and
    iii. the difficulties faced by the OIDCs in earning suffi-
         cient foreign exchange to finance the oil imports
         which they will need for a long time, in order to
         maintain an acceptable rate of economic growth.

    B. Production and Reserves

        There are approximately 28 developing countries which
are net oil exporters (OXDCs). Their production and reserves
are shown in Table II-7 below. Thirteen of them are members
of the Organization of the Petroleum Exporting Countries
(OPEC). Among the others, it now seems likely that Peru will
be a small net exporter for some years. But Bahrain and
Bolivia are more or less self-sufficient and may not have been
net exporters in 1979.

        In addition to being net exporters of oil, several of
the countries have very large reserves of natural gas, notably
Algeria, Indonesia, Iran, Nigeria, Qatar, Saudi Arabia, the
United Arab Emirates, Malaysia, Mexico, and possibly Kuwait
and Venezuela. These reserves are, for the most part,
undeveloped but represent a major potential source of energy

for the importing countries. This source could eventually be
a factor in smoothing the transition away from oil. (See
Section G below.)

TABLE II-7: CRUDE OIL PRODUCTION & RESERVES IN OXDCs, 1979

	Production	Proven Reserves at Year-end
	(thousand b/d)	(billion barrels)
TOTAL OXDCs	34,881	491.4
OPEC Countries	30,919	440.3
Algeria	1,240	8.4
Ecuador	214	1.1
Gabon	204	2.0
Indonesia	1,595	9.6
Iran	3,117	58.0
Iraq	3,451	34.0
Kuwait	2,511	65.2
Libya	?,066	23.5
Nigeria	2,302	17.4
Qatar	506	3.8
Saudi Arabia	9,527	169.1
UAE	1,830	30.3
Venezuela	1,356	17.9
Other OXDCs	3,962	51.1
Angola	140	1.2
Bahrein	50	0.2
Bolivia	32	0.2
Brunei	255	1.8
Cameroon	32	0.1
Congo	59	0.4
Egypt	510	3.1
Malaysia	285	2.8
Mexico	1,593	32.5
Oman	295	3.0
Peru	195	0.7
Syria	170	2.0
Trinidad & Tobago	223	0.7
Tunisia	102	2.3
Zaire	21	0.1

Total crude oil production in OXDCs reached 35 mm b/d in 1979, of which 31 mm b/d were produced by OPEC countries. Total proven reserves at year-end 1979 were 490 billion barrels, approximately three-quarters of the world's total reserves. A small number of other developing countries benefit from the oil trade by importing crude oil, processing it in intermediate refineries, and exporting the products. These countries are Bahamas, Bahrain, Netherlands Antilles, Singapore, and South Yemen. Two of them (Bahamas and Netherlands Antilles) also have trans-shipment terminals. Finally, relatively minor benefits accrue to six transit countries which collect transit fees or tolls on movements of crude originating in another country for export to third country destinations. These are Jordan, Lebanon, Panama, Syria, Turkey, and Egypt, although the pipelines are not currently operating through Jordan and Lebanon (mid-1980). Both Egypt and Panama benefit from canal tolls on oil cargoes in transit and tankers transmitting in ballast on the return leg of the journey. Panama is also an important bunkering point, as are some of the "intermediate" refineries mentioned above.

Of the 28 exporting countries, 12 have potential for significant expansion of either oil or gas production or both. Of these, 11 produce well over 1 mm b/d of oil each. They are the only countries which are of much interest to the importing countries for the purposes of reaching an accommodation which will facilitate an overall global energy policy. The others are either too small or do not appear to have any promise for significant expansion.

The 12 countries referred to above are Algeria, Indonesia, Iran, Iraq, Kuwait, Libya, Nigeria, Qatar, Saudi Arabia, United Arab Emirates, Venezuela, and Mexico. All of them, except for Mexico, are members of OPEC. To some extent, they share the development problems of other developing countries. But there are four main areas that directly concern energy which would have to be the subject of an accommodation between the industrial countries and some or all of the 12 exporting developing countries, if the objectives of both are be be reconciled in a mutually advantageous way. These areas are:

   i.   exploration and development of oil, particularly heavy oil, and secondary and tertiary recovery projects,

  ii.   development and commercialisation of natural gas reserves,

 iii.   the conservation of oil and gas resources, and

  iv.   the treatment of financial assets held in the North by the capital-surplus oil-exporting countries.

Each of these issues will be touched upon below along with other important factors affecting relations between the OXDCs and the industrial North.

C. The Importance of Sovereignty

Any approach to a global energy policy can only hope to be successful if the countries of the industrial North fully comprehend the importance which developing countries generally, but in this instance, oil-exporting countries in particular, place upon their sovereignty. The industrial countries of the North, none of which has in recent times been subjected to colonial occupation and exploitation, view their own sovereignty in a relaxed manner, and indeed take it largely for granted. By the same token, they tend to view the importance which developing countries attach to sovereignty as exaggerated, and largely emotional. They suspect that emphasis on it by politicians from Third World countries is merely empty rhetoric, designed to massage the amour propre of their people. But, in fact, as far as OPEC countries are concerned, the memory of colonial and semi-colonial domination remains fresh in people's minds. Of the present 13 member countries of OPEC, eight were European colonies or protectorates until well after the Second World War, another had been militarily occupied by the Allied Powers during the war, and the remaining four were nominally independent, although the independence of two of these was more a matter of form than of substance.

The references to sovereignty, which form part of the Solemn Declaration of Algiers of March 1975 by the Conference of the Sovereigns and Heads of States of the OPEC Member

Countries, are not therefore to be taken lightly. The
following quotations are taken from the third and fourth
paragraphs of the Declaration:

> (The Sovereigns and Heads of State of the Member
> Countries of OPEC) stress that world peace and pro-
> gress depend on the mutual respect for sovereignty
> and equality of all member nations of the interna-
> tional community, in accordance with the UN charter.
>
> The Sovereigns and Heads of State re-affirm the
> solidarity which unites their countries in safe-
> guarding the legitimate rights and the interests of
> their peoples, re-asserting the sovereign and
> inalienable right of their countries to the owner-
> ship, exploitation and pricing of their natural
> resources, and rejecting any idea or attempt that
> challenges those fundamental rights and thereby the
> sovereignty of their countries.

The Solemn Declaration of Algiers is of particular
importance because it is the only occasion on which the heads
of state of OPEC countries have met to formulate and put
forward their points of view with respect to the development
of their principal natural resource. It still remains largely
representative of their views.

As far as their oil resources are concerned, the
producing countries attach a special importance to the notion
of sovereignty. The reason is that, until recently, their oil
was being produced in accordance with a series of concession
agreements which completely removed the industry from any kind
of national control, so that the country itself was entirely
excluded from any decision related to investment and expansion
plans, levels of production, destination of export, or indeed
of any important matter whatsoever. Their sole remaining
rights were to tax revenues in accordance with a formula that
could not be changed without the consent of the
concessionaire. In fact, in the Middle East and Africa, the
governments were not even entitled to information concerning
the price at which their oil was being sold for export (taxes
being levied on a notional price set by the companies
themselves, without consultation with the governments
concerned).

The concession agreements had been voluntarily entered into by previous governments, and numerous revisions of a relatively minor kind had in fact been introduced into them by mutual agreement with the concessionaire. But on key decisions, the concession agreements were becoming, in the view of the host governments, increasingly burdensome and anachronistic as the host country and its government developed and became more sophisticated. Hence, the view was widely held that the concession agreements, which were of unusually long duration (all in the Middle East lasted until at least near the end of the century and one to the year 2025), and not subject to the jurisdiction of local courts, were "unequal treaties" virtually imposed upon them by the oil companies with the backing of their home governments who, at the time, were immeasurably stronger in political terms.

When the events of the early 1970s brought to a head trends which had been gathering force during the previous decade, resulting in a virtually complete transfer to the governments of control of the industry in their countries, these governments felt for the first time that they had achieved in substance what they had previously claimed as their right in theory, namely the right of permanent sovereignty over their natural resources (which had been, in fact, the object of an earlier United Nations resolution). They have now exercised these rights for the past seven years, including the right to make or at least control all decisions concerning investments, the level of production and export prices.

Having once gained the substance of sovereignty over their petroleum resources, the governments of producing countries naturally view with great suspicion any attempt by the industrialised importing countries to draw them into political agreements which would once more limit their freedom of action with respect to supply and price. The derogation to sovereignty which the concession agreements with the oil companies represented having been eliminated, it is not, in the governments' view, to be simply replaced by a new limitation to be introduced into international agreements made, this time, essentially with the governments of the oil companies' home countries. This is the real background to the unremitting hostility which OPEC has shown towards the International

Energy Agency, created by the industrial importing countries
to coordinate their energy policies as a counterweight to
OPEC. It is also an important part of the broad background to
the difficulties inherent in any general accommodation with
the OXDCs.

D. Depletion and Transition

The central problems for all of the principal OXDCs
are a) the depletion of their oil and gas reserves and b)
economic   transition   from   dependence   on   their   petroleum
resources to a diversified and developed economy.   Both of
these problems exist in widely differing degrees among the
exporting countries.   As far as depletion is concerned, the
following table gives some indication of the disparities among
them by showing the ratio of crude oil production in the year
1979 to proved reserves at year-end 1979 for the main 12
exporters.

TABLE II-8:   RATIO OF CRUDE OIL PRODUCTION TO PROVED RESERVES:
END 1979

COUNTRIES	RATIO OF CRUDE OIL PRODUCTION TO PROVED RESERVES: END 1979
Indonesia	17
Algeria	19
Nigeria	21
Qatar	21
Venezuela	21
Iraq	27
Libya	31
United Arab Emirates	45
Saudi Arabia	49
Iran	51
Mexico	56
Kuwait	71

Clearly,   the   countries   which   have   been   relatively
well explored and whose ratio of current production to proved
reserves is in the low twenties or less have ample reason for
concern.   Indonesia, Algeria, Nigeria, Qatar, and Venezuela
all fall in this category, and all of them are anxious to

stimulate further exploration, although Qatar has limited acreage to offer. But their approach to the problem differs from country to country: Algeria and Indonesia have been signing exploration and production agreements with foreign oil companies; policy in Nigeria appears at present (mid-1980) to be uncertain as reorganisation of the country's petroleum administration continues; while Venezuela is attempting to carry out all exploration through its own national company.

In two instances, the above table is misleading. First, it shows Iraq with a rather low ratio of current production to reserves (27), whereas in fact the geological prospects in Iraq are very good, though little data is available on recent discoveries. It is best classified as a country with ample possibilities for expansion. It may be noted that spokesmen for the country have on occasion stated that assistance from industrialised countries in increasing exploration and development (especially of heavy oils) is among their objectives in any future dialogue. The second misleading feature of the table is that Libya is shown with a relatively high ratio of current production to reserves (31) whereas in fact there is serious concern in Libya over depletion, and the country has been signing a limited number of exploration and production agreements with foreign companies. It should be noted that Libya has in the past experienced sustained production levels of well over 3 mm b/d (compared with its present 2 mm b/d), and that over-production of certain fields was an important factor in determining government policies and attitudes towards the foreign oil companies in the early 1970s.

Taken as a whole, this group of countries has a keen interest in stimulating further exploration; but it must be said that in most cases the acreage is attractive enough to permit them to attract foreign risk capital, if they so wish, on reasonable terms, as is being done in Indonesia, Libya, and Algeria.

The remaining countries, namely the United Arab Emirates, Saudi Arabia, Iran, Mexico, and Kuwait, can all afford to take a more relaxed view about the proving up of further reserves, though here again substantial differences exist within the group as to prospective acreage. The United Arab Emirates and Kuwait have limited possibilities for

finding large new oil deposits, and policies are consequently
highly conservationist. Saudi Arabia, Iran, and Mexico, on
the other hand, still have highly prospective unexplored
acreage (this is less true of Iran than the other two
countries). Their interest therefore lies more in a slow-to-
moderate pace of exploration, a remark which must be qualified
by other policy considerations, notably in the case of Iran.
In any event, their need for outside assistance is either
non-existent in their own opinion (Iran and Mexico) or already
proceeding satisfactorily (Saudi Arabia).

Closely linked to the question of depletion, and
underlying nearly all policy concerns of OXDCs highly dependent on oil, is the transition that all of them must sooner or
later make to a more balanced and diversified economy. In
some countries, notably Venezuela, the investment of oil
revenues in economic diversification has been a constant preoccupation and policy since before World War II. Today, most
of the major exporting countries are vitally concerned with a
diversified economic development which will permit continued
overall economic growth, once oil revenues start their
ultimately inevitable decline.

The present unparallelled prosperity of the principal
OXDCs obscures the fact from the rest of the world that, in
the long run, the transition from dependence on oil to other
sources of energy will ultimately be infinitely more difficult
for them than the consumers. It is most unfortunate, though
perhaps natural, that as far as any energy dialogue is concerned, the attention of the North has been largely focussed
on the question of prices rather than the economic development
objectives of most of the major OXDCs, a field which would
provide much more room for future dialogue.

Senior officials of the Organisation of Arab Petroleum Exporting Countries (OAPEC) and of OPEC itself have
repeatedly pointed out that in their view the energy problem
must be faced in the context of the economic development of
the oil-exporting countries. The transition period into which
the world's energy economy will soon be entering will take on
markedly different proportions in the North. In the countries
of the industrial North, the major concern is whether the
supply and price of energy will impose a serious constraint on
the growth of the economy;   but most scenarios, despite

pessimism over the level of unemployment, do not include major political and social upheaval. In the OXDCs, on the other hand, the major concern is not with an eventual slowing down of growth once production starts to shrink, but rather with the effects of a steady decline in the economy and the political and social upheavals that would almost certainly accompany it.

Economic development and industrialisation within the life span of existing oil and gas reserves are major objectives of most of the principal exporting developing countries. But this is not true for three of them (apart from some downward integration into local refining petrochemicals and LNG), namely Kuwait, United Arab Emirates, and Qatar. All three now appear to have understood the futility of attempting to industrialise arid and sparsely populated areas devoid of suitable infrastructure and far removed from the main industrial markets. After some attempt at industrialisation in the 1960s, Kuwait was the first to understand this and make a conscious decision to prepare for transition by a careful program of investment abroad, mainly in the form of indirect investments (though more recently there appears to be increasing emphasis on direct investment). This decision seems to have been taken even before the first large increase of oil prices in 1973-74. In Qatar and the United Arab Emirates, the initial reaction to the increase in prices was, as earlier in Kuwait, to draw up plans for industrialisation which included a number of expensive projects not directly related to the oil and gas industries. More recently, however, there has been some disillusionment with this policy, and neither country has within the past year approved any new major industrial project not directly related to oil and gas.

In rather general terms, the implications for supply and price of the depletion and transition problems which will be faced by all OPEC member countries in the medium or long-term reflect somewhat different approaches by different members of OPEC.

Countries already producing close to their physical limits and without great hope of an expanding reserve base in the future, such as Algeria, Indonesia, Libya, Nigeria, as well as all the minor producers, will tend to place increasing emphasis on obtaining the maximum price. Conservation is an

important part of overall oil policy, but because they have
already attained a certain level of spending based on production levels close to the maximum, they have limited scope for
cutting back.

Venezuela lies in an intermediate position because,
while its conventional oil resources place it on a par with
countries such as Algeria and Indonesia, it still has vast
hydrocarbon resources in the Orinoco petroleum belt to
develop. Hence, for Venezuela, the transition is a matter not
only of a transition to a diversified economy, but also from
conventional petroleum resources to the heavy oils of the
Orinoco, which are capable of supporting production at a level
of 2 or 3 mm b/d for a period that is indefinite (about three
hundred years) for all practical purposes. Hence, a certain
ambiguity surrounds Venezuelan policy towards supply and
price, since it sees its relations with important consuming
countries, both at the commercial and technical levels, as
lasting indefinitely into the future.

At the other end of the spectrum are the countries
which still have an ample resource base relative to their
current and immediately prospective needs—notably Iraq,
Kuwait, Saudi Arabia, and the United Arab Emirates. The chief
emphasis of petroleum policy in these countries is bound to be
on conservation, because the accumulation of financial
surpluses which must be held outside the country is politically undesirable and, so far, economically unprofitable.
Consequently, these countries, like Venezuela, also see themselves in a much longer-term relationship with the major
consuming countries, although mainly at the commercial level.

In summary, between the two groups of countries there
is therefore a sharp distinction of emphasis between the
attitudes towards supply and price, and towards the consumer.

E. The Supply and Price of Oil

There are a number of interrelated factors which
affect the decisions of OXDCs with respect to the supply and
price of oil. The most important of these is at present the
question of conservation, but others include investment
policies, the security of financial assets held abroad, and
political factors.

i. Conservation Policies

The most important factor determining the supply of
oil from the principal OXDCs is conservation, meaning in this
context a policy of production restraints, designed primarily
not to maintain price but to prolong for as long as possible
the economic life of the country's petroleum reserves, with
due regard to a level of government revenues which permits
continued economic growth. This is possibly the most widely
misunderstood aspect of OXDC policies—it being too easily and
too commonly assumed by observers in industrial countries that
the so-called conservation policies of producing countries are
a mere camouflage for price maintenance. Consequently, over
the past few years, these observers have found their expectations repeatedly frustrated when surpluses appear on the
market without leading to a serious weakening in what they
suppose to be a conventional cartel seeking to maximise
revenue. In practice, several countries have been only too
happy to reduce production, and thereby reduce surplus
revenues which can neither be spent profitably at home nor
invested safely abroad.

Production ceilings in the OPEC area at present (mid-
1980) are in aggregate about 6 mm b/d lower than already
developed capacity, and probably about 15 mm b/d below maximum
potential capacity.

ii. Investment Policies

To a large extent, policies governing investment in
exploration and the development of producing capacity are a
facet of conservation policies viewed in the long run. Unim-
portant in the short-term, they are critical in the medium and
long-term because, if and when conservation policies are
relaxed to allow production to catch up with already developed
physical capacity, the result of past investment policies will
impose a constraint that cannot be overcome except with a
considerable time lag.

Policies vary from country to country. At one
extreme is Kuwait, where there has been no investment in the
development of new capacity for some years and only very

limited investment in exploration.   The present exploration
activity is oriented mostly towards the discovery of gas.

The most notable and important example of muted
investment policies in the development of new capacity and
exploration is, of course, Saudi Arabia where plans originally
laid a few years ago by Aramco for the development of capacity
up to 20 mm b/d have been successively scaled down.   There
are, at present (mid-1980), no plans to develop capacity
beyond 12 mm b/d by the year 1985.   By and large, however,
other member countries of OPEC and other exporting developing
countries are pursuing active exploration policies, some of
them indeed quite vigorous.   These include, as noted above,
Indonesia, Algeria, Libya, Mexico, Venezuela, and probably
Iraq, although not much is known about the level of activity
in that country.   In some of them, vigorous exploration is
accompanied by ceilings on present production.

iii.   The Security of Financial Assets

Some six OPEC countries (Saudi Arabia, Kuwait, UAE,
Qatar, Iraq, and Libya) have been consistently in surplus on
current account during the 1970s.   The financial assets which
they have consequently accumulated abroad could be as much as
$300 billion (net of private and public transfers), most of it
held in dollars and much of it in short-term notes.   These
funds are vulnerable both to inflation and to political action
(i.e., blocking).   Since the producing countries with large
funds invested abroad are largely confined to Saudi Arabia,
Kuwait, and the United Arab Emirates, their vulnerability is
clearly a matter of limited importance for OPEC as a whole,
but it is of major importance to the countries concerned.   The
issue has attracted a great deal of attention in recent years,
because it is clear that, if sufficient guarantees could be
given to Saudi Arabia in particular as well as to the other
two countries, some of the constraints on production reflected
in the countries' conservation policies and investment
policies would be either entirely removed or greatly attenuated. Hence, some observers have seen the question of financial security for the assets of the producers held overseas as
the key to avoiding production restraint in the future.

A number of different schemes have been mooted, most
of them centred on the issue of long-term bonds indexed in

such a manner as to compensate for inflation. Some of these proposals have come from the producers themselves, particularly (several years ago) from Iran when the country expected to remain in surplus for some time. More recently, nearly all of the proposals have come from sources in industrial countries. Among the difficulties in establishing such inflation-proofed bonds is the political difficulty in the US necessarily associated with the creation of a special class of investor who would have privileges not extended to others. Conversely, the producing countries feel that such bonds are more easily identified than other financial investments and therefore more politically vulnerable to freezing as well as less mobile in the short-run. These fears may be more theoretical than practical, but they nevertheless exist and colour the attitudes of the surplus countries.

There are a number of other obstacles, which vary from country to country, placed in the way of the financial surplus countries and inhibiting their investments abroad. There are, most notably, constraints in several countries, either of a statutory or political nature on the acquisition of assets (especially, the making of direct investments), as well as tax considerations which tend to inhibit the investor. The removal of some of these obstacles would no doubt represent a positive step as far as the capital-surplus countries are concerned and could be an element, though not a major one, in any rapprochement between the oil-exporting countries (or some of them) and the industrial countries of the North, particularly the US.

iv.   Political Factors

The Arab-Israeli conflict is, without any doubt, one of the most important of the obstacles in the way of any general agreed solution to the energy problems between the exporting developing countries and the industrial ones. It is rarely discussed openly and candidly; but it should constantly be borne in mind that no permanent solution or agreement will be possible as far as energy is concerned, until a solution is found to the Palestinian problem which is acceptable to a majority of the petroleum-producing Arab states. The dependence of the West in general and the US in particular on imported oil is seen by the Arab countries as one of the few potent weapons which they can bring to bear in their favour to

solve the problem of the Palestinians. It is idle to think
that this weapon will be abandoned in order to reach a broad
energy agreement on the economic and financial issues
involved. Nothing could be more unrealistic; and the only
apparent point in any "dialogue" or preliminary talks on the
economic and financial issues seems to be to prepare the
ground for an energy agreement once a broad political settlement can be achieved, if ever, on the Palestinian issue.

F. Factors Determining Pricing Policies

        The setting of oil prices has, in the past, been
largely a pragmatic affair, with the exporting countries
reacting to market forces which they themselves have in large
measure created through the enforcement of conservation
policies curbing production for reasons other than price-
support. There are, however, underlying objectives which find
general agreement among the exporting countries, despite (or
perhaps because of) their vagueness when it comes to concrete
detail. Essentially, OPEC pricing policies aim at shifting
the price of oil upwards to the cost of alternative sources of
energy. Neither the cost nor the supply volumes that such a
price would bring out is specified, although, again in vague
terms, many of the producers tend to think of the cost of
alternatives as being represented by gasification of coal in
the western US in relatively modest quantities with a number
of other alternatives being produced at below this cost, in
particular steam coal, nuclear power, shale oil, oil from the
tar-sands, LNG from outside the OPEC area, possibly some deep
gas, and at the margin, some of the exotics such as green
petrol.

        Of less fundamental importance, there is now firm
agreement within OPEC that the price of oil should escalate to
keep pace with inflation. Most member countries are in agreement that the deflator should be an OECD index of export
prices, possibly in combination with an index that gives some
measure of the increase in the price of services in OECD
countries. There is also general agreement in OPEC countries
that the speed at which the price of oil should move up from
its present level to the (undefined) cost of alternatives
should be pari passu with the growth of GNP in real terms in
the OECD area. The rationale for this linkage is that the
growth in GNP is both a measure of ability to pay as well as

an indication of the time span within which the alternatives will be needed. If GNP grows fast, the alternatives will be needed sooner, and the price of oil will have moved up correspondingly quickly.

Opinion is divided on the desirability of establishing price ceilings. Most, though not all, exporting countries feel that a price ceiling is, in principle, desirable, partly to maintain order in the markets, and partly to prevent premature development of alternatives. However, those countries that recognise the desirability in principle of a price ceiling are themselves divided among the ones that believe a price ceiling can be administered and those that believe it is impractical because it would not be respected for long and that, therefore, any attempt to impose one is futile and divisive.

Finally, it may be remarked that OPEC, at any rate, sees the administration of prices as entirely manageable and a matter which pertains exclusively to the seller at the political (though not commercial) level. It is not a point which is open for negotiation with the industrial countries, except in the case of the rather far-fetched hypothesis that industrial countries would agree to regulate the prices of their own exports of manufactured goods and food to the producing countries.

G. Natural Gas

Of growing importance and concern among the OXDCs is the future development of their natural gas reserves. Among the OXDCs, twelve countries either already possess or have excellent prospects for natural gas in large exportable surpluses. They are Algeria, Indonesia, Iran, Iraq, Kuwait, Nigeria, Qatar, Saudi Arabia, the United Arab Emirates, Venezuela, Brunei, and Mexico. The latest published proved reserve figures for natural gas are shown below for the countries mentioned, but there is little doubt that they vastly underestimate the true position of these countries, in particular with respect to the recent discoveries of large gas deposits in Qatar, Saudi Arabia, and Venezuela. In addition, Kuwait is confident that its deep drilling program will encounter large reserves of gas.

TABLE II-9:   PROVED NATURAL GAS RESERVES

Countries	Trillion Cubic Ft.
Algeria	132
Indonesia	24
Iran	490
Iraq	28
Kuwait	31
Nigeria	41
Qatar	60
Saudi Arabia	93
UAE	21
Venezuela	43
Brunei	8
Mexico	59
TOTAL	1,030

The above countries account for 63% of the world's gas reserves (excluding CPEs), and their aggregate reserves are equivalent to 170 billion barrels of oil, or about twice as much as the combined oil and gas reserves of Canada and the US together. As noted above, they are (with the possible exception of Iran) possibly greatly understated.

Saudi Arabia's gas program will, when completed, utilise virtually all of the associated natural gas produced with its oil. The country is already recovering 300,000 b/d of natural gas liquids, and the stripped gas will be used as fuel for electricity generation, seawater desalination, and feedstock for petrochemicals, as well as reinjection for pressure maintenance to the maximum extent technically possible. The large discoveries of non-associated gas which have been made are not being developed. Saudi Arabia, having accounted for virtually all of its associated gas production and because of its very large liquid hydrocarbon reserves, can afford to take a relaxed view of the development of its non-associated gas resources and does not consider them a problem for the near-term future or an important element in its relations with industrial countries.

This is not true of most countries, particularly
Algeria, where natural gas reserves are more important than
oil and where massive investment has already been made in LNG
facilities. For Algeria, the question of natural gas pricing
is, at the time of writing (mid-1980), a highly controversial
issue and the government's stand on pricing has practically
brought gas shipments to the US to a halt and greatly reduced
shipments to European destinations. Plans to build a pipeline
overland through Tunisia and undersea to Sicily and Italy are
well-advanced and may be followed by a pipeline to Spain.

Other exporters of gas include Indonesia, Brunei,
Libya, the United Arab Emirates, and Mexico, all of them
except Mexico in the form of liquefied natural gas (LNG) and
natural gas liquids (NGLs). For the most part, however, these
exports are merely scratching the surface of the various
countries' natural gas potentials. As crude oil production
reaches a peak in some of them, there will be increasing
efforts to mount export-oriented projects. A major problem,
of course, is that with gas, unlike oil, the production and
liquefaction phases cannot be prudently undertaken and
certainly not financed without at the same time making provision for the long-term sale of the gas (a 15-20 year contract
seems to be the norm), with provision for the shipping facilities in the form of LNG carriers, reception facilities at the
port of unloading, and regasification plants. Shipment of LNG
in large quantities to the markets therefore necessarily
implies, at the commercial level, agreement on price over the
long term, a coordinated investment program encompassing the
whole chain of operations from production of gas in the
producing country to regasification of LNG in the consuming
country and involving the producing government, operating
companies, purchasing companies, the government of the
importing country, and financial institutions.

In view of the very large reserves of natural gas now
being discovered in the oil-producing countries and the much
greater difficulties involved in their development for export,
it is clear that they must be a further element in any global
energy strategy.

H.   Policies Towards Oil-Importing Developing Countries

        The policies of OPEC member countries and some other
OXDCs towards the OIDCs are now acquiring some sharpness of
definition.   The recommendations of OPEC's Ministerial
Committee on Long-Term Strategy were unanimously adopted by
the full Conference when it met in Saudi Arabia in May 1980.
Briefly, these recommendations envisage the following measures
with respect to OIDCs:

a.   OIDCs are to be guaranteed supply of all their domes-
     tic oil needs at no more than official government
     prices, receiving priority over supply to industrial
     countries.

b.   For the better off among the OIDCs (countries such as
     Brazil, Singapore, South Korea, Taiwan, and Hong
     Kong), bridging loans are to be made available at
     essentially commercial rates to cover periods of
     balance-of-payments difficulties caused partly by
     increases in oil prices.

c.   Soft loans and grants are to be made available to
     other OIDCs to provide financing for the development
     of indigenous energy sources in the longer-term, as
     well as broad-based lending on concessional terms for
     specific projects not necessarily related to energy.

        As far as pricing is concerned, OPEC policy has
consistently rejected a generalised system of two-tier pricing
for the following reasons:

a.   it renders the aid element virtually invisible,
b.   fear of leakage into other markets, and
c.   differential pricing ties the amount of aid to the
     volume of oil imports, regardless of the country's
     actual needs. It also gives the impression that high
     oil prices are chiefly responsible for the economic
     problems of the OIDCs. In fact, OPEC country aid has
     been extended to a number of countries which are
     either close to oil self- sufficiency or are them-
     selves net exporters, such as Egypt and Zaire.

Nevertheless, there has been some limited selling of oil on a two-tier price system with concessional prices to developing countries by Iraq and Venezuela. Venezuela's sales have been mainly to the Central American and Caribbean importing countries. Among the recent examples of sales to OIDCs at concessional prices is the agreement between Mexico and Venezuela to set up a system to supply the Central American and Caribbean importing countries with all of their domestic requirements of oil at prices which will, in the final analysis, equate to a discount of 33% on the official government price.

OPEC countries have recently been giving about $4-5 billion per year in official development assistance to other LDCs through a variety of national and international institutions, including notably the OPEC Fund for International Development.

Table II-10 sets out the OPEC aid record during 1976-1979. The figures shown are net disbursements of concessional aid and exclude financial flows at commercial rates. On average, it amounts to about 2% of aggregate GNP in the OPEC area. Current proposals within OPEC envisage a sharp escalation in the flow of aid to other LDCs, although no specific sum has yet been fixed. Multilateral aid is now running at about $2.5 billion per year.

An important part of this would be earmarked for the development of energy resources in other LDCs with emphasis on exploration for hydrocarbons. This proposal runs parallel to the proposal put forward by the World Bank for the creation of a separate affiliate, which would be financed partly by industrial countries through the World Bank itself and partly by OPEC member countries. Its funds would be exclusively devoted to the development of indigenous energy resources in developing countries.

At the time of writing (mid-1980), it is an open question whether the two proposals can be fused, but it is indisputable that this is one area where the interests of industrial countries and OXDCs fully coincide. The industrial countries, by assisting LDCs to develop their indigenous energy resources, will free up oil supplies from the OPEC area and thereby increase import availability as well as reduce pressure on price. The OPEC countries similarly have an interest in assisting other LDCs to become as close to energy self-sufficiency as possible, since this would reduce their need for economic aid and would also attenuate the pressure on supplies from OPEC countries that wish to lower production rates in order to conserve.

TABLE II-10

NET DISBURSEMENTS OF OFFICIAL DEVELOPMENT ASSISTANCE
BY OPEC COUNTRIES

	1976	1977	1978	1979
	(US$ million)			
TOTAL Bilateral and Multilateral	5,586.8	5,846.8	4,344.0	4,708.2
Bilateral Aid in:	4,532.8	3,887.5	2,970.4	3,519.7
Europe	14.9	5.0	n.a.	n.a.
Latin America	9.6	—	n.a.	n.a.
Africa	1,535.7	1,428.3	n.a.	n.a.
Middle East	1,337.4	1,253.3	n.a.	n.a.
Other Asia	1,464.8	510.7	n.a.	n.a.
Others	170.4	690.2	n.a.	n.a.
Multilateral Aid through:	1,054.0	1,959.3	1,373.6	1,188.5
Non-OPEC Agencies & Funds	222.8	214.9	n.a.	n.a.
Arab/OPEC Agencies & Funds	831.2	1,744.4	n.a.	n.a.

I. Conditions for New Dialogue Between Producers and North

From the outset, producing countries have insisted that any discussion of energy with the industrial countries should be linked to discussion of other problems of developing countries and issues between North and South. Thus, to quote again from the Algiers Declaration,

The Sovereigns and Heads of State declare that, parallel with and as a counterpart to the efforts, guarantees and commitments which the OPEC Member Countries are prepared to make, the developed countries must contribute to the progress and development of the developing countries through concrete action and, in particular, to achieve economic and monetary stability, giving due regard to the interests of the developing countries.

In this context, they emphasise the necessity for the full implementation of the program of action adopted by the United Nations General Assembly at its Sixth Special Session.

In discussing the conditions for an international conference in which energy would be discussed, the Algiers Declaration stated that:

The agenda of the aforementioned Conference can in no case be confined to an examination of the question of energy. It evidently includes the questions of raw materials of the developing countries, the reform of the international monetary system, and international cooperation in favour of development in order to achieve world stability.

The reference was, of course, to the conference which became known as the Conference on International Economic Cooperation or the North-South Dialogue of Paris. The question of linkage touches upon a whole series of issues between North and South, chief among them being commodity price stabilisation, aid commitments by developed countries, implementation of an effective food program, the transfer of technology, access to industrialised countries' markets for the manufactures of developing countries, protection against the depreciation of financial assets held by OPEC countries in the industrialised ones, the security of those financial assets, and the reform of the international monetary system.

It was evidently unrealistic to hope to ram through reforms on all these issues on the back of the relatively limited "guarantees and commitments which the OPEC Member Countries are prepared to make." The CIEC Conference ended in failure, although participants claimed to have made progress

in the sense of gaining deeper insight into each other's
points of view. Nevertheless, OPEC's position has hardened in
the ensuing years, partly because the industrial countries
appeared to have made a reasonably comfortable adjustment to
the higher level of prices of 1973-74; partly because the
problem of recycling funds was overcome without major difficulties; and partly because they saw little possibility of any
major concession being made on the part of the industrial
countries who believed that competition and inflation would
erode the price of oil over a period of time. In addition,
the absorptive capacity of OPEC Member Countries themselves
proved greater than anyone anticipated. Hence what had seemed
to be problems requiring an urgent solution turned out to be
manageable. OPEC discovered that it had less leverage than it
had believed, but also that the industrial North was much more
capable of absorbing large price increases than had been
thought.

The second price explosion of 1979-80 has not caused
anywhere near the same degree of alarm as felt in 1973-74,
although in absolute terms the increase has been greater and
the difficulties of recycling may not prove to be so easily
managed.

J. The Allocation of Supplies

In an increasingly tight market, which is the
situation generally anticipated for the mid to late 1980s, it
seems quite possible that OPEC may feel constrained to
allocate supplies of crude oil internationally if the pricing
mechanism does not by itself clear the market. One of the
reasons why there should be doubt about the ability of the
pricing mechanism to function is the lack of easily
substitutible supplies for crude oil and an absolute need for
oil if economic growth is to continue. To some extent, the
doubt stems from the situation engendered in 1979 at the
height of the Iranian supply crisis when most of the
industrial nations were fully supplied with crude, mainly at
contract or official government prices, while some developing
countries had difficulty obtaining sufficient crude supplies
or could only obtain sufficient supplies at the spot market
price which was well above official government prices (at
times, about twice as high as the Saudi Arabian official
government price).

It now appears that OPEC member countries may be embarking on an embryonic system of supply allocation. As part of its long-term strategy, OPEC has, as mentioned above, agreed that supplies to developing countries at the official government price should be guaranteed by the organisation, and that a mechanism should be established in order to implement this recommendation. Thus, supplies to LDCs would take priority over supplies to industrial countries in times of shortage. This means, of course, that any shortfall would have to be administered by reducing the amounts of oil available to one or more industrial countries, presumably through a central coordinating office. As far as is known, no steps have yet been taken to establish such a mechanism. But if the guarantee is to work, then some such body would have to be in place, before any supply crisis were to arise again or ad hoc measures were hastily worked out.

Along the same lines, the Venezuelan/Mexican agreement (also referred to above) allocates supplies at a certain price to countries of Central America and the Caribbean. The allocation covers domestic requirements of petroleum only and does not include oil required for processing and re-export, nor for international bunkers at certain points such as the Panama Canal. However, it does involve establishing what domestic requirements are, and this means that some kind of coordinating body must be created to work out the mechanics of the system.

Obviously, allocation of supplies in favour of a given set of consumers is not likely to raise vigorous protest from them, although there is probably room for dispute on the part of those who believe they should receive more. Allocation away from another set of consumers is, however, a different matter. As far as is known, there has as yet been no protest, formal or informal, on the part of industrial countries with respect to the implications of allocation in favour of the LDCs at their expense. Presumably such protests will not be long in coming, if and when the threat of an allocation system appears more imminent and more real than at present, because it is a matter which could be interpreted as affecting national security in the consuming countries. If there is general acceptance among industrialised countries that the aggregate global supply cannot be rapidly expanded, then it would seem that there might be room for exporters and

importers to discuss the mechanics of supply allocation, at
least on an ad hoc basis and for a limited period of time.
Some thought should be devoted to tackling this problem before
it is too late for anything to be done about it. It scarcely
needs saying that, should producer-exporters resort to a
supply allocation scheme on a global basis, the scope for
serious conflict with the industrial importing countries is
almost without limit.

3. INDUSTRIALISED COUNTRIES

A. Introduction

The strong economic growth of the industrialised
countries during the 1950s and 1960s was fuelled by cheap
abundant energy. Domestic coal production gave way to low-
cost oil, either domestic as in North America or imported as
in Western Europe and Japan. Oil production in developed and
developing countries and its pricing, shipment, refining, and
marketing were controlled by international oil companies which
were typically US, British, Dutch, and French. The growth in
the international trade and consumption of oil continued at a
rapid pace during the two decades. Reliable access to cheap
imported oil was scarcely doubted.

This complacency was upset in the 1970s. Industrialised countries now face an era of high-cost oil, whether
domestic, as in the North Sea and the frontier and heavy oils
of North America, or imported. Production pricing and increasingly destination of oil exports from OXDCs are now
controlled by their own national oil corporations. These
countries seek further control over downstream operations at
home and abroad. Meanwhile the major oil companies have lost
their dominance in the international market and their role as
wholesalers to third parties. They are joined in the market
by an array of other purchasers, including refiners, traders,
and national oil companies of industrialised countries. The
growth in international oil trade has virtually disappeared.
So has reliable long-term access to imported oil.

From the viewpoint of industrialised countries, the
decade of the 1980s remains fragile. These countries are
faced with essentially three dangers: short-term oil supply
disruptions; continued medium-term reliance on oil imports;

and long-term depletion of world oil supplies entailing a delicate management of the transition to new energy sources. The dangers are evident.

Faced with such concerns, the industrialised countries are forced to take into consideration the strategic nature of oil in their economies. Today there is an over-riding concern expressed by all the industrialised countries for secure and assured supplies of oil at what they see as reasonable prices. This is part of the current concern over high inflation and unemployment: stagflation. The energy problem, while not the sole cause, is a key component especially with such large outward flows of money to pay for oil imports.

Conservation and accelerated development of new and renewable energy sources are cures for the long-term transi-tion. In the short-term the industrialised countries are faced with the need to deal with potential crises before the transition can take place. For oil, such efforts include demand restraint, emergency sharing arrangements, stockpiling, and import target ceilings.[a] In times of more acute crises, there have also been favourable responses from the OXDCs, in the form of short-term production increases.

B. Energy Diversity of the Industrialised Countries

Part and parcel of the concerns of industrialised countries is that they have diverse interests. Their energy supplies may range in source from complete self-sufficiency to utter dependence on imports. These differing degrees of import dependence are true not only for oil but also for other energy forms. This diversity itself can create strains and even divisiveness among industrialised countries themselves.

The United States has a fundamental concern with world strategic relations, above all with the Soviet Union. It is a nation rich in natural resources and yet woefully dependent on imported oil since the 1970s. Its imports repre-sent about one-quarter of international oil trade. This dependence is evidently detrimental to its economic and stra-tegic strength. It has a vital interest in the stability of the Middle East, where it has the dilemma of supporting different foreign policies and economic aims: containment of

Soviet designs, support for Israel, and secure long-term access to oil supplies. High-cost oil imports hurt its international financial balance, except to the extent that it can entice back petrodollars at attractive (high) interest rates and can export economic and military goods and services. Oil imports also weaken the US's political and strategic freedom to manoeuvre. A creative US energy policy is a top priority concern for all industrialised countries. A solution can only be achieved through the obvious two-pronged policy of improved conservation and accelerated development of energy resources.[b]

Both Canada and Australia are rich in natural resources. Both are federated states where ownership of natural resources is an issue between the federal Government and the provinces or states, and this has far-reaching implications for the formation of energy policies.[c]

Canada is energy self-sufficient though it has become a net oil importer. Its production of conventional light and medium Western crude oils is perceived to have reached a plateau, and medium-term prospects are for increasing net oil imports. However, the longer-term prospects for oil are good, as production from frontier offshore oil, heavy oil, and synthetic oil from tar-sands looks very promising. Moreover, the potential for other energy resources is large, particularly gas as well as coal, hydro, and uranium.

Australia is sitting on a power-house of coal and could become a very large exporter; it is rich in natural gas; and it produces about 70% of its oil consumption. On balance it is a substantial net energy exporter.

New Zealand has a relatively small economy, and its energy strength lies in hydroelectricity, gas, and condensate. It imports most of its oil but is making efforts to reduce this dependency.

South Africa's energy strength lies in coal, and it looks likely to become a large exporter. It has restrained its demand for oil imports for strategic reasons and relies heavily on synthetic oil from coal.

At the other end of the scale is <u>Japan</u> which has very small known domestic energy resources. So it is the world's second largest importer of oil and also a large importer of coal and gas. It is accelerating efforts to find indigenous offshore hydrocarbon resources, but a major concern is the issue of jurisdiction over such resources with neighbouring countries. It has pursued an active nuclear power program, but that is way behind official hopes. Present prospects are that Japan is likely to remain dependent on large oil imports, which it will have to finance through its strong export sector. With the demise of the third party oil market, Japan has perforce reshaped its oil import conduit in 1979 from reliance on major oil companies to Japanese trading companies. Japan meanwhile has entered into the high-priced spot oil market. To alleviate its worst anxieties about its dependence on oil in an uncertain future, Japan has adopted policies of building significant oil stocks.

To diminish its energy dependence on a relatively few Middle Eastern countries, Japan is pursuing policies of diversifying its oil import sources (i.e., Indonesia and PR China) and substituting imports of other energy forms from a range of countries. It has created the Japan National Oil Corporation (JNOC) to strengthen oil and gas exploration efforts abroad and has encouraged private Japanese interests to do likewise.

Countries within <u>Western Europe</u> are not homogenous in economic, social, or cultural structure. Some countries such as FR Germany, Sweden, and Switzerland have high per capita income, and others such as Turkey and Yugoslavia have much lower ones and for some purposes are grouped with the developing countries. Economic wealth is also concentrated. Just four countries (France, FR Germany, Italy, and the United Kingdom) account for two-thirds of GNP in Western Europe and indeed 28% of that in all OECD countries.

From an energy viewpoint there is an utter diversity of sufficiency in energy resources within Western Europe. Seven countries are highly import-dependent, importing over three-quarters of their energy supplies: Belgium, Denmark, Greece, Ireland, Italy, Luxembourg, and Portugal. Another eight import more than half their supplies: they include the two large economies France and FR Germany as well as Austria, Spain, Turkey, and the hydro countries Finland, Sweden, and

Switzerland.   This group includes some of the strongest
economies and one of the weakest (Turkey).   There are just two
more countries which import more than one-quarter of their
supplies: Iceland (strong in domestic hydro and geothermal
energy) and Yugoslavia (strong in domestic lignite, hydro, and
some oil and gas).   There are also significant differences in
capital stock and energy end-use between these countries.
Nevertheless, Western European countries have banded together
politically, economically, and for defence through a number of
international organisations.

One Western European country imports less than one-
quarter of its total requirements: the United Kingdom, which
is self-sufficient in energy other than hydrocarbons and is
heading rapidly for self-sufficiency in oil and gas (though it
imports North Sea gas from Norway).   Finally two countries are
net energy exporters: Netherlands and above all Norway.   Both
show concern to extend the life of their hydrocarbon reserves.
The Dutch gasfields are mature and could decline in output,
and exports are being phased out.   Rotterdam is also the Euro-
port and key port of entry to the energy infrastructure of
Europe.   Norway has just opened offshore areas north of 62°
for exploration; this is an untouched, technologically difficult frontier region of unknown prospects, for which fingers
are crossed in hope.

All Western European countries have a fundamental
interest in reducing their vulnerability to supply disruptions.   They are seeking ways of reducing their dependence
through increased energy conservation and production.   Britain
and Norway are now consolidating their successes in finding
and developing oil and gas in the North Sea.   European efforts
are now gearing up for offshore exploration in frontier areas
such as north of 62°, west of the Shetland Islands, and the
Western approaches, and are continuing in the Mediterranean
Sea.   Onshore prospects do not look likely to yield significant bonanzas.   All new fields reduce import dependence for
the successful nations, but this leaves open the policy issue
of how far these successes directly benefit other Western
European countries in terms of secure long-term access.   There
has been great debate how far North Sea oil policies should be
determined on national or regional criteria.

Meanwhile, West European countries are seeking to develop other energy sources. But there are serious constraints of a political, social, and environmental nature to accelerated development of conventional energy sources. It is not easy to reverse decisions of the 1960s and reopen or start new coalmines in countries which have dismantled their coal industry. There are physical and environmental barriers to further substitutional expansion of new hydro sites. Some governments have pursued the nuclear power option but are encountering much public opposition.

C. Institutional Efforts to Coordinate Industrialised Countries' Energy Policies

i. OECD

Industrialised countries quite early on made an effort to deal in a concerted manner with energy policy. Shortly after World War II, the OEEC (OECD's predecessor) set up a system of emergency-sharing for coal allocation. Efforts were also made within OECD prior to 1973 to set up a system for emergency oil allocation and energy policy coordination.

ii. EEC

The EEC's first organisation was the European Coal and Steel Community (ECSC), and since the ECSC's inception the EEC has worked towards a common energy policy. The European Commission, however, does not seek to have everything in the energy sector regulated on a centralised basis at the Community level. The largest part of the Community's energy strategy can only take place on a national level. Thus the Commission aims at coordinating and supplementing efforts of national governments with Community-wide measures.[d]

iii. IEA

The Arab oil embargo and the jump in international oil prices in 1973-74 led to the Washington Energy Conference in February 1974, and the creation in November 1974 of the International Energy Agency (IEA). This is an autonomous body within the OECD, established to implement the International Energy Program. Its membership has risen and now comprises 21

out of the 24 OECD members.[*]   IEA countries account for some
93% of developed countries' energy consumption and 60% of the
world's consumption. The IEA has the roles of i) promoting
energy conservation and the enhanced development of secure
energy supplies and ii) ensuring the adequate distribution of
oil supplies in an emergency.

Basic elements of IEA members' cooperation on an
International Energy Program include:

a. cooperation to reduce excessive dependence on oil
    through energy conservation, development of alterna-
    tive energy sources, and energy RD&D;

b. an information system on the international oil market
    and consultation with oil companies;

c. cooperation with oil-producing and other oil-consuming
    countries, with a view to developing a stable inter-
    national energy trade as well as rational management
    and use of world energy resources in the interests of
    all countries; and

d. a plan to prepare against risk of major disruption of
    oil supplies and to share available oil in event of
    emergency.

It has established a useful oil market information
scheme and over 40 cooperative RD&D projects covering
conservation, coal technology, nuclear and fusion power,
hydrogen production, and renewable energy sources (including
solar, geothermal, biomass, ocean, and wind).

IEA also functions as a consultative organ with a
clear mandate on substantive energy issues. Such work has led
to a process of understanding and cooperation on an area of

[*]   Australia, Austria, Belgium, Canada, Denmark, FR Germany,
      Greece, Ireland, Italy, Japan, Luxembourg, Netherlands,
      New Zealand, Norway, Portugal, Spain, Sweden, Switzerland,
      Turkey, United Kingdom, and the United States. The other
      three OECD countries are Finland, France, and Iceland,
      while Yugoslavia has associate status.

concern to industrialised countries. It is a process by which countries can bring public pressure to bear on each other on energy policy, following guidelines outlined in treaty obligations. While France is not a member of IEA, it receives its information and has an input by way of the EEC and OECD.

D.   The Second Oil Shock, 1979-80

After the first shock of international oil price increases of 1973-74, most industrialised countries were lulled into complacency by the subsequent erosion in real oil prices and more comfortable oil market to 1978. It took the second oil shock of 1979-80 to awaken the consciousness of decision-makers in these countries to the pressing nature of energy-related issues, particularly oil.

It is true that governments of these countries as a whole were in general agreement in the mid-1970s on the likelihood of ever-increasing difficulties in obtaining energy supplies from the mid-1980s onwards. This was reflected in the IEA Governing Board's communiqué in October 1977: the world, it said, is confronted with the serious risk that in the 1980s it will not have enough oil or other energy available "at reasonable prices" unless present energy policies are strengthened. Such dangers, it felt, would lead to severe world economic, social, and political repercussions. It said that member countries must help reduce this risk by strong and sustained policy to make effective use of energy resources, while emphasising less depletable energy sources; that member countries should act promptly on energy policies; and that their policy response should be concerted. At that 1977 meeting, the Governing Board first introduced a target ceiling on IEA oil imports. Import ceilings were also set up within the EEC.

But the international oil market turned slack in 1978. The expressions of concern for the energy future by industrialised countries' governments in 1977 gave way to a sense of relief.

In contrast to this slackening, the supply and demand balance in early 1979 was precarious. The Iranian oil disruption broke up the complacency of industrialised countries and heralded the arrival of the supply constraints of the 1980s.

It brought home the message to industrialised countries of their alarming dependence on increasingly uncertain oil supplies. It highlighted the difference between a crisis of supply and one of rapid real price increases.

In 1979 other OXDCs increased output towards capacity to help ease the crisis. Meanwhile, oil consumption and stockbuilding in industrialised countries grew apace. That spring IEA countries agreed to reduce demand on world markets by 5% from anticipated "pre-Iran" levels. This action was matched by similar agreement by EEC countries (i.e., including France). At the Tokyo summit of the Seven and the EEC summit in June 1979, the participating countries reaffirmed these actions by agreeing i) to oil import targets for individual countries, and ii) to discourage trading on the oil spot market which was overheating.

Both IEA countries and the Seven summit countries also agreed to a set of principles on energy pricing, conservation, development of coal trade, expansion of nuclear capacity, RD&D, and the development of alternative sources of energy. IEA countries agreed to a yearly review of their progress in achieving long- term aims and commitments.[e]

Despite all these measures aimed at concerted action, there was strong competition for oil. International oil prices surged during 1979, pushed upwards by both the momentum and uncertainty of the Iranian situation and by panic buying. Oil companies and traders bought heavily on the spot market at prices approaching $40 per barrel (i.e., several dollars above official export prices) in an effort to replace oil previously available through traditional supply channels. FR Germany, Japan, and Switzerland were able to buy oil with their strong currencies. Transactions at spot price grew rapidly to become 25-30% of international oil trade, as opposed to the 3-5% previously characteristic of the spot market. Meanwhile, the differentiation between long-term and spot deals became increasingly blurred in oil supply contracts.

The US imposed a $5 entitlement program in May 1979 to entice back Caribbean oil which they believed was being diverted from them to the more profitable Rotterdam market.

Competition thus led to a doubling of oil prices during 1979. This contributed to lower economic growth and higher inflation and unemployment, while it added no new oil to the market. It only highlighted the weaknesses of the industrialised countries to deal with rapid real price increases, for which no policy or emergency mechanism existed.[f]

E. Impact of Oil Price Increases on Industrialised Countries' Economies, 1979-80

The rise in international oil prices during 1979-80 contributed adversely to the overall level of prices, balance-of-payments, and economic activity in the industrialised (and other oil-importing) countries. The OECD ministerial communiqué of June 1980 suggested the likelihood that by end-1981 "the direct and indirect effects of the oil price rise will be to pull real income in the OECD area down $400 billion, more than 5%, below what it would otherwise have been. They will also push inflation up by several percentage points and swing the balance-of-payments to a deficit of about $75 billion in 1980 compared to a $10 billion surplus in 1978. For the developing countries, added to the depressing effects of the oil price increase, there will be the impact of the slowdown in the OECD economies which constitute their principal markets."[g]

i. Inflation

Taking into account price increases of oil produced outside the OXDCs, the IMF estimates that the direct impact on the general level of prices in oil-importing countries from 1978 to 1980 might be about $4\frac{1}{2}$%.[h] This pass-through could take about a year to be completed. In addition, there are indirect (secondary) effects of the oil price increases. These include (a) price increases which result from higher wage demands subsequent to higher retail oil prices and (b) price decreases for non-oil goods which may possibly result from lower economic activity induced by the oil price increases. Moreover, prices of energy products other than oil have typically risen parallel to those of oil.

Hence, the total impact on the overall level of prices is considerably greater than the direct impact of oil

import prices themselves. Inflation in oil-importing
countries is passed on in prices of exports of goods and
services to developing countries including OXDCs. Inflation
in industrialised countries hurts everyone; this pleases no
one and creates conflict in matters of North-South trade.

At the OECD ministerial meeting in June 1980, it was
noted that priority will be given to containing the current
surge of inflation "which has resulted mainly from the external shock of higher oil prices." It would be a serious error
to relax tight monetary and fiscal policies until the current
surge in inflation has demonstrably been brought under control
and the consequences of higher oil prices are fully absorbed.

At that meeting the OECD Secretary-General stated
that "the policies we shall have to follow to cope with our
inflation and energy problems are bound to make life more difficult for the developing countries.... We must be concerned
lest the required adjustments tax the fragile economic,
social, and political systems of these countries beyond the
breaking point. Paradoxically, action to mitigate the impact
of slowed OECD growth on developing countries is more difficult, in the current circumstances, but it is very much in our
own economic--and wider political--interests to do all we can
to lighten the load on the developing countries." The immediate policy priorities are clear, he continued:

- We must keep our markets open.
- We must be ready if need be to strengthen the financial
  system to cope with the expanded financing needs of the
  developing countries.
- We must increase our aid, particularly to the poorer
  developing countries.

ii. Reduced Economic Growth

The rise in oil prices from 1978 to 1980 has raised
the export earnings of OPEC countries by about US
$170 billion. Of that amount, the IMF estimates that the
industrialised countries would absorb something like
$155 billion.[h] This diversion of industrialised countries'
purchasing power into oil imports will be deflationary on
their real economic activity. As a rough guide to the size of
the direct deflationary impact, the increase in their current

account deficits (goods, services, and private transfers) during this period will be about $80–85 billion. To this should be added the short-term deflationary effect of domestic oil price increases. Together, they are estimated by the IMF to represent a direct impact of about 2% of GNP in oil-importing countries. In addition, there are short-run multiplier effects of a deflationary nature. However, for some countries this estimate may be too high, to the extent that they use funds recycled by OXDCs to international markets.

Globally the oil-importers' deficits are the counter-part of the surpluses of the capital-surplus oil-exporters. Although each oil-importing country has powerful reasons for wanting to expand exports and restrain imports, they cannot all succeed simultaneously while the oil surpluses persist. The attempt to do so through uncoordinated domestic deflation-ary policies will slow world economic growth even more. Because of their weight in the world economy, the World Bank advocates that industrialised countries should maintain growth to the extent that this is compatible with addressing problems of inflation, recognising that this involves large deficits.[i]

There is a great disproportion between different groups of countries, in as much as industrialised countries have great ability to consume oil, while not all OXDCs have the ability to buy a balancing value of goods and services. The additional flow of saving to the OXDCs that cannot be used domestically in the immediate future must be recycled effi-ciently, so as to offset the decrease in saving and to sustain investment in the rest of the world. The net short-run impact will be deflationary for the world as a whole and more so for the oil-importing countries. In the longer-run, adjustment of investment spending will occur, and exports of goods and services to OXDCs will take place. Both effects will reduce the initial deflationary effect of the oil price increases.

Oil-importing countries must tackle problems of adjustment among themselves, caused by their differing depen-dence on oil imports and their differing ability to attract foreign capital. Adjustment to oil price increases worsens the tendency to stagflation in industrialised countries. Workers resist a reduction in real income by demanding infla-

tionary wage increases.   Government attempts to moderate
inflation through monetary restraint may lead to recession, as
real interest rates are forced up and investment falls.

Global economic adjustment in the 1980s is generally
expected to prove more difficult than during 1974-78.   First,
as noted by the World Bank, capital surpluses of some OXDCs
could stay at a high level for longer than in 1974-78, because
a) OXDCs may pursue more conservative development programs and
hence expand imports less rapidly than previously and b) the
real price of oil is widely thought likely to rise.   Second,
the prospects for capital flows are less favourable.   Third,
the industrialised countries face more serious difficulties
than during the mid-1970s.   No quick economic recovery can be
expected.   Governments have decided that inflation must come
down before rapid growth may be resumed, and that deflationary
measures must be pursued.   Productivity has slowed sharply for
reasons including incomplete adjustment to higher energy
costs, sluggish investment, and a mismatch of skills in the
labour market, which cannot be rectified easily.

iii.   Current Account Deficits

A sustained recovery of the world economy from the
slowdown expected during the next few years will in the World
Bank's view depend largely on policies pursued in three areas
of international concern: energy, trade, and capital flows.
It notes that all economies will have to adapt to higher
energy prices.   The long-term outlook is uncertain, but a
prudent energy policy should assume that real energy prices
will rise for the foreseeable future.   What happens to prices
will be determined by trends in energy conservation and production.   It also comments that most industrialised countries
will run current account deficits in 1980.   How they respond
to these deficits will largely determine the climate for world
trade.   If they all simultaneously attempt to restrain imports
while boosting exports, shrinking markets for each others'
exports will defeat their purpose, and world trade and output
will suffer, as happened in acute form in the 1930s.   Avoiding
an excessive slowdown in world trade and output in the early
1980s requires that industrialised countries run larger
deficits, and for longer.

OECD ministers agreed in June 1980 that "member countries, as a group, will have to accept a large but diminishing current account deficit, corresponding to their share of the counterpart of the OPEC surpluses, for some time to come. All countries will have to pursue policies designed to reduce inflation and to promote structural adaptation to higher energy prices. Those countries which have no difficulty in external financing should refrain from taking policy measures specifically aimed at reducing current account deficits."

The present size of current account balances and the prospect for their continuation raises important issues for global financing. In the IMF's view, the main financial problem could be the recycling of funds from the major financial markets to the smaller industrial countries as well as OIDCs. Much of this recycling has been done through medium-term loans by commercial banks. This worked well in the past but could be constrained in the future. While the current account balances of major industrial countries may not be a source of concern for recycling, the smaller industrial countries may need to make a prompt start to a medium-term adjustment of their economic structure, in order to finance their current account deficits. Industrialised countries have a large combined deficit which is expected to remain large for a number of years. Attempts by any one country to cut its deficit can only increase the deficit of other countries.

F.   Recent Energy Strategies of Industrialised Countries

In May 1980 EEC's European Council[j] passed a resolution on Energy Policy Objectives for 1990, while in June 1980 first the OECD ministerial meeting and then the Seven agreed on some comparable energy policy objectives. The comparability is not surprising, given that four of the Seven are EEC members and, except for France, all are IEA members. Moreover, all EEC and IEA countries are members of OECD.

i.   Energy Pricing Policies

Having said that "the oil price increases in 1979-80 are severely damaging the world economy" and stressed "the serious damage that would be done by further large and sudden oil price increases," the OECD meeting in June 1980 and the

preceding meetings of the EEC and IEA stressed reliance on the
price mechanism.   The EEC said that consumer energy prices
should "reflect" the world market, taking account of longer-
term trends, and that one determinant should be the cost of
replacing and developing energy resources.   The Seven stated
that domestic prices for oil should "take into account"
representative world prices.

Energy pricing policies in industrialised countries
are complex problems. Oil-importing industrialised countries
are almost all pledged to using the price mechanism as part of
their energy policies.   But such a tool, as with taxes,
tariffs, and quotas, is linked to a range of domestic
policies. At least one Western government has fallen due to
this issue. Indeed, some believe that taxes and use of the
price mechanism are detrimental to the fight against inflation. Yet there can be little doubt that energy prices which
reflect the long-run replacement costs of oil would be
extremely useful in solving the energy problem.

ii. Official Stockpiling

Industrialised countries have stockpiled crude oil
and products, often as part of treaty obligations which set
legal minima.   Official stocks are seen as a buffer from
crisis. But, as said earlier, rapid stockbuild can help force
up prices.   Indeed it may lead to undue confrontation when
seen as a political lever. Given the strategic nature of such
stocks, they would presumably be rarely run-down.   The
stockbuild places an upward pressure on the market, however
inevitable it may be.   Panic buying by oil importers can hit
international trade in time of crisis. Equally severe are the
similar pressures on oil supplies from consumer stockbuilding,
such as the topping up of gas tanks.

Concerted and constructive stock management policies
are central to both good crisis management and good relations
with OXDCs.   For example, IEA and EEC governments in December
1980 advocated that oil supply deficiencies resulting from the
Iran-Iraq conflict should be met by drawing down stocks rather
than buying in an overheated spot market.

It should be added that stocks may not solve the
further problem of product imbalances.   This occurs when

refiners lack flexibility to procure their desired slate of crude oils, whose yield would match the market pattern for refined products. This leads to gluts of some products and deficits of others, with consequent storage problems.

iii. Emergency Oil-Sharing Arrangements

Stocks form part of mechanisms under the auspices of the OECD, EEC, and IEA for the emergency allocation of oil. The IEA mechanism, for example, provides for triggering the allocation of oil on the basis of consumption patterns, domestic production, and other factors, if supply should fall below 7% of a set norm. Demand restraint and stock drawdown are elements in the allocation system. Such an allocation would be quite serious in terms of both cause and effect.

The 1979 oil disruption indicated the need for measures to be worked out for shortfalls less than the 7% level. The EEC terms such a state of affairs a sub-crisis. Like the IEA, it has begun to outline both voluntary and mandatory allocation measures for such sub-crisis. In May 1980, the IEA set up yardsticks and ceilings both to manage structural change to new energy sources and to deal at short notice with a deterioration in the oil market, i.e., sub-crises of supply. Such measures are designed to permit monitoring and quick action.

iv. Oil Import Ceilings

Some constructive steps were taken by the IEA Governing Board in December 1979, which agreed to establish specific oil import targets for individual countries for 1980, tightened import goals for 1985, and agreed to rigorous monitoring. It also agreed to develop an equitable system of adjustment of targets if the oil market tightens up, and to continue coordinating their stockbuilding programs to avoid putting undue pressure on world oil supplies.

The IEA and EEC agreed separately to examine possible means for bringing more stability into oil markets, including a registration system for all international oil traders and a code of conduct for behaviour in oil trading, which would be enacted in times of erratic oil market behaviour.

The IEA countries' overall ceiling was set for 1980 at 24.5 mm b/d (or 23.1 mm b/d excluding bunkers) and for 1985 at 26.2 mm b/d (or 24.6 mm b/d excluding bunkers), compared with estimated imports of 24.0 mm b/d in 1979. The target for 1980 was easily met, given the decline in oil consumption. The target for 1985 looks achievable, provided that oil consumption in major industrialised countries continues the decline of 1979-80.   But the target is also too high, as future oil import availability to industrialised countries could be reduced by import demands of OIDCs and Eastern Europe and by possible export policies of OXDCs.

At the IEA ministerial meeting in May 1980, members saw potential for substantially under-shooting the 1985 target, by 4 mm b/d in the Secretariat's view, a view noted in June 1980 at the Venice summit meeting of the Seven.   Members agreed to continue efforts to reduce oil imports beyond 1985.

v.   Increased Energy Efficiency and Accelerated Non-oil Supplies

In mid-1980, the EEC and the Seven separately agreed on the need for improved energy conservation and accelerated supply and the use of energy other than oil.   The Seven estimated their potential at 15-20 mm b/d o.e. during the decade.

Both EEC and the Seven expected that oil would be reduced by 1990 to 40% of total primary energy consumption. The Seven expected that their collective oil consumption would be significantly below present levels so as to permit a balance between supply and demand at tolerable prices.   They also envisaged that the energy coefficient could be reduced by 1990 to 0.6, while the EEC's guideline is 0.7 or less; the difference may reflect the greater room for energy saving in North America.

Coal has become a great expectation as a substitute for oil.   The IEA in May 1979 followed up its 1978 report on Steam Coal: Prospects to 2000 by establishing its Principles for Action on Coal and setting up the Coal Industry Advisory Board, thus beginning efforts to strengthen coal trade and production.   These efforts were subsequently endorsed at the Tokyo summit of the Seven in June 1979.   In early 1980 the World Coal Study (WOCOL) was published, which advocated increases over the next 20 years in world hard coal production of 2.5-3 times and in steam coal trade of 10-15 times 1979 levels. More ambitiously, the Venice summit of the Seven expressed the intention of doubling their coal production and use by 1990, and the IEA ministerial meeting of May 1980 sought recommendations for a similar doubling.

The replacement of oil by coal to any degree requires increased expenditures for infrastructure and coal burning facilities. Industrialised countries envisage the need for the US, Australia, and Canada to build up export capability, while Western Europe and Japan would conversely build up import capability. There are serious constraints to the development of coal (see Chapter I). They include the lack of consensus on environmental issues, for example air pollution and the accumulation of CO_2 emissions in the atmosphere. It is conceivable that these constraints could rival those for nuclear energy. Despite these constraints, there is likely to be a substantial increase in coal demand and output.

The leaders of the major industrialised countries have supported nuclear energy, as stated at the Venice Summit. Indeed, French energy policy has emphasised nuclear energy as the major thrust of its effort. But the industrialised countries' aspirations have encountered a whole range of serious difficulties, and there has been no slackening of resistance to this form of energy (see Chapter I). For example, even the partial victory of the "yes" side in the March 1980 Swedish referendum has not ended opposition there and only indicated a desire to see nuclear energy be phased out.

vi.   Structural Readjustment

The future economic success of industrialised countries depends largely on how well they manage the energy problem. They are increasingly vulnerable to uncertain supplies of energy. Illustrations are the recent accident at Three Mile Island, the New York blackout, the 1979 Iranian oil disruption, and the 1980 Iran-Iraq conflict. The challenge for the 1980s will be to find effective strategies for dealing with an oil balance, in which exports from OPEC countries are at best expected to remain constant or could even decline, assuming that the present structure is here to stay. The real issue at stake for industrialised nations is how do they avoid destructive competition in the face of a tightening oil market. They have need to develop means for equitable burden-sharing.

Energy is a ubiquitous factor in the modern economy. This produces problems for the industrialised countries, because energy has for so long been taken for granted as being in sufficient abundance to permit growth. Now it must be seen as a constraint, at least for the medium-term. Such an energy-related upheaval has not taken place since the wood shortages of the seventeenth century in Europe. Great difficulties remain in convincing large segments of the population that the crisis is real. Successful conservation depends on such a realisation. In a sense, there is need to show that quality of life and reasonable expectations can still be met in a conservation-oriented world. However, there must be a change in some values. The structural change needed in the industrialised countries is very deep. But these changes are being made.

Policy solutions in most industrialised countries are perforce turning to increased energy efficiency and to the long-term possibilities for new and renewable energy forms to the extent practicable. Democracies face three severe political problems in the energy field.

The first is due to the inevitability of elections and resultant promises. The tendency is to attempt to find short-term solutions for long-term problems, in short, palliatives.

The second is the ability of interest groups to receive a hearing, which is a fundamental right in democracies. This creates a political context for energy policy in which various interests battle on energy issues. The validity of any particular interest group may or may not be correct, but such activity does complicate the process of energy decision-making.

The third and perhaps most crucial is the difficulty in improving people's understanding of energy-related issues and the need for better practices in energy use (see Chapter III.1.B).

Countries with sizeable dependence on energy imports will be concerned to have good relations with exporters, in order to keep continued and uninterrupted long-term access to imported energy at prices they consider reasonable and predictable.   Industrialised countries are likely to pursue increasing diversity of energy import sources.   They have also typically sought some degree of control over their destiny by setting up their own national oil companies and researching the merits of direct oil purchases from oil-exporting countries.   Finally, most industrialised countries now show concern for a revived dialogue with OXDCs.

G.   North-South Dialogue from Northern Viewpoint

i.   Conference on International Economic Cooperation

In 1974 the IEA appeared to most OPEC countries to symbolise the confrontation inherent in the energy crisis. But it was not intended by most IEA participants to be confrontational.   For its part, France's reluctance to parti-cipate reflected its preference to dissociate itself from the apparent confrontation and instead to pursue bilateral arrangements with OPEC countries.

These different perceptions were reinforced by the CIEC conference of 1975-77.   That conference, called at France's initiative, ended in qualified failure.   One cause was the North's reluctance to deal with all issues of concern to North-South relations.   Instead, the North preferred to discuss the issue of primary concern to itself, energy.[k]

The final report of the CIEC conference pointed out the areas of agreement and disagreement.   Regarding energy, agreement was reached on a few simpler matters:

a.   an assessment of the availability and supply of commercial energy,
b.   a recognition of the depletable nature of oil and gas and the need for transition to renewable sources of energy,
c.   the necessity for conservation and increased energy efficiency,
d.   the need to develop all forms of energy, and

e.   general conclusions and recommendations for national
     action and international cooperation in the energy
     field.

Disagreement was pointed out on the real substantive issues,
including:

a.   energy prices and OXDCs' purchasing power from energy
     export earnings,
b.   accumulated revenues from oil exports,
c.   financial assistance to bridge external payments'
     difficulties of oil-importing countries,
d.   recommendations on resources within the UN Law of the
     Sea Conference, and
e.   continuing consultations on energy.

ii.   Subsequent Efforts towards Cooperation

     Fortunately, cooperation has begun to replace confron-
tation.   Some real efforts have been made to cooperate on
non-political technical subjects.

     The 1978 IEA Workshop on Energy Data in Developing
Countries included participation by OXDCs and OIDCs.   The IEA
has a current RD&D project with Mexico in the field of geothermal energy.   The 1979 OECD report on renewable energy
technology for developing countries was also an effort to find
means of technical cooperation devoid of politics.

     The EEC has begun a concerted effort to provide
financial and technological assistance to OIDCs.   Such efforts
were embodied in the Lomé II convention of October 1979.   It
agreed on cooperation between the European Community and 58
African, Caribbean, and Pacific nations on a broad range of
issues, including the field of energy.   However, this did not
include Latin America.   In fact, EEC aid in the energy field
in absolute terms is second only to the World Bank.   In a more
political sphere the EEC is renewing efforts for a Euro-Arab
dialogue.

     At their Venice summit meeting in June 1980, seven
major industrialised countries advocated increased financial
aid for energy to OIDCs, and an international energy financing

facility to undertake it.[*]   They asked the World Bank to
examine the adequacy of the resources and mechanisms now in
place for the exploitation, development, and production of
conventional and renewable energy sources in OIDCs.   This
includes the possibility of establishing a new affiliate or
facility by which it might improve and increase its lending
program for energy activities.   They asked the World Bank to
explore its findings with oil-exporting and industrial
countries.   The Seven welcomed the Brandt Commission report
and undertook to consider its recommendations carefully.

iii.   Renewed Interest in North-South Dialogue

        There is a growing realisation that a) economic
disaster in the industrialised countries and b) the well-being
of developing countries both affect the whole world.   The
North-South dialogue in its several for is an effort to deal
amicably with issues of joint concern to both industrialised
countries and developing countries, whether they be
oil-omporters or exporters.

        In 1980 the OEDC, EEC, IEA, and the Seven separately
called for a constructive consumer-producer dialogue.   In
recent months a number of industrialised countries have
expressed increasing interest in resuming some kind of
North-South dialogue.   This looks likely to be the underlying
theme in summit meetings in 1981, including a) the mini-summit
of about 25 developed and developing countries planned for
October 1981 in Mexico City, and b) the Seven industrialised
countries' meeting of July 1981 in Ottawa.   This is all
additional to attempts to launch the UN global negotiations on
international economic cooperation for development.

        There have been many difficulties in reaching a
consensus even among industrial couontries in the field of
energy, but there has been willingness to overcome them.   A
North-South dialogue will encounter similar difficulties, but
much can be achieved if there is a comparable willingness to
solve them as among the industrialised countries.   The work

___

[*]   Canada, France, FR Germany, Italy, Japan, United Kingdom,
      and the United States.   All except France are members of
      IEA.

already begun on technical cooperation, in areas devoid of
political content, presages well for the future.

4.   CONVERGENCES AND CONFLICTS

A.   A Review of Interests--National and Global

i.   The National Energy Interests of the OIDCs

To begin with, it is basic to the national security
of most OIDCs that they have enough oil to meet the needs of
their economies. Typically, this means a quantity growing at
perhaps 6% p.a., to support their rapidly growing modern
sectors and in some cases to meet needs in their traditional
sectors that depleting woodfuels can no longer fill.   It is
also important that oil imports be made available on financial
terms which will not leave the OIDCs with crushing debt
burdens.   Most OIDCs are in the midst of a transition from
traditional fuels to more modern fuels.   At the same time,
they must soon make a transition from oil to renewable and
other more plentiful sources.   Each of them needs to learn as
soon as possible what these successor sources will be, and
whether they can shift directly from traditional fuels to
those successors without an intervening period of oil use.

ii.   The National Energy Interests of Oil Exporters

These nations would like to maximise their earnings
from oil exports.   It is not clear whether this can be done
best by changing prices frequently and in small increments to
charge what the market will bear, or by permitting prices to
fluctuate wildly as they did in the 1970s.

A second related goal is to protect the value of
their export earnings, perhaps by accepting payment in a form
whose value is maintained by large oil importers or the IMF,
and perhaps by converting such earnings into investments at
home, in industrialised countries, or in insured investments
in the Third World.

A third closely connected goal is to keep control of their oil resources--a control won only recently and hence jealously guarded. This includes control over prices, production rates, and allocation among consumers.

Fourth, oil exporters need to make a transition to the post-oil era. This means that their economies must be strong enough to withstand the reduction in earnings from oil exports. It also means that energy sources must be available to take the place of oil for internal use in these countries.

A fifth goal which they have expressed is to expand their internal oil-producing capacity. This will give them greater knowledge about and control over their oil resources.

At least some oil exporters are eager to gain access to markets in industrialised countries for their processed raw materials and manufactured exports. This includes such goods and services as oil shipping, fertilisers, and other petro-chemicals.

Several of them are concerned that demand from the industrialised countries is forcing them to produce oil at a faster pace than is warranted either by the goal of maximising oil extraction or by their economic goals. Hence, they support the idea of oil conservation especially in the large industrial countries.

Finally, oil-exporting countries and OPEC countries as a group have called for reforms in the international economic order. From time to time experts from oil-exporting countries have suggested that any negotiations on oil must be linked to such reforms.

iii. The National Energy Interests of Industrialised
      Countries

      The chief energy concern of the industrialised
countries is to have a reliable supply of oil. Some of them
hope to achieve this by securing a political commitment from
one or more producers. Others have urged that productive
capacity be expanded in their own jurisdictions, or elsewhere
in the world.

      Another energy goal common to most of these countries
is to achieve orderly prices for oil. Orderly prices
according to some views have meant cheap prices. But
increasingly, the view is heard that orderly prices may mean
rising real prices along a trend line that avoids sharp fluctuations.

      A third energy goal is to make a non-traumatic trans-
ition from oil to renewable and other more plentiful energy
sources.

iv. The Common Energy Interests of the World Community

      The first goal shared by all nations is to keep the
world economy performing well. To do so requires several
successful efforts.

      The second goal shared by the community of nations is
to make the transition from oil to renewable and other more
plentiful sources of energy before physical shortages of oil
have inflicted damage on the world economy.

      The third common goal is to resolve our common energy
problems in ways that protect the world's ecosystems, notably
the planet's forests, soils, streams, lakes, oceans, and air.

B. Converging and Conflicting Approaches to these
    National and Global Goals

      Insofar as international actions are concerned, four
steps are essential:

    i. to ensure an adequate supply of oil to each nation,
   ii. to keep the prices of oil orderly,

  iii. to keep the trading system open, and
   iv. to keep the foreign exchange earnings of capital-
        surplus countries recycling throughout the global
        economy.

In addition, actions by nations (particularly the largest economies) to avoid inflation and recession are critical to the health of the world economy.

We will briefly examine each of these four international actions, and identify those approaches to each which are likely to cause conflict, and those where the national interests of the several parties are likely to converge.

i. Ensured Supply of Oil

In the medium to long-term, the least contentious approach to a reliable supply of oil is to expand world oil production capacity. Judging from the stated position of the several parties, oil-exporting nations very much want to expand their capacity; clearly OIDCs would like to do the same; many industrialised countries are providing incentives to their people to do likewise; and OPEC nations have expressed preliminarily their interest in joining other nations to start a new program to help OIDCs develop their oil and other energy resources. In sum, a major program to expand world oil supply should be relatively non-controversial.

Another approach to energy supply reliability applicable to the OIDCs would be to help finance their oil imports. Even if world oil supply is adequate, a number of OIDCs may be threatened with supply shortage for want of financing to pay for oil on terms they can afford. There is no great disagreement in principle over the proposition that the world should help OIDCs finance their oil imports. One somewhat controversial proposal is that exporters should sell oil to OIDCs at world prices but on long-term credit at low interest rates (much as the US does with food under P.L. 480). Another proposal that has generated nothing but opposition among oil exporters is for them to sell oil to OIDCs at special low prices.

A very controversial approach to supply reliability is the proposal that oil producers agree to an international covenant that limits their unilateral control over oil products and exports. OPEC countries, long frustrated by having their oil in foreign hands and only recently having won control, are exceptionally sensitive about any proposals which would reduce their unilateral control over their oil.

The method of ensuring supply reliability being followed by the largest industrial oil importers is to make bilateral arrangements with individual oil exporters. For example, the largest importer, the US, gives particular attention to its bilateral relationships with Saudi Arabia and Mexico. Likewise, Japan and the several European countries rely on bilateral understandings with oil suppliers. There are two defects in such an international system. First, it is not clear that any of these bilateral understandings would last in the event of a serious shortfall in supply. One can anticipate keen competition in such an event, and it is likely that producers would tend to review their own positions anew, seeking to serve their own self-interest, rather than considering themselves bound in perpetuity by past understandings. The second defect is that a system of competing bilateral understandings tends to leave small importers and financially weak countries out of account.

The industrialised country members of the International Energy Agency have also sought to improve their oil supply reliability by agreeing among themselves on an emergency system of allocating oil in the event of a shortfall. Some industrialised countries have begun a program of stockpiling oil, but this has prompted OPEC nations to threaten retaliation because they do not wish to lose any of the leverage given them by the dependence of oil importers.

Finally, OPEC's Long Range Strategy (which is still under review) suggests that developing countries be given priority over the industrialised countries in the allocation of oil. OPEC officials are giving thought to the mechanics of an allocation system to give effect to this intention.

It is not easy to find a short-run reliable way to correct this patchwork of arrangements. Even if OPEC were willing to agree to a long-term binding guarantee not deliberately to cut supplies below a stated level, it would require an unusual degree of discipline among its members for the agreed supply level to be met.   Nevertheless, because of the importance of reliable supplies of oil, the dialogue between oil exporters and importers should not cease to search for acceptable formulae that would help.

The one step which would be effective and probably could be agreed upon is to launch a program to expand oil production capacity in OPEC and non-OPEC countries.   This would take several years to bear fruit.   Meanwhile, oil importers must live with a degree of uncertainty, a condition that could be improved relatively quickly by conservation efforts.

ii. Orderly Prices for Oil

Many experts believe that the level of oil prices is not as important as the sudden, unpredictable, and uneven pace of change.   While they accept the need and desirability of continuing increases in real prices, they believe that the inflationary impact could be substantially reduced if these price changes occurred in small, predictable increments.   It must be conceded, however, that a large strand of thought in the governments and publics of the North believes that the problem is one of absolute levels of oil prices; that the OPEC "cartel "is forcing artificially and unjustifiably high prices.   This does appear to be a declining point of view, as the weight of opinion grows that prices are in fact determined by the buyers' competition for available oil and that the official prices set by OPEC countries merely confirm what the market has already determined.

Some proposals have been made, which would help gradually to moderate prices and would have a good chance of being accepted.   These include proposals a) to cut demand for oil by conserving and by increasing the production of alternatives to oil, and b) to increase oil supplies by stepping up exploration in all prospective countries.

The most controversial proposal is that there should be multilateral negotiations of a price formula which would be binding upon oil exporters.   The reaction of these nations to such a proposal is as negative as their reaction to proposals for a negotiated formula for oil supply and for similar reasons: having only recently gained a degree of control over the prices of oil, they do not want to lose it.

OPEC countries are reviewing the merits of introducing a system of unilateral orderly increases in oil prices, linking them to the rate of inflation and growth of real GNP in industrialised countries. The formula would constitute a floor price for oil rather than a ceiling or a target. But if the ceiling is the result of competition among buyers (as suggested above), perhaps the floor price would not be far from the ceiling.

OPEC has prepared a table indicating the price at which oil would have sold, if the floor price had represented the actual price since 1974.

TABLE II-11: FLOOR FORMULA PRICE 1974-80

YEAR	INDEX (1973:100)	PRICE ($ per barrel)
1974	116.8	10.84
1975	136.5	12.66
1976	143.0	14.80
1977	164.4	15.50
1978	195.5	17.82
1979	223.8	21.19
1980	...	24.25

Note: Index is the aggregate of inflation, exchange rates and GNP changes. The base is the actual price for 1974; other prices are derived by applying index.

Source: Petroleum Intelligence Weekly, May 12, 1980, Supplement.

This clearly shows a much more orderly price progression than the prices which actually prevailed. The unilateral price formula could be of value to world economic stability, if the floor were to approximate the ceiling. Vigorous efforts by all parties to expand productive capacity of energy and to restrain demand would help ensure that it did.

iii.   An Open Trading System

If shortages and price gyrations of oil cause recession, unemployment, and foreign exchange crises, some
countries will be tempted to impose restrictions on imports.
This could trigger retaliatory trade barriers that would
greatly magnify the damage to the world economy. Even without
such oil-induced disturbances, trade barriers already exist
which are especially burdensome to developing countries that
do not have economic strength to protect themselves. Quotas
are imposed on some imports from developing countries, and so
are tariffs which escalate with the degree of processing or
fabricating. This is burdensome to countries which hope to
move from exporting raw materials to finished or manufactured
goods but find their exports of such goods penalised. Several
proposals have been made, including elimination of tariff
escalation, and rebates to developing countries of all
revenues collected from tariffs on imports from those countries. Because of rising unemployment, industrialised
countries will find it politically difficult to accept proposals which would accelerate the rate at which their workers
are displaced by imports. Tariff rebates may be less controversial, but it would be difficult to ensure that they were
not offset by matching cuts in aid programs.

Proposals have been made and partially adopted which
would support the health of the world economy by smoothing out
price swings of raw materials and ensuring to some extent that
such prices were not too low. These commodity agreements have
been difficult to operate, although there is not much opposition to them in principle.

iv.   Money Recycled Efficiently

Recent rises in oil prices together with sustained
demand will mean that total costs of oil traded internationally in 1980 will come to about $290 billion. This is
more money than oil exporters can spend in the short run.
Thus, surplus foreign exchange in 1980 (before official
transfers) in the hands of major oil exporters is estimated by
the IMF at about $115 billion. This is mostly in the hands of
half a dozen capital-surplus exporters: Saudi Arabia, Kuwait,
Qatar, UAE, Iraq, and Libya. The corresponding deficits are

basically in the industrial countries ($52 billion), some
minor OXDCs ($6.5 billion), and OIDCs ($62 billion).   Unless
these surpluses are moved quickly into use, the result will be
economically depressing, like a giant tax suddenly imposed
without matching expenditures.   Recycling can take place when
the surplus dollars are borrowed by persons or institutions
that invest them, or when the owner of the surpluses invests
them directly.   Over time, the surplus countries' demand for
imports will also reduce the surplus, but this does not help
in the short-run.   Much of the surplus will be recycled
routinely by the banks where it is deposited.   They lend it to
investors, especially in the industrialised countries.   But a
large part of the deficit is in the OIDCs.   Unless a propor-
tionately large share of the surpluses is recycled to the
OIDCs, the tax-like depressing effect would hit them and be
radiated to the rest of the world.   But banks may be reaching
the limits to which they can prudently lend to such countries,
and in many cases those countries have never established
credit in the industrialised countries' money markets.

        A number of ideas have been evolving to deal with the
recycling problem.   To begin with, the industrialised
countries could greatly expand the movement of funds to
creditworthy Third World nations, by establishing a facility
to rediscount debts of such countries held by the banking
system of industrialised countries.

        For years, ideas have been discussed involving World
Bank participation in a program to guarantee against default
the bonds of Third World countries which are placed directly
on the public bond markets of Northern countries.   Proposals
are also being discussed to expand the IMF's activities in
deficit countries.   Each of these three general approaches
would be of most use to countries which can afford to pay
commercial rates.   Except for the IMF, these sources would be
available only to countries which have established credit
ratings in international money markets.

        At least two kinds of proposals would be useful to
countries without established credit and without ability to
pay commercial rates.   One would be for an established institution such as the World Bank or IMF to make loans with very
low interest rates and long repayment periods to such
countries.   The Fund or Bank might borrow the money for those

loans directly from the surplus countries. Another approach
is represented by the OPEC staff proposal to expand the OPEC
Special Fund into an international aid agency with capitalisation of $20 billion. These are only a few of the many ideas
that have been suggested for recycling funds. The main job
will, of course, continue to be done by the private banking
system. None of these ideas is particularly controversial.
But it is by no means certain that any satisfactory program to
recycle funds will be approved, because the self-interest of
the economic powers in recycling money is not widely perceived
outside the ranks of monetary specialists.

C. The Goal of Making a Transition to More Plentiful
    Energy Sources

        The entire world shares the problem that oil and gas
will one day be depleted. It therefore shares the goal of
making a transition to renewable and other more plentiful
sources of energy before oil and gas supplies fall short.
Four actions can help in this transition: i) to conserve
energy, ii) to find more oil in order to allow more time for
the transition, iii) to find, invent, develop, and deploy
alternative energy sources, and iv) to adjust the price of oil
and other energy forms relative to one another. In addition
to these four worldwide actions, OPEC nations have a special
problem of preparing their economies for the loss of revenues
in the post-petroleum era. These five topics are discussed in
the following paragraphs.

i. Conserve Energy

        Proposals to conserve energy in the industrialised
countries enjoy widespread lip service, backed by less widespread willingness to take hard actions. Speed limits, penal-
ties on gas guzzlers, limits to space heating and cooling, and
investments in improved energy efficiency by saving oil and
gas will give the entire world more time to convert to oil's
successors. Even proposals to help capital-poor Third World
countries make such investments enjoy some popularity, because
of the growing understanding that a barrel of oil conserved in
any nation contributes to the energy security of all nations.
Even more directly, it contributes to the financial strength
of the conserving country.

ii. Find and Develop Oil and Gas

Vigorous exploration and development will not find oil and gas where it does not exist, but at least it will help find what does exist. This in turn will provide more time to make the transition to non-oil energy systems.

It is generally estimated that about as much oil remains to be found as has been found; so the search for oil is very much worthwhile. Both OXDCs and OIDCs complain that not enough is being done to expand their oil and gas production capacity. Thus proposals to expand oil production capacity, wherever in the world conditions are favourable, should be welcomed in OXDCs, OIDCs, and industrialised countries. Forward momentum is very possible on this front, as is indicated by OPEC countries' proposal for a special facility to help develop domestic energy in developing countries and the favourable response of seven industrialised countries at the Venice summit meeting.

By way of caution, if a great deal of oil is found, there will be a temptation for complacency to resume and for the transition to stop in its tracks, unless thought is given to restraining production and preventing declines in real oil prices.

iii. Find, Develop, and Deploy Alternatives

For some applications, the practical alternatives to oil and gas may be conventional energy forms such as coal, nuclear, or hydroelectricity. In others, they may be unconventional forms such as windpower, solar heat, solar cells, biogas, or gasohol. In still others, they may be improved traditional sources such as fast growing woodfuels, more efficient charcoal kilns, or improved animal traction. Any of these developments will help the world to make the transition to oil's successors. The sooner these alternative sources are put in place, the less danger there will be that oil and gas will run short and damage the world's economy, and the more oil and gas there will be left in place for non-energy purposes over the centuries ahead. Vigorous action will be needed.

To find conventional alternatives such as coal will take private incentives and, in some cases, government encouragement. To develop hydro will call for major capital inputs. To invent, develop and test non-conventional renewable technologies will take government and private RD&D efforts on a large scale. To market these technologies will take the combined and cooperative efforts of governments and private entrepreneurs. To develop and make available improved traditional energy will call for important investments by public bodies working cooperatively with local institutions and individuals.

Fortunately, there is no opposition in principle to these programs. Major obstacles are government budget restraints, lack of trust between investors and public authorities, and imperfect understanding of the common stake in the success of such programs.

iv. Prepare the Oil Exporters' Economies for the Transition

Oil exporters have needs similar to other countries in terms of expanding oil capacity, conserving oil (waste is apparent in some of these countries), and finding and deploying alternatives to oil. But oil exporters have another special transition problem: their economies have become dependent on earnings from the export of oil and gas. Their import bills for machines, food, and services have soared. At the end of the oil era they will lose the oil revenues and need other economic activities to take their place, by earning equivalent revenues or producing import substitutes. Hence one finds on OPEC nations' agenda for negotiation the goal of obtaining "free access to the markets of developed countries for refined products and petrochemicals; access to existing and new advanced technology and know-how needed by OPEC countries for development of their industries; ...the location of energy-intensive industries in areas of natural gas production in OPEC countries; ...and the lifting of trade barriers on non-oil exports from oil-producing countries" (PIW, May 12, 1980, Supplement).

v.   The Role of Prices in the Transition

Rational pricing is critical in every step of the transition from oil and gas to successor energy sources.   If prices are too low, the less accessible deposits of oil and gas will not be sought or, if found, they will not be exploited.   Secondary and tertiary production will not be pursued. Heavy oil will be left underground.   In short, the right price is important to finding more oil.   It plays an equally important role in the conservation of oil.   In many cases it cost money to save energy (insulation, new machinery, etc.).   An investor (e.g., a homeowner or a businessman) typically will calculate how much money he will save annually by investing in energy efficiency; and he will make the investment if it will pay off in a short period but not if it takes many years.   If the price of energy is high, the annual savings are greater; and so it may pay to make an investment which would not be warranted when energy prices are lower. Virtually the same calculations are at play when entrepreneurs consider investments which would replace oil.   If a solar hot-water heater is paid for in five years by saving natural gas, some may regard it as a good investment, but not if it takes 15 years.   The investment decision may depend on the price of natural gas.

Pricing is likewise important to OPEC countries' effort to prepare for the decline of oil. So long as gasoline sells for $0.12 a gallon, it is likely that their economies will quickly become deeply dependent on petroleum, making it that much harder for them to make the transition.

D.   The Goal of Preserving Earth's Ecosystems

Certain of the world's ecosystems may be threatened by the energy choices made by nations, businesses, and individuals.   Forests and other ground cover are threatened in some places by the demand for woodfuels.   Deforestation and devegetation in turn may lead to soil erosion, reduced watertables, downstream siltation, flooding, and desertification. The construction of large dams for hydroelectric power destroys river valleys and in some cases may bring waterborne diseases to a region.   Nuclear plants may lead to ocean dumping of low-level radioactive wastes, which are a threat of unknown proportions to ocean life.   They involve a) threats of nuclear accidents which may make an area uninhabitable for long periods, and b) the problem of how and where to dispose permanently of spent fuels. Finally, decisions to move to a coal economy or to synthetic liquid fuels made from coal or shale bring the likelihood of an increase in the earth's CO_2, together with a possible warming trend which could cause great dislocations on earth.

Although the issue of the earth's life systems is clearly important to all nations, it has not generated as many proposals or as much intense diplomatic interest as issues of oil price and supply or of a New International Economic Order. There would probably not be much controversy generated by proposals to protect and renew forests, to safeguard the oceans against radioactive dumping, or to study carefully the impact of building large dams. Clearly more information is needed on the problem of CO_2 and nuclear spent fuel disposal before international action can be seriously discussed. But these are energy-related issues that may profoundly affect all of us or our descendants. There is strong convergence of interest in protecting the earth's ecosystems.

E.   Maximising OPEC's Economic Gains

Each of the more pressing demands of the oil-importing and industrialised countries has been dealt with in the three preceding sections. But the oil exporters have a strong interest which has not been covered: namely to maximise their economic gains. They wish to optimise their oil revenues. They wish to protect the value of these revenues. Probably most important of all, they wish to keep control of their oil resources.

i.   To Optimise OPEC Revenues

Much more study is needed to answer the question how OPEC countries' earnings can be maximised. How far could they cut production and raise prices without causing economic damage which would harm their own earnings? Clearly the health of oil-importing countries' economies is important to them. How can prices rise, without bringing substitutes into play and harming OPEC earnings? We cannot answer these questions; but interestingly, if the OPEC Long Range

Strategy Report's index had been applied from 1973 to 1980 (as the actual price rather than the floor price), OPEC countries would have earned a cumulative $1,306 billion compared to the $1,218 billion they actually earned, an increase of $88 billion (Table II-12).

TABLE II-12:   OPEC OIL PRODUCTION AND REVENUE

Year	Production	Actual		Indexed	
		Price	Revenue	Price	Revenue
	(million b/d)	($/bbl)	($ billion)	($/bbl)	($ billion)
1973	30.9	3.39	38.2	3.39	38.2
1974	30.7	11.28	126.4	10.84	121.5
1975	27.0	11.02	108.6	12.66	124.8
1976	30.7	11.77	132.3	14.80	166.3
1977	31.0	12.88	145.7	15.50	175.4
1978	29.8	12.93	140.6	17.82	193.8
1979	30.7	18.64	208.9	21.19	237.4
1980	28.0	31.00	317.7	24.26	248.6
		TOTAL	1,218.4		1,306.0
		Difference		87.6	

Source: US Department of Energy, for production and actual price; PIW, Special Supplement, May 12, 1980 for indexed prices.

The irony is that this formula may also have been better for oil-importing nations. Although the annual cost of oil would have been greater by about $11 billion, we believe that this would have been more than offset by two factors: i) the oil price in 1980 might have been an indexed $24.26 rather than an estimated $31, and ii) the price path might have been predictable, smooth, and orderly. There might not necessarily have been any large increases in real prices, followed by declines and sudden steep rises. Less disturbance would have been caused to the global economy. Perhaps the formula may offer part of the answer to the apparent conflict between OPEC countries' desire to optimise earnings and oil-importing countries' desire for orderly pricing. But it does not resolve the conflict between OPEC countries' desire to keep unilateral control over their oil and gas and oil-importers' desire for assured supply.

ii. To Protect OPEC Revenues

The second step in optimising OPEC countries' economic welfare is to protect the value of their earnings. One of the forces which has discouraged capital-surplus exporters from producing more oil has been the fact that oil in the ground (appreciating in value) is a better investment than money (depreciating in value). It is asking too much of these exporters that they should sell more oil than necessary to cover their import needs and to hold the balance in money, unless the value of these funds can be protected.

One approach to protecting their value is to make it easy for OPEC countries to invest surplus funds in profitable ventures in industrialised countries. Some OPEC countries have shown interest in investing downstream, e.g., in shipping, refining, and distributing oil. This would also give capital-surplus countries a stake in keeping a reliable flow of oil to oil-importing countries and thereby keeping their own investment earnings healthy, a clear convergence of interests.

A second approach is to encourage OPEC countries to invest in OIDCs, where some of the highest-paying investments are to be found. The problem is that such investments may be risky. Reasons include less-developed economic infrastructure, immature money markets, unknown consumer demands, and sometimes uncertain government policies towards foreign investors. Hence OPEC countries may be unwilling to invest in OIDCs, unless means are found of sharing these special risks with other countries or international institutions, again a clear convergence.

OPEC countries are eager to put their surplus earnings into investments at home, including fertiliser plants, petrochemicals, oil refineries, and manufacturing plants. To the extent that such investments are in industries which already have unused productive capacity and therefore displace plants in the North or in OIDCs, there will be contention. This kind of problem needs to be worked out on a case-by-case basis.

Another idea for protecting surplus earnings is to pay them in bonds or other securities whose dollar value increases with the decline in the purchasing power of the dollar. A somewhat related proposal is that they be paid in SDRs. The SDR is valued according to a formula which includes the 16 leading currencies (five leading currencies as from 1981). Since a decline in value of any one of these currencies tends to be offset by corresponding gains in others among the 16 currencies, the SDR is unusually stable in value. Moreover, there is less risk that any sovereign government might freeze an OXDC's account, because the SDRs would be held on deposit with the IMF. This approach would also have the effect of strengthening the IMF's role in world banking. None of these ideas generally provoke any great opposition in principle.

Of course, even with all these proposals OPEC earnings would not be completely without risk. Insecurity is to some extent unavoidable not only for oil exporters but also for oil importers. The best one can hope for is to reduce it and make it more manageable through international cooperation.

iii. To Retain OPEC Control

The third related objective of OPEC countries is to keep control over production and pricing of oil and gas. As noted above, they are especially sensitive on this point, because of long history of foreign control. They do not regard the issue of control over oil price and volume as negotiable in any eventual dialogue with oil importers.

It was suggested above that the indexed price formula (if an actual price target rather than a floor) could help resolve the price impasse, as it would be better for all parties than what has happened. The problem is whether it will approximate the actual price.

So long as there is no major interruption in oil supply and there are efforts by major oil importers to restrain demand, there is good prospect that the floor formula will become the actual price formula because the floor price will be continually revised upwards and may press against what the market will bear. But if major cut-offs do occur and demand outstrips supply, then the actual price is likely to exceed the formula price. This will be hard to prevent, even if there were a global negotiated and "binding" obligation upon OPEC nations to restrain prices. The spot market might simply become active, and the amount of oil moving at official prices (which might indeed not exceed negotiated prices) would decline.   It is very difficult to prevent any nation or entrepreneur (oil importers as well as exporters) from charging what a hungry market will bear.

Regarding control over production levels, OPEC countries' desire to control their own resources is in conflict with oil importers' desire for an assured supply. The Brandt Commission has suggested that "oil-exporting countries... assure levels of production and agree not to reduce supplies arbitrarily or suddenly..." We believe that such an agreement is plausible if it is matched by such a commitment by oil importers to meet some of the demands of OPEC countries discussed above.

F. Prospects for a Negotiated Settlement

The convergent interests of all parties are powerful indeed. They include such basic goals as keeping national and international economies healthy, making a transition from societies based on oil to those relying on different energy sources, protecting the earth's life systems, and satisfying the special demands of oil exporters so that progress towards the other goals can proceed. The conflicts do appear formidable, although they are fewer and less important to the life and health of the world and its inhabitants. They include the strong desire of OPEC countries to keep control over oil price and production, which is to some extent in conflict with oil importers' desire for certainty of supply and orderly prices. It is conceivable that OPEC countries, having developed a floor price formula, might be willing, in exchange for concession by oil importers, to prescribe a formula for a price ceiling or for a price target where the actual price would fall within the ceiling and floor. We believe it possible that negotiations between OXDCs and oil-importing countries could develop a formula to provide some insurance to oil importers against capricious supply interruptions. Given the importance of the stake which all nations have in cooperating, it is certainly worth continuing the dialogue in search of agreement.

CHAPTER III: GLOBAL OPPORTUNITIES

This chapter discusses global opportunities in several areas, taking into account convergences and conflicts between the parties involved. There are opportunities in managing the remaining decades of oil, such as a) finding and developing oil and gas in the OIDCs, polar regions, and deep ocean water, and b) conserving oil production and consumption and improving efficiency in energy use. There are opportunities in pressing ahead with the transition from oil to other energy sources and technologies.

1. MANAGING THE REMAINING DECADES OF OIL

A. Development of Oil and Gas in the OIDCs

The development of oil and gas resources in OIDCs is one of the few areas where there is, in principle at least, a clear convergence of interest between industrialised countries, oil-exporting countries, and the OIDCs themselves. Indigenous production of oil and gas in the OIDCs benefits all countries. Industrialised countries stand to gain because additional production in the OIDCs will take some of the pressure of demand off limited supplies from exporting countries-- a consideration to be weighed in the context of OPEC's guarantee to give priority of supply to other developing countries. The oil-exporting countries stand to gain from the decreased pressure on their depleting reserves and from fewer demands for financial assistance related to oil imports of the OIDCs. And of course the OIDCs stand to gain enormously from the balance of payments relief that increased production of indigenous energy would bring (oil imports will probably account for 40% of the OIDCs' merchandise exports this year).

Exploration for oil in developing countries is very far from having responded adequately to the price rises of 1973-74 and 1979-80. There are a number of reasons for this which are set out below, but the salient statistics on the exploratory and development record before and after the 1973-74 price rises should first be recalled.

The average number of seismic party-months in OIDCs (including some countries such as Zaire and Peru which have

recently become small net exporters of oil) actually declined
by 8% during the three-year period 1976-78, as compared with
the years 1970-72, prior to the price rises. The decrease in
seismic activity was in the order of 35% for OIDCs in Africa
and 20% in Latin America, partly offset by an increase of 25%
in Asian OIDCs. Worse still, in all three areas, activity in
1978 was substantially lower than for the three-year average
1976-78, indicating still decreasing exploratory interest. In
contrast, seismic party-months in the US and Canada were at an
all-time high in 1978, up 64% over the 1970-72 annual average.
Table III-1 below sets out the relevant data in party-months.

TABLE III-1:   SEISMIC PARTY-MONTHS IN OIDCs, 1970-78[a]

OIDCs in:	1970-1972	1976-1978	Year 1978
	(average number per year)		
Africa	178	116	114
Asia	356	446	424
Latin America	601	478	394
Total	1,135	1,040	932
cf: US & Canada	3,124	4,458	5,116

[a]Oil-importing developing countries as of 1979.

It may be that exploratory interest will pick up
after the 1979-80 price increases, though this is difficult to
predict. However, in line with the geophysical exploration
trends shown above, there has been a decline in exploratory
(wildcat) drilling in African and Latin American OIDCs since
1970, though this has been more than offset by a substantial
increase in activity in Asian OIDCs. In absolute terms, the
figures remain depressingly low: 339 wells drilled in 1970 and
390 in 1978, one thirty-fifth of the number drilled in Canada
and the United States. Table III-2 shows exploratory wells
drilled in OIDCs by major area in 1970 and 1978:

13. DEVELOPED AND DEVELOPING COUNTRIES: GEOPHYSICAL ACTIVITY, SEISMIC PARTY-MONTHS,1970-1978

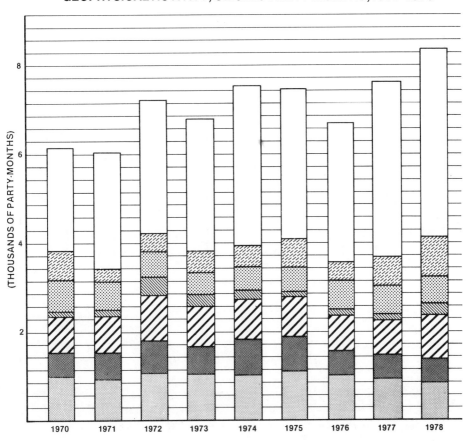

UNITED STATES

CANADA

WESTERN EUROPE

OTHER DEVELOPED

OPEC COUNTRIES

NON-OPEC:

    OXDCs

    OIDCs

Source: AAPG Bulletin, October 1979.

14. DEVELOPED AND DEVELOPING COUNTRIES: NUMBER OF WILDCAT WELLS DRILLED, 1970-1978

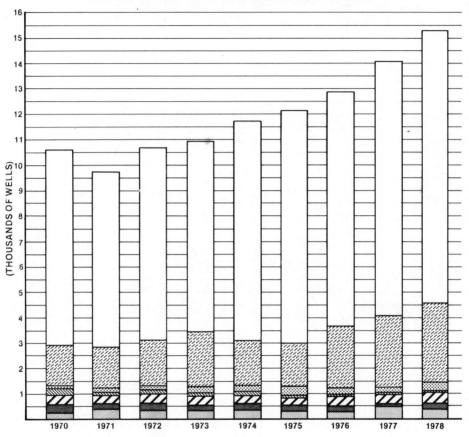

UNITED STATES
CANADA
WESTERN EUROPE
OTHER DEVELOPED
OPEC COUNTRIES
NON-OPEC:
    OXDCs
    OIDCs

Source: AAPG Bulletin, October 1979, and Oil and Gas Journal, Annual December issues, 1970–1976.

TABLE III-2: NUMBER OF EXPLORATORY WELLS DRILLED IN OIDCs[a]

OIDCs in:	Year 1970	Year 1978
Africa	53	41
Asia	13	121
Latin America	273	228
Total	339	390
cf: US & Canada	9,252	13,821

[a]Oil-importing developing countries as of 1979.

The total number of rigs active on both exploratory and development drilling on the other hand has increased fairly rapidly since 1971 (data unavailable for 1970), at a rate of almost 8% per year—but from a very low base. As of 1978, they numbered 296 and have continued to rise since then, reaching a total of 328 in June 1980. Table III-3 below shows the comparison between 1971 and 1978:

TABLE III-3: NUMBER OF RIGS ACTIVE IN OIDCs[a]

OIDCs in:	March 1971	December 1978
Africa	9	26
Asia	51	103
Latin America	103	167
Total	163	296
cf: US & Canada	926	2,460

[a]Oil-importing developing countries as of 1979.

A measure of the inadequacy of the exploratory effort is the minimal result so far obtained. Of the more than 120 countries which were OIDCs in 1979, only eight[*] were producing oil from fields discovered during the eight years 1970-77. Moreover, that production only amounted to 320,000 b/d. In comparison, import requirements of the OIDCs (excluding southern Europe) are about 4.5 million b/d. Thus, on the average, discoveries during each of the eight years contributed only 40,000 b/d to total production in 1979. If this performance cannot be improved in the future, annual growth of indigenous production will be less than 1% of import requirements, and the gap between production and imports will widen.

Even if one includes countries which have become small net exporters since 1970 (Congo, Cameroon, Tunisia, Zaire), total production in 1979 from 1970-77 discoveries aggregated only 425,000 b/d, or 53,000 b/d each year. If one also includes the handful of success stories which have become net exporters since 1970: Angola, Egypt, Gabon, Malaysia, Oman and Trinidad & Tobago (apart from Mexico which already knew in 1970 that it could develop an export surplus whenever it chose), total production in 1979 from 1970-77 discoveries rises to only 1.3 million b/d, or only 164,000 b/d each year. The data is shown in Table III-4 below.

These results can only be described as wretched. They are very far below the annual increment in oil demand in OIDCs. Unless great improvements can be made in discovery rates, import requirements will continue to grow, or demand (and probably economic growth) will have to be severely constrained through lack of foreign exchange to pay for the imports.

In brief, exploration worldwide in 1978 reached record levels. By far the most part took place in North America. A relatively small amount took place in OIDCs. The lion's share was in those of them which produce oil. Exploratory efforts were very small in OIDCs which do not produce oil, no more than 130 seismic party-months (1.5% of

---

[*]   Excluding Argentina, for which insufficient data are available.

15. DEVELOPED AND DEVELOPING COUNTRIES: RIGS ACTIVE, 1971-1980
(end of month)

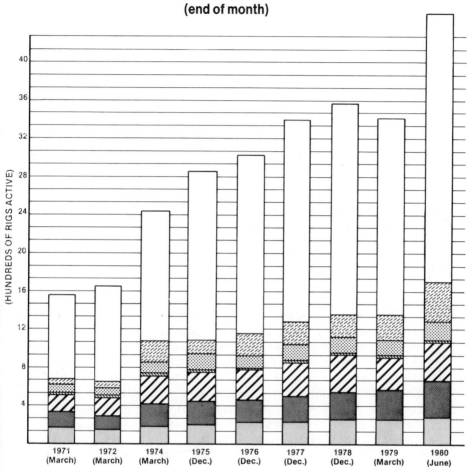

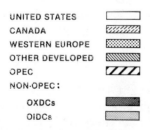

UNITED STATES
CANADA
WESTERN EUROPE
OTHER DEVELOPED
OPEC
NON-OPEC:
    OXDCs
    OIDCs

Source: Hughes Tool Co.

TABLE III-4:
OIL PRODUCTION IN 1979 FROM OIDCs OF 1970 AND 1979

	OIDCs 1979[a]	OIDCs 1970[b]
No. of fields discovered, 1970-77	34	83
	(thousand b/d)	
Crude production in 1979 from 1970-77 discoveries	323	1,309
Ditto, average annual increment	40	164
Average size of field	11	16

[a]Countries which were OIDCs in 1979.
[b]Countries which OIDCs in 1970.

the total for developed and developing countries) and 63 wells
(0.4% of the total).

It is possible that lead-times are so great that it
is still too early to judge the response in the exploratory
effort to the 1973-74 price increases.   For example, four
major countries--Argentina, Brazil, Chile, and India--have
reversed long-standing policies, and have only recently, or
are only now, bringing in foreign oil companies to assist in
exploration.   However, the weight of the evidence so far
(reflected in the statistics above on geophysical exploration
and drilling activity) suggests that the response to price
increases is rather low, and that there are a number of
constraints on exploration which cannot be overcome, or which
can only be partially overcome, through the normal economic
incentive provided by high prices and the expectation of even
higher ones to follow.   These constraints are examined below.

i.   Poor Geological Prospects

The most intractable constraint of all is, of course,
when a country has poor geological prospects.   But this is not
as straightforward a matter as might seem at first sight.
What constitutes a poor geological prospect is a matter of
judgement.   The improvement of geophysical exploratory tech-

niques during recent years means that much of the previously obtainable seismic data is open to reinterpretation and that many of the areas already explored need to be reexplored with more modern equipment. It is possible that the higher prices of oil would provide sufficient incentive for this reassessment to take place in the normal course of events. In some instances, however, lead-times may be substantially shortened with assistance from non-commercial sources. This is because in the establishment of private sector companies' priorities, countries with a _prima facie_ presumption of poor geology, based on prior exploration, may rank rather low.

ii. Boundary Disputes

In a few instances, boundary disputes between countries are holding up exploration for hydrocarbons. Examples are Malta and Libya, Greece and Turkey, Vietnam and Indonesia, Colombia and Venezuela. The high price of oil, far from helping to get exploration under way in these disputed areas, is likely to aggravate them; and if outside assistance can help at all, it must come at the political level in the form of mediation.

iii. Monopolisation of Acreage

In a few countries, the government has granted concessions over very large areas, sometimes virtually the whole of the area of any geologic interest, to a single company or to a single consortium of companies. This acreage is then explored very slowly, because the concessionaire company is generally willing to devote it to only a relatively small amount of money each year, possibly no more than enough to cover the operations of one rig. The exploration effort is therefore held up until, in the usual course of events, relinquishments from the main concession make more acreage available to other companies (though usually the least attractive).

iv. Government Policy and the Legal Framework

A number of countries have traditionally been hostile to the participation of foreign oil companies in the exploration and production phases of the industry. In Latin American countries in particular, government policy, as reflected in the countries' laws, has resulted in the exclusion of foreign private companies from exploration; and exploration and production of oil have been reserved exclusively to the national oil companies. This is true also of some other countries outside Latin America, notably until recently India. But as noted above, there has been a change in policy during the past few years in several of the largest developing countries, which are now turning once more to foreign oil companies for assistance in the exploratory effort.

In other instances, government policy has tended to discourage exploration by setting conditions which are unacceptable to many foreign companies, either because of burdensome fiscal terms or because of other factors, such as performance bonds or minimum work programs considered too high by the companies.

Finally, another aspect in which government policy sometimes contributes to a slowing-down in exploration for hydrocarbons is through indecision or simply inability on the part of the government to implement its policies efficiently. Indecision may reflect internal differences within the government, sometimes as between government qua government and the national oil company. Lack of ability to implement a policy usually stems from inexperience in such matters as deciding what type of contractual arrangements are most suited to the country and its geology, as well as poor judgement of what will attract foreign companies.

v. Political Risk

Related to government policy is the question of the degree of political risk involved for the foreign oil company. Usually, if the geology is attractive enough, the political risk tends to be highly discounted. But in cases where the geology is moderately attractive or only marginally so, the political risk may be determining in either deterring some companies from taking any interest whatsoever, or in making those companies which are interested take only minimal exploration commitments. In some cases, drilling contractors are reluctant to undertake assignments for the oil companies with concessions in certain countries, unless they are insured by the companies against the risk of either having their equipment confiscated, or finding that they cannot get export permits for it once it has completed the exploration program for which it was committed to the country.

vi. Industry Structure

Among the most important constraints on hydrocarbons exploration in OIDCs is the structure of the international oil industry. Local capital and know-how are not available in the OIDCs, and foreign companies must therefore be relied upon.

Historically, companies with an interest in exploring in Third World countries have come mostly from the United States and, to a lesser extent, from Canada and a few European countries. All of them have had and continue to have their main base of operations in their home countries, either as producers or refiner-marketers or both. Their interest in Third World oil has been first and foremost access to cheaper crude oil supplies for their markets in the industrial countries, and they have practically never had interest in exploration for oil to satisfy the local markets.

Usually, such local markets have been too small to rank in a company's order of priorities, as it surveys the likely geological prospects around the world and matches up its own resources against them. There have been exceptions, such as Brazil, Argentina, and India. But in the vast majority of OIDCs the minimum size of geological prospect which attracts the foreign company is generally larger than the whole of the domestic market. The smaller deposits, which may satisfy local markets and be extremely important to the Third World country itself, are of little interest to companies big or small, because opportunities elsewhere are more attractive in terms of lead-time, in terms of limited technical and management resources available to a given company, and in terms of the size of the potential reward.

Indeed, in recent years, the balance of alternative opportunity has, if anything, swung against Third World countries as progressive decontrol of crude prices in the US and investment opportunities in Canada have made exploration there more attractive than previously, thus drawing away some of the resources that might otherwise have gone to Third World countries. It seems doubtful if many Third World countries will ever be in a position to attract companies prepared to

mount more than a minor exploratory effort (one or two rigs)
in searching for fields whose potential production is not
likely to be more than 2-3,000 b/d.

- - - -

        The combination of the factors enumerated above and,
in particular, the structure of the industry, present a strong
argument in favour of stimulating exploration through other
means, whether out of official development assistance funds or
otherwise. Some programs are already under way through the
World Bank and the OPEC Fund for International Development,
and proposals for larger programs are being considered.

        The World Bank's current program of loans and grants
to Third World countries for energy-related projects amounts
to US$13.2 billion through 1985, of which $2.7 billion are to
be dedicated to petroleum. The Bank has proposed that these
sums be doubled and that an energy affiliate be created which
would raise much of the additional money required.

        OPEC has approved in principle the creation of a
joint fund with industrial countries to encourage energy
resource development and general economic development in Third
World countries. Action on this proposal is likely to be
delayed until the present conflict between two OPEC members,
Iran and Iraq, is resolved.

        A regional project is under way in Central America
and the Caribbean, under which Mexico and Venezuela have
agreed to soft loans to nine countries with especially favourable conditions if the loans are used for developing indigenous energy resources.

        Finally, there are a number of bilateral assistance
projects, such as the financing by FR Germany of eight exploratory wells in Bangladesh, the loan by Algeria of a rig to
Tanzania to drill a certain number of wells, and the agreement
by Mexico to drill a number of exploratory wells in Costa
Rica.

        These are encouraging signs that the importance of
the problem is starting to be recognised. But a much greater

effort must be made if OIDC production of oil and gas is to be significantly expanded in the next two decades.

B.   Energy Efficiency and Conservation

One of the major international themes at this time is the prospect that energy problems will seriously limit the economic growth of oil-importing countries, whether developed or developing. There is an overwhelming necessity for a major structural readjustment to improve efficiencies and conservation in the use of energy if energy supplies are going to be enough in most countries to support reasonable expectations of economic growth.

The largest potential source of energy supplies is the saving which can be derived from improved efficiency in energy use. This is the greatest positive solution for the global energy scene.

The world is faced with the choice of being forced into doing "less with less" or facing up to the challenge of doing "more with less." The phrase "energy conservation" to some people has a negative connotation of deprivation and cuts in standards of living, which have acted adversely on the political enthusiasm to grapple with the issue of restraining energy demand. The positive approach is the phrase "improved efficiency." There is a broad array of measures which can be taken. Some of them can have a more effective economic return than investments in high-cost energy supplies. In the past, they have not excited much attention. But now the signals of price and income constraints as well as some government incentives are beginning to be acted on by intermediate producers and consumers.

The largest absolute savings in energy consumption can and must be made in the industrialised countries. Their efforts will have the greatest impact on reducing unsupportable pressures on world oil supplies and on easing the transition to alternative energy sources. But it will be imperative for OIDCs to make similar efforts if their economic prospects are not to be jeopardised. Even for the OXDCs, there are concerns to stretch out the life of oil reserves not only by pacing their oil production but also by curbing domestic oil consumption through conservation measures and substi-

tution of other fuels such as gas; these latter steps free oil
for export to finance economic development.

i. Industrialised Countries

The industrialised countries are highly concerned at
the prospect that energy supply constraints may dampen
economic growth. The analysis in Chapter I drew attention to
the latest expectations that energy supplies available to
industrialised countries during the next two decades might
expand only slowly (in the order of 1.5-2.0% p.a.). The
energy coefficient targets expressed by the IEA, EEC, and the
Seven at the most recent round of summits are probably over-
generous.[*] The EEC is using 0.7 as a minimum in its
guidelines for 1990, and the Seven and IEA expect the
coefficient to be about 0.6. A central theme is the need to
decouple the growth rate of energy demand from that of
economic activity, if the latter is not to be lower and energy
prices higher than sought.

The long-term prospects for large improvements in
energy efficiency could be very promising. This is not easily
quantified. But several recent studies have suggested that
energy supplies at today's level or even lower could support
reasonable economic growth through the next two or three
decades. They include several studies for the United States
(CONAES,[b] Ford/RFF,[c] Harvard Business School,[d] RFF[e])
and one for the United Kingdom (Leach et al[f]).

During the 1980s there is every prospect of a highly
uncomfortable transition to the subsequent era of increased
supplies of alternative energy to imported oil. Any
encouraging recovery in economic growth in oil-importing
countries could be nipped in the bud by the resultant
acceleration in demand for imported oil, sharp increases in
its real price, inflation and consequent deflationary
government policies, together with the danger of restrictive
trade practices. In other words, if there is inadequate

[*]   The ratio expresses the percentage annual change in
primary energy consumption to that in real GDP. It is, of
course, a highly rough and ready concept, and analysis has
to be in-depth to be useful.

improvement in energy efficiency, there will be an economic downturn as a result of the energy constraint.

This has been part (though only part) of the story for industrialised countries since 1973. Price increases of imported oil have upset their balance-of-payments and level of economic activity, even in countries such as the United States where imports do not comprise a large segment of the economy. Industrialised countries are under great pressure in the short as well as the long-term to reduce oil imports by increasing efficiency in energy use. This is even true of countries with a strong export sector such as FR Germany and Japan, and of countries relatively self-sufficient in energy as Britain, Canada, and Norway which will thereby benefit by a slower depletion of domestic resources.

The prerequisite to improved energy efficiency is a realistic adoption by the public of a conservation-oriented society. It has been proven that more can be done with less, but the perceived effects of conservation are as important as the realities. This is the cause of the slow progress on conservation. More incentives are needed. The US and Canada have traditionally had larger houses, larger cars, and in general built more spread out cities, in contrast to other industrialised countries. To reverse such trends is diffi-cult. There is undoubtedly a formidable obstacle in changing lifestyles and values to orient industrial society to a more energy efficient value system.

As mentioned in Chapter II, improved efficiency requires an apropriate carry pricing policy. All energy forms should be priced at their long-run marginal cost, which for most industrialised countries is the cost of imported oil. It is irrelevant that this cost is determined in the interna-tional market place. That is the going price of incremental energy. Too often one form of energy or another is subsidised at prices controlled below marginal cost; and hence the right price signals to consumers are missing which would have guided them towards more energy-efficient practices or towards alter-native energy forms. Retail gasoline prices in North America are still less than half than in other industrialised countries. In a number of countries, natural gas prices and electricity rates still reflect average rather than long-term

marginal costs, and declining block tariffs are still quite
widespread.

If higher energy prices result in unwarranted profits
to producers and inequities to low-income consumers, these
problems can be addressed by solutions other than general
price subsidies; solutions include investment incentives and
windfall profits taxes for producers or relief measures for
particular groups of consumers. If the price level for energy
in oil-importing industrialised countries is below that of
imported oil, it is usually unhelpful to restrict the increase
in domestic energy prices to a rate lower than domestic inflation; or else real energy prices are just eroding, and the
right signals are not reaching the consumer. The IEA's Review
of 1978 pointed out that industrial countries are reluctant to
allow energy prices to increase or to impose energy taxes
because of the effect on domestic inflation and industrial
competitiveness. Yet as the Seven at Venice now point out,
market forces should be supplemented where appropriate by
effective fiscal incentives and administrative measures. They
also point out that energy investment will contribute
substantially to economic growth and employment.

There is a multitude of means to improve energy
efficiency. They are listed in a number of publications
including the annual IEA reviews and also in a recent study by
Shell International on "Energy Efficiency."[g] An IEA
ministerial conference in October 1977 endorsed a series of
principles for energy policy and referred to a list of
suggested conservation measures. Subsequent meetings of the
IEA, EEC "energy" council and the Seven have added new
measures and principles.[h] The potential benefits can be
high but are hard to quantify. Those listed in the Shell
publication are believed able to reduce overall energy per
unit of economic activity by roughly 15-30%.

In residential and commercial sectors the greatest
results are achievable from the integrated design of new
buildings and from strengthened building codes. Next come
insulation, reduction of draughts, effective incentives for
retrofitting programs, minimum energy efficiency standards for
appliances, boiler improvements, improved automatic controls
for boilers and central heating, good heat management, waste
heat recovery, heat pumps, and double glazing. Other measures

include regulatory limits of indoor temperatures in summer and winter and of hot water temperatures, individual room thermostats, individual metering of gas, electricity, and hot water, wind screening by trees, solar hot water and solar space heating, switching off unused lights, closing curtains, and district heating from power stations' waste heat (where economically viable).

In the transport sector, measures include incentives for public transport, mass transit systems, and increased use of rail freight. They also comprise smaller cars, minimum fuel efficiency standards, engine improvement, car weight reduction, drag reduction, and use of micro-processes to improve driving. Steps to rationalise production and marketing can eliminate cross-hauling. Other measures include speed limits, car pooling, mini-buses, improved routing, closed town centres, debottlenecking, and reduction of urban sprawl.

In the industrial sector the greatest results come from the integrated design of new processes. Next come effective incentives for energy-saving investments, the correct choice of energy type, good combustion technology, recovery of waste heat for pre-heating and space-heating, insulation, replacing steam by direct-firing techniques, cogeneration of heat and power, heat management, improved maintenance, improved buildings, manufacture of goods which last longer, and recycling of used materials.

In the energy sector, measures include incentives and regulations for district heating, cogeneration of heat and power, greater use of waste heat and waste products, full-cost tariffs for electricity generation, and domestic oil prices at prevailing world market levels.

The measures are evident, but the steps to implement them are slow. Certain "house-keeping" measures can be taken quickly, such as reduced road speeds and reduced use of indoor heating in winter and air-conditioning in summer. Others require capital investment of differing degrees. It takes time for past investment to be replaced. Hence there is the burden of existing infrastructure and the delay in installing new capital stock.

Delivered energy costs are only a small part of total costs, whether in the residential, commercial, transport, or industrial (other than energy-intensive) sectors. The effect of energy price increases has been diluted in the final delivered cost of economic goods. Inflation has augmented this dilution. The crux of the problem is with final consumers, who account for about half the energy used. But these consumers have to make the requisite energy-saving investments, and most demand a very short pay-back time (say 2-3 years). They will therefore probably not touch good investments which require long-term amortisation. Governments need to make conservation attractive to individuals by reducing or subsidising the cost of conservation investments or by raising the cost of oil. There is also great potential in mandatory energy labelling; this permits consumers to choose products, taking into account energy costs.

A commonly used indicator of energy intensity is the aggregate ratio of a nation's energy consumption to GDP. The energy/GDP ratio provides a rough-and-ready but useful monitor of progress in conservation for individual countries or regions, as long as it is measured over a sufficiently long period of years. Some results seem to have been achieved since 1973, particularly in the last two years. Exxon's "World Energy Outlook" of December 1979 sees evidence that industrialised countries are at last reducing the energy intensity of their economies compared with the 1960s, perhaps by 6% in 1978 for the United States and 3% for other industrialised countries.[i]

Let it be said that the energy/GDP ratio should be used with great care in comparisons of one country's performance with another's, as it is not a good international measure of economic or energy efficiency.

Regarding economic efficiency, energy is only one input into the total of goods and services which comprise GDP. Inputs of capital, labour, and materials are much larger. Regarding energy efficiency, the energy consumed in a country relative to its GDP is affected by the economy's industrial composition. Thus a developed country dependent on energy-intensive heavy industry will use more energy than one dependent on agriculture.[j,k]

Nevertheless, international comparisons can be helpful at the sectoral level, provided they are treated as indicative and qualitative rather than precise and quantitative.

A nation will have a more energy-intensive economy than elsewhere when:

  i) In the residential/commercial sector:
     a. its housing units are larger,
     b. the share of single dwelling units is larger,
     c. the climate is colder;
 ii) In the transport sector:
     a. fuel and power prices and costs are lower,
     b. the passenger-mile volume relative to GDP is larger,
     c. the fuel economy of its passenger car fleet is poorer,
     d. the share of public transport is lower,
     e. freight-transport volume relative to GDP is larger,
     f. the share of rail, pipelines, and waterways in freight transport is lower;
iii) In the industrial sector:
     a. the share of extraction/manufacturing is greater;
 iv) In the energy sector:
     a. the role of electricity is greater, and
     b. energy supply self-sufficiency is higher.

Even having allowed for economic structural differences among countries, energy intensities do differ significantly, particularly between North America and other countries.* The differences are particularly striking in passenger transport and industrial processes. The US consumes about 50% more energy relative to GDP than Western Europe or Japan. This higher energy intensity is reflected in almost all sectors, though more in some than in others; the greatest difference is in the transport sector (60%). As between

---

* It is important to make international comparisons of GDP using purchasing power parities rather than exchange rates; this has become more practicable through the recent series of studies of the UN International Comparisons Project (Kravis et al.).

Western Europe and Japan, there is considerable difference in all sectors except transport. Such differences between nations complicate efforts to coordinate policy and often confuse public perceptions.

It should come as no surprise that intensity in energy use in North America is by-and-large higher than in other industrial countries. There are great differences in energy prices, structure, geography, resources endowment, population, and tastes. However, some of these characteristics are showing signs of change, through higher energy prices or policy measures (taxes or subsidies) to restrain demand. Shifts towards enhanced fuel economy in cars, improved central heating practices, and use of public transport could reduce the North American/European differential by 15-20%.

There has been a great reduction since 1973 in the growth of energy consumption in industrialised countries. In part, this has been due to slower economic growth and at times recession, augmented by milder winters in some years. At the same time, there are also perceptible improvements in effi- ciency of energy use. Nevertheless, as noted in the IEA's Review of 1978, the merit of energy conservation continues to be under-estimated in most countries. There has been too much reliance on information and voluntary action. Policy measures have often been held back by insufficient government funding and staffing and by government perceptions of economic and social constraints. In a few countries, comprehensive conser- vation programs are in place, but elsewhere most programs are inadequate. The EEC "energy" council in May 1980 passed a resolution including "Guidelines for a Basic Energy-Saving Programme," which cover fuel efficiencies in all economic sectors.[1]

Strong action has typically not been adopted in contrast to the emphasis on accelerated development of energy supplies. The outlook for further substantial improvement is dimmed by failure to press aggressively for new conservation measures. There is great cause for concern that energy efficiency may be improved at too slow a rate in industrial- ised countries. Much more could be done to reduce energy demand without hampering economic growth, although the fear of doing so holds back industrialised countries.

In the residential/commercial sector, most industrialised countries have thermal efficiency standards of varying scope. Mandatory and, in some cases, stringent building codes for all new buildings are in place in the Scandinavian countries, FR Germany, and Italy, and are being prepared in Canada. The greatest savings could be obtained from retrofitting existing buildings. The IEA's 1978 Review comments that very strong and comprehensive programs are still limited to three countries (Denmark, the Netherlands, and Sweden). The EEC has initiated community-wide recommendations and directives on retrofitting and rational use of energy in non-industrial buildings. In other countries there has been some strengthening of incentive programs. But elsewhere, programs have been accepted more slowly than hoped. In most countries, public funds for retrofitting are still very modest.

The introduction of steps to improve energy use has proven particularly slow in the transport sector. The necessary policy measures are known but are politically and socially not easy to implement. The greatest scope for improvement is in North America with its historical reliance on large powerful cars for personal transport in spread-out cities. Mandatory fuel efficiency targets have been set there and were strengthened in 1978. Voluntary programs have been announced by FR Germany, Japan, and the United Kingdom. Most industrialised countries outside North America tax gasoline heavily and vehicles by weight.

But in most industrialised countries retail prices of gasoline declined in real terms during the four years to 1978, giving the wrong price signals to the consumers. Since then, real prices have probably ceased eroding and may even have risen. Gasoline prices remain a politically sensitive issue.

Increased efforts are being made to expanding public transport systems. Their improvement is vital for energy saving. But their quality of service had typically been allowed to deteriorate with the fast expansion in the use of private vehicles, particularly in North America. But government action still for the most part looks half-hearted. There remains huge scope for expanded public transport in most countries.

In the industrial sector there appears to be increasing awareness of the financial benefits from improving efficiency. This is particularly evident in energy-intensive industries such as aluminum and steel-making. Some countries have adopted voluntary energy-saving targets for energy intensive industries, for instance Canada, Greece, Japan, and the United States. Governments have introduced incentives for energy-saving investments in a number of industrialised countries. Nevertheless, the IEA's Review of 1978 comments that efforts to promote energy conservation in industry should be expanded, given that this sector is the largest energy user and is expected to show the greatest growth in energy consumption in the next decade.

In the energy sector, efforts are being made to reduce energy losses in electricity generation, transmission, and distribution. Some countries have introduced incentives to encourage a) waste heat recovery, b) use of district heating, and c) combined production of heat and electric power. Peak and seasonal electricity pricing have been adopted by many countries. But there remains great scope for improvement in this sector.

ii.   Developing Countries

There is need for a big increase in the technical efficiency of energy use in developing countries--using less primary fuels for each unit of useful output. Understandably, however, many people in the developing countries (as in the North) associate conservation with sacrifice and a lower standard of living. Some people in the developing countries also believe that the talk of energy conservation is motivated by a Northern desire to hold consumption down in the South, so that the North will have more.

Although it is true that there is much more waste in the industrialised countries than in the developing countries, it does not mean that the OIDCs should not make every effort to use energy more efficiently. In fact, the logic of energy efficiency is even more powerful for developing countries than the developed nations. To begin with, the price and availability of energy being what it is, the poor countries can least afford energy waste. Second, using energy efficiently does not mean reducing economic growth or giving up pleasant

activities.   Energy conservation can be achieved without affecting economic growth and living standards.   Third, because
the developing countries are building new economic structures
at a rapid pace, attention to energy efficiency can make a big
difference in their total energy bill sooner rather than
later.   Finally, conservation and increasing efficiency of
energy will enable the OIDCs to save resources that can be
used for other development activities.

Basically, energy conservation in the OIDCs is
different from that in the industrialised countries.   The
problem in the latter is to a significant degree related to
luxurious use of energy and energy-intensive goods.   In the
OIDCs the problem is one of inefficiency in energy use.
Inefficient cooking equipment wastes wood; poor harnesses and
carts waste animal traction; older, poorly maintained vehicles
waste gasoline; inefficient industrial layouts waste oil and
electricity.   The problem is fundamentally one of poverty or
the lack of skills and capital to improve the level of
efficiency.   In areas of waste there are opportunities for
OIDCs to take a range of conservation measures.

2.   MANAGING THE TRANSITION FROM OIL TO OTHER SOURCES

A.   Accelerated Development of Energy Resources

Oil is the major energy source used in to providing
high temperature heat.   It is easily transported and stored.
But it is no longer low-priced in international trade.   Nor
are most new sources of liquid hydrocarbons cheap to develop
and produce.   The old era of low-priced oil has gone.   Oil
will increasingly have to be reserved for premium uses such as
transport and chemicals.

Higher international oil prices have created urgent
challenges to shape new national energy policies in
oil-importing countries, as has the problem of deforestation
particularly in developing countries.   The desire for relief
from the insecurity of imported oil is a powerful motive for
governments to promote domestic energy supplies even if they
are more costly than imported oil, and most are not.   Even
more fundamental is that long-term prospects suggest
increasing constraints on conventional depletable energy
supplies, above all oil.

The pressing needs to find and develop new sources of oil as well as to conserve in its use have been described in Section 1 of this chapter. Strenuous efforts will help by providing more time for the transition to a broader array of energy options.

The next two decades will be faced with an era of transition towards the next generation of energy sources and technologies. There is need to keep energy supply options open wherever possible. All planning must allow for uncertainty. The world needs a diversity of energy sources; as there is a diversity of energy needs and as there are uncertainties surrounding each individual energy source. There is a danger of being locked into short-term palliatives. Hence a wide range of every kind of research and development is needed to retain flexibility of technical options. Moreover, some changes to the energy mix could be made today with little adjustment to the existing capital stock. But more radical changes will take time to make the necessary structural adjustments to the economy.

Yet, developed and developing countries alike have limited financial, technical, and manpower resources to devote to energy. Not every energy process can or should be pursued; each must be economically, socially and environmentally justifiable.

The range of energy sources is very wide, as was already discussed in Chapter I. It includes deposits of very heavy oil, tar-sands, and shales, as well as oil in polar regions or beneath deep water. Then there are enhanced recovery processes to improve the recovery of oil-in-place from existing and new fields beyond that from primary and secondary methods. Discovery of small fields will continue and may accelerate in many countries well into the next century; their cumulative impact could be great, and their support to economies including those of oil-importing developing countries will be significant.

Natural gas is likely to make an increasingly large contribution to world energy supplies during the next two decades. Its potential looks far greater than had been surmised in earlier years. It has similar advantages to oil, except that it is less easy to store and has less transport flexibility. Its role is likely to grow up to the limit set by supplies, as it is after all a depleting non-renewable resource.

Coal is plentiful but mainly limited to bulk heat end-uses, particularly electricity generation. Extending its range of applications presents a challenge. There are great opportunities for expansion of its use, but there are also serious economic, financial, and environmental uncertainties surrounding the pace of its development.

Electricity is versatile in application, easy to use, and can be generated from a variety of sources. The main ones today are fossil fuels, hydro, and nuclear power. Coal is becoming an increasingly favoured source for new power stations and existing thermal stations. The use of hydroelectricity is expected to continue growing, particularly in Canada and developing countries. Nuclear power has expanded fast. But the future expansion of both coal and nuclear could be constrained by a wide range of concerns in a number of industrialised countries. (See Chapter I.)

In view of the perceived constraints on accelerated development of the conventional forms of commercial energy, much more serious attention is now beginning to be paid to the development of oil, gas, and coal supplies from non-conventional sources, as well as to the energy Cinderellas: conservation and renewable energy sources.

Oil-importing countries need to take long-term steps towards a) improved energy use and b) supply alternatives to conventional oil supplies.

The Seven at Venice, the EEC, and the IEA all expect or have set guidelines to reduce oil as a share in energy consumption from 50-53% to 40% by 1990. Indeed the Seven foresees its collective consumption of oil to be below present levels by 1990 so as to permit a balance between supply and demand. IEA and the Seven sanguinely foresee by 1990 a doubling in the use of coal and an increase in the use of nuclear energy. The Seven have specifically said that their potential to increase the supply and use of energy sources other than oil over the next ten years is estimated at the equivalent of 10-20 million b/d o.e. daily. They agreed that

no new base-load, oil-fired generating capacity should be
constructed save in exceptional circumstances, and that the
conversion of oil-fired capacity to other fuels should be
accelerated.   Increased efforts are pledged to encourage oil-
saving investments and oil substitution by all means including
fiscal incentives.

B.   Research, Development, and Demonstration

        Much use can be made of existing technologies.   But
in the long-run new and better technology must be developed
for energy conservation and supplies.   This points to the
fundamental importance of well-directed national programs for
energy research, development, and demonstration (RD&D).*

        The ultimate goal of energy RD&D is to meet the long-
term needs for energy and to open technological solutions to
energy problems for incorporation into energy policy.   Hence
energy policy should provide clear guidelines for RD&D, and it
should take better account of the supply and conservation
options offered by RD&D.

i.   Industrialised Countries

        Not surprisingly, much of the work worldwide on
energy RD&D programs is being done in the industrialised
countries, by both governments and the private sector.

        Virtually all the industrialised nations, except
France, are now members of the IEA, which introduced in 1977 a
system of annual reviews of its member countries' energy RD&D
programs.   By 1980 it had published a report on energy RD&D
strategy for member countries and three annual reviews of
national programs.[a,b]

        The IEA report of 1980 on "Energy RD&D: a Strategic
View" contains some significant policy guidelines for its
member countries.   Its conclusions for RD&D planning are that

---

*   The following paragraphs on energy RD&D in the industrial-
    ised nations draw greatly on publications of the IEA,
    European Community and UN Economic Commission for Europe.

the need for imports of conventional oil will decline during the years to 2020. During the first two decades the decline is mainly due to conservation and existing technologies, while thereafter new technologies for liquid fuels should begin to make a significant contribution. Nevertheless, the rate of decline in oil imports would continue to leave countries vulnerable to supply disruptions. The contribution of new energy technologies before 2000 may not reduce oil demand enough to avoid supply constraints, unless their introduction is accelerated.

The impact of new technologies for conservation can be as significant as new ones for supply. The report attaches high priority to RD&D efforts for coal and nuclear power. Some new technologies for renewable energy will begin to make substantial contribution before 2000. But those for non-renewable energy will provide most energy needs for the balance of this century, even if efforts are accelerated to introduce renewable ones.

The conclusion is that the pace should be accelerated to develop and bring new energy technologies to commercial use. A strategic view must be taken of requisite near-term action, taking into account their state of development and potential importance. Some technology will be at the exploratory stage, some at the stage of pilot-scale experiments, some at that of large-scale demonstration, and finally some ready to be brought into commercial use. Virtually all energy technologies have environmental impact, and this should be taken into account at all stages of their development.

The deployment of new technologies can be affected by a wide range of non-technical issues. There is the need for rational pricing signals to assist the proper introduction of new technologies as well as conservation. If energy forms such as oil, gas, or even electricity are subsidised at prices below their long-term marginal costs, consumers have little incentive to move to alternative energy forms which may be lower in cost but are priced to cover that cost. Social impacts need to be well considered. So does the availability of skilled labour, raw materials, infrastructure, land, and water.

The IEA annual reviews assess how adequate the scope and character of national programs are in meeting energy needs, and they identify steps to strengthen these programs. All these countries have stated in some form or other their policies or aims for energy RD&D programs. But their statements are often so general that they offer little guidance to the long-term decision-making necessary for these programs. Countries need at least to define priorities by technology areas. They should also identify which of these priority technologies they would try to develop themselves and which they would import.

Is the aggregate level of present effort in industrialised countries enough to provide new technologies in time to offset the depletion of conventional resources and the risk of disruption to oil supplies? This looks unlikely at the present pace of development.

The annual reviews illustrate that IEA countries have increased their government support of energy RD&D substantially, by 113% in real terms from 1974 to 1978. The United States is dominant; its funding represented half the total in 1978 and grew particularly strong (by over 200%) during the period. Hence the growth in other IEA countries was much less (45%), and some even spent less in 1978 than in earlier years. The size of the effort varies greatly from country to country. Population, type of economy, and energy intensity inevitably lead to different efforts.

Official funding of energy RD&D in industrialised countries is dominated by nuclear programs. In 1978 IEA governments devoted 31% of these funds to conventional nuclear fission, 20% to fast breeders, and 9% to nuclear fusion.

In contrast, they allocated less than 9% to renewable energy (solar, wind, ocean, biomass, and geothermal). Moreover, the United States accounts for about three-quarters of the renewables effort. There are considerable differences of national view as to the potential of renewable energy technologies. Most of the funds for renewable energy are spent on large-scale applications that will be of little use to rural people who need decentralised energy sources.

The effort devoted to coal technology continues to increase. But in the IEA view these increases are not enough to provide a proper balance of coal RD&D relative to other conventional fuel systems.

By far the greatest government efforts are spent on supply technologies. In 1978 IEA governments allocated only 6% of their energy RD&D budgets to conservation. These efforts look woefully small. RD&D financed by private industry is thought to be much greater in this area. Moreover, some official funding of RD&D into energy-related supporting technologies (power conversion and transmission, energy storage, environmental protection and safety, energy systems analysis, and basic energy research) has some impact on conservation improvement.

Industrially financed RD&D makes an important contribution to national programs. It is much directed towards product improvement. But it includes significant work on technologies for energy conservation, enhanced recovery of hydrocarbons, and some supporting technologies. The IEA reviews comment that RD&D on non-conventional oil deposits still receive less emphasis by governments and industry than their worldwide potential would warrant.

The RD&D results could be greatly increased without corresponding cost increases if there were reliable arrangements made for exchanging information, materials, and personnel, and for pooling research results.

In this regard, it is of interest that in 1979 an International Energy Technology Group was created under the auspices of the EEC and OECD/IEA, with participation from 14 industrialised countries. Its purpose was to define priorities by technology areas in the field of new energy sources, to examine current and planned projects, and to look for potential areas of international collaboration. The Group came up with four main conclusions. First, a program of commercialising new technologies is needed. Second, international cooperation is needed in areas where commercialisation is not possible without government support, specificaly coal liquefaction, heavy oils, tar-sands and shale, biomass, high calorific coal gasification, natural gas liquids, and coal combustion. Third, there is need for government efforts to

reduce risk and improve financial incentives. Fourth, there
is need to monitor the commercialisation of new energy
technologies.

Recently, multilateral programs have been initiated
by the UN agencies and international financial institutions to
assist developing countries in their efforts to make the
transition from oil to other energy sources. The UN Conference on New and Renewable Sources of Energy in 1981 will focus
especially on these issues.

Industrialised nations have expressed willingness to
assist developing countries bring into use technologies
related to renewable energy, as at the Tokyo summit meeting of
seven major countries. Such initiatives could have great
potential.

This is also a two-way street, as some developing
countries have been making significant technological breakthroughs, from which industrial countries have much to learn.
Examples include Brazil's program to produce liquid fuels from
biomass and PR China's production of biogas units to produce
gas and fertiliser from animal and vegetable wastes.

ii. Developing Countries

For the developing countries, alternative energy
includes small-scale, decentralised renewable energy, as well
as commercial energy used in the modern sector such as gas,
oil, coal, and large-scale electricity from whatever source.
It includes inherently decentralised renewable energy sources
(DRE) such as wind, flowing water in small streams, biomass,
and sunshine. These energy sources have characteristics that
make them especially interesting for Third World countries.

First, they are inherently decentralised to the rural
areas where most Third World people live (except for Latin
America where slightly less than half live in rural areas).
This is important because the distribution of centrally
produced energy (e.g., electricity and diesel fuel) to rural
areas has proved to be a problem in many countries. A World
Bank report of 1975 estimated that only 4% of the rural people
of Africa lived in areas served by electricity and the pace of

extension seemed very slow (World Bank, "Rural Electrification," p.17).

Second, the costs of certain technologies to collect and use DRE are not expected to rise as rapidly as oil, and the costs of at least one technology (photovoltaics) are expected to decline. In most regions one or more of these renewable sources are likely to be plentiful.

Third, the long-term future of oil does not seem bright and even the short and medium-term outlook is uncertain. This adds to the interest in technologies that can collect and convert into usable form the generally very ample renewable supply of locally available energy.

Despite these evidences of promise especially for application in remote areas, renewable energy needs a great deal more research and site testing before its full promise becomes evident.

The concepts and technologies developed in laboratories need to be tested in actual village sites in order to learn reliably how well they work, what they cost in terms of actual village work performed, how well they are accepted, operated, and maintained by the people and institutions of the villages, and how best they can be introduced into villages. In addition there needs to be a great deal of survey work to learn of the quantity and reliability of various kinds of primary energy present at the village level in the Third World. This would include surveys of the wind regimes at various sites, small stream flow data, insolation, and estimates of biomass.

Optimally, research, site testing, and collection of data on local energy availability should be conducted by one or more institutions of each developing country. This calls for financial and technical support for those institutions by industrialised countries and international donor agencies.

A growing amount of research and development of DRE is under way in the laboratories of industrialised and developing countries. The bulk of the funding for this kind of work comes from industrialised countries, and most of the actual laboratory work is done in those same countries. There is an opportunity for mutual benefit if Northern RD&D funds were used to finance certain kinds of DRE research in the developing countries. In some cases the costs would be lower, while the research results could be equally or more effective for the Northerners who were to finance the work. There would be an added benefit that Southern RD&D institutions would be strengthened as a result.

There is room for strengthening existing or creating new international machinery to deal with this topic. Proposals have been made for an International Energy Institute (Kissinger, UN Seventh Special Session), a "Global Energy Research Centre" (Brandt Commission Report), a Solar Energy Fund (Overseas Development Council), or a Fund for Renewable Energy Enterprise (Lovins et al., Foreign Affairs, July 1980). Such a proposed new institution might be a research center, a leader agency knitting together the various renewable energy researchers into a network, a central information bank, a monitor and critic of existing research, a fund to finance promising RD&D in the Third World, or a combination of the above and other ingredients.

Beyond research, site testing, and primary energy data collection, there will soon be a need for mechanisms to finance the distribution to Third World villages of the kinds of technologies that are proved in laboratories and site tests to be the most promising. In many cases the best distribution system may be private entrepreneurs who see a chance to make a profit by selling equipment and providing spare parts, training, and repair services to keep it functioning. In other cases the distribution system may need to be governmental. In either case, government action may be needed to collect information, provide financing, and train people to help technologies move from laboratories and test sites to widespread village use.

Offers by industrialised countries to conduct a major new program of assistance to Third World countries for DRE could form part of a package for negotiations of oil and related subjects. This might also be linked to initiatives now under consideration by OPEC and industrialised countries to help OIDCs find and develop indigenous energy resources.

3. MEETING THE ENERGY NEEDS OF DEVELOPING COUNTRIES

Human material progress is dependent upon the use of energy. Without sufficient amounts of energy in usable forms and at affordable prices, there is little prospect for improving the conditions of the majority of the people in the world. The inability of the poor to use adequate and efficient energy lends to low productivity and low incomes. And because of their low incomes, the poor cannot afford to use more and high quality energy to increase their productivity and they remain poor. They are in a vicious circle.

In many countries the oil price increases have most seriously affected the poorest segments of the societies. For instance, the sudden increases in international oil prices have affected the retail price and availability of kerosene, the commercial fuel mostly used by the poor. When kerosene became expensive the poor returned to using wood and charcoal, thereby driving the prices of these commodities up. Because energy costs take a very high percentage of the poor's income, the price increases tend to be very damaging. Furthermore, it was the poor who were the first to be laid off as a result of curtailed industrial activities that followed the oil price increases. Agriculture has also suffered from higher fuel and fertiliser costs creating food shortages and higher food prices that mainly affect the poor. In order to be able to pay for the increasing oil prices, many countries were forced to cut back on imports of other essential commodities, thereby lowering their growth rates. The drop in economic growth affected the poor seriously in countries which seek to alleviate poverty through higher growth.

The consequences of heavy reliance on non-commercial fuels is also negatively affecting the poor. In addition to the price increases for wood and charcoal, the expanding deforestation, devegetation, declining water tables, soil erosion, silting, and flooding are leading the shortages in food supplies with consequences of hunger and famine to the poor. Deforestation also leads to desertification with all its consequences on the ecosystem in general and food and firewood production in particular.

The energy problems of developing countries are so serious and so complex that they cannot be tackled without

massive help from the international community. Assistance is
needed by the LDCs to overcome energy related constraints to
their development efforts.

A. Assistance in Energy Development

The energy problem is basically a global problem.
The availability and price of oil, for instance, affect most
every country. It is in the self-interest of every nation to
see that as many countries as possible find and develop oil,
develop substitutes for it, and conserve energy. This will
prolong the availability of oil, so that the world has time to
develop successors to oil. Moreover, the world's ability to
find successors to oil depends on the quality and amount of
RD&D of new technologies and on the efficiency with which
different countries coordinate such work. The Third World's
participation in RD&D projects and the strengthening of its
RD&D capabilities will contribute to this global effort.
Furthermore, our planet's energy problem, if not well managed,
may lead to mounting ecological damage. It is in the interest
of every nation to prevent such damage.

The developing world stands in need of help, and the
international community can render timely and essential assistance for energy development in the Third World. In the
following paragraphs we will point out some of the types of
actions that donors can undertake.

B. A Basic Energy Assessment

To begin with, sound policies depend on a good grasp
of the relevant facts about resource availability and demand,
consumption   pattern,   development   strategy,   technological
capability, etc. In other words, good energy planning begins
with a comprehensive and detailed energy assessment.

The easiest and least valuable way to conduct an
assessment is for aid-giving agencies to send technicians who
prepare the assessment and turn it over to the host country.
A harder way but one that is incomparably more valuable is for
host country technicians to prepare the assessment with the
help of experts from the industrialised countries. Beyond the
clear developmental value of developing host country assessment skills, confidence, and pride, an additional reason for

favouring this approach follows from the fact that any assessment begins to obsolesce the day it is written. To be relevant, an assessment must be continually updated and re-evaluated as resource estimates, prices, development plans, and technologies change. Since aid donors cannot supply permanent assessment teams the best course is to help the host country develop the institutional ability to make its own continuing assessment.

A number of energy assessments have been undertaken under various aid programs. A common failing of such assessments has been that they have ignored or treated inadequately the non-commercial and especially the rural energy scene. Above all, they have not dealt adequately with the paramount Third World energy problem, that of fuelwood. The Third World institutions that will make future energy assessments should be adequately equipped to treat these neglected areas.

A good assessment of present and prospective energy supply and demand is only the starting point for energy policy planning. The developing countries need institutions and experts who can evaluate these facts, identify alternative courses of action, weigh them, and choose among them. This is a task that is too intimately connected with internal political, social, and economic factors to be performed by outsiders. But outsiders can advise, and they can help train a corps of technicians who can supply the analysis needed.

Before undertaking the project demand for energy in the future, one needs a reasonably accurate estimate of current demand and consumption patterns. With respect to modern sectors of developing countries, where energy is distributed in a formal market, there is some information, although it is markedly less complete and reliable than comparable data in the industrialised countries. But for the traditional energy sector—mostly rural areas but including urban slums as well—the picture in the Third World is quite different. There is virtually no quantitative information on traditional energy consumption, since most such energy is used directly by the gatherer of the fuel or owner of the animal and never enters into a formal market place; hence, the concept of demand is not very applicable. The first need is to learn something about current energy use in the traditional areas.

But even if complete and reliable information on the present use of energy were available, there would be special problems in making projections in the Third World for several reasons. To begin with, there is the problem of predicting the pace of economic growth, a problem that is similar to but greater in intensity than that faced in industrialised countries. This is because economic growth in developing countries which produce primary goods fluctuates even more than in industrialised countries.

Even more of a problem is presented by another variable, the development strategy chosen by the developing country. For example, a national decision to emphasise import-substituting or labour-intensive exporting industries will call for different kinds and amounts of energy than a commitment to agriculture and rural development. Moreover, the pace of population growth and the rate of migration to urban areas are also variables that pose problems. The rate of decline in available traditional fuels and the rate at which people substitute modern energy sources for traditional fuels also complicate assessment efforts. While virtually nothing precise is known about the speed of this substitution, the direction is generally clear: it nearly always takes the form of oil. One final complication in projecting is that so little is known about the potential for conserving energy in the Third World. It is possible that a concerted effort to improve efficiency of energy use could yield greater results in the short run than any equivalent effort at producing more energy.

All of these complications suggest two courses of action. First, countries must have their own capabilities to make projections, because projections must be constantly updated. The reason for this is that several of the variables discussed above are volatile and must be reassessed frequently. If a donor country were to send a team in to make a projection of demand, that projection would begin to become outdated as soon as it was completed. To be sure, some out-side help will be needed in many cases and that suggests our second course of action: the outside assistance should come from those who—in addition to knowing energy—are steeped in those developmental variables that make projecting so compli-cated in the Third World. A person whose entire experience has been in making energy demand projections in industrialised countries would have to acquire a great deal of knowledge about developing countries before he would be of much use in making a projection in a developing country.

C. Exploring and Producing Oil and Gas

One of the promising methods of alleviating the energy problem in the medium-term is to help develop indigenous energy resources in the OIDCs. Oil and gas exploration and development offer excellent opportunities for foreign assistance in the energy field. Some geologists claim that more than 40% of the world's prospective oil reserves is in these countries. Yet, only about 5% of the world's investment (excluding centrally planned economies) in petroleum exploration—virtually all of which is private investment—now takes place in the non-OPEC developing countries. The industrialised countries can, therefore, encourage the exploration and development of oil in the OIDCs. Because many private companies, for various reasons, have shown reluctance to invest in oil exploration in many of these countries, their governments can encourage them to undertake the investment. This could be done by such measures as guaranteeing the investment, giving tax breaks, and providing soft loans. In situations where the foreign companies are not attracted to invest at the initial stages, international institutions can help the host countries to take all or part of the risk of exploration.

Because technological capacity is one of the things that the OIDCs lack, there is a need for the industrialised world to help in the development and application of various technologies. In the exploration for petroleum, one area in which the developed countries can help is in undertaking the very important geological and geophysical surveys. The survey information is very valuable in negotiations between governments and the companies that might be interested to invest. Both sides will have a better knowledge of the prospects and probable commercial value of any oil and gas that may be found. Accurate knowledge of what they have to offer will also strengthen the bargaining position of the countries concerned.

An important task in this area is meeting the urgent need of these countries to train their nationals as engineers, geologists, and others capable of performing geological and geophysical surveys and interpreting results. Once commercial scale reserves are found, training is needed for engineers and chemists able to produce and refine oil, and oil economists and lawyers able to produce the analysis on which a sound development policy can be based. Such training and institution building activities should be included among the highest priorities of bilateral and multilateral aid programs.

OPEC countries could also help in the effort to develop the oil reserves of the OIDCs. OPEC can help the developing countries by advising them on how to get the best possible deals from the oil companies, by providing finance for initial surveys and exploratory drilling, by giving them advice on contractual matters, and by cooperating with other international institutions, like the World Bank, which promote the exploration and development of oil in the LDCs. OPEC can also enter into joint ventures in co-financing oil development with oil companies and/or developing country governments.

D. Developing Substitutes for Oil

In the long run, developing more plentiful substitutes for oil in developing countries will be more important than finding or conserving oil. Energy sources like coal and hydroelectricity where they exist could be utilised more extensively. Other renewable energy sources could also be developed.

Although coal is vastly more abundant than oil and gas, its development in the OIDCs faces a number of serious problems, including lack of data on the resource base, heavy infrastructural and other requirements, and serious environmental hazards. Assistance from bilateral and multilateral agencies could help developing countries make surveys, train personnel to undertake basic tasks such as preparing the technical and economic analysis to determine whether and if so how to develop their coal supplies, and help secure the financing required to do so.

With over 60% of the world's major hydroelectric potential located in the developing world, hydroelectric development will continue to have a significant future role. Because conventional hydroelectric projects are typically very large, they face both capital availability constraints and the problem of concentration of demand for their large power output. Although the number of large hydropower projects cannot be expected to increase very rapidly, such plants will be an important electric power alternative, especially to oil-powered thermal power plants. This warrants increased aid in preparing project plans to seek financing as well as larger capital resources for loans to worthy projects.

An even less exploited potential for water power lies in the many possibilities for medium-sized and even small installations. This is especially relevant, given the predominantly rural distribution of most developing countries' populations. Aid programs can provide funds for preparing feasibility studies of hydrosites, identify suitable locations, and finance dams and power installations.

The most prevalent form of energy now used in most developing countries is renewable energy. Even for the world as a whole, renewable sources in old and new forms will eventually become the dominant energy sources. The research and development of small-scale renewable energy technologies need much greater attention and funding. An effort of great value in assessing the real worth of renewable energy resources could be a special international cooperative program for RD&D on DRE that could substitute for and eventually succeed some uses of oil. The technology would, of course, be available for application anywhere in the world, but the justification for such a program should acknowledge that the earliest and perhaps most frequent application of the resulting technology probably would be in the Third World.

A related area of mutually beneficial cooperation on new and renewable energy resources is the testing and demonstration of renewable energy equipment on the farms and in villages, market towns, and urban slums of the developing countries. Such tests and demonstrations are essential steps in the evolution of DRE technology. Because many of the LDCs do not have the financial resources, the technological know-how and the institutional capabilities to undertake such activities, assistance from donor agencies is highly valuable.

Aid agencies can also help in the dissemination of information and distribution of new technologies. As the

intended beneficiaries are mainly the poor, rural dwellers of
these countries, the development of efficient distribution
methods is highly crucial. Aid agencies can be helpful in the
marketing and distribution process in a number of ways.

First, they help the country to gather the facts on
local needs, preferences, and primary energy availability.
Surveys will be needed of such conditions as available local
stream flow, sunshine, wind, and organic materials in order to
determine what DRE devices might be usable in a particular
locality. The aid input might take the form of funds and
advisors to help indigenous institutions to conduct the
survey.

Second, aid programs could help build or strengthen
essential institutions, such as extension services, small
credit services, and marketing facilities. Aid programs could
also help finance imports of DRE equipment and provide local
currency for small credit programs. In all cases, great
effort should be made to strengthen the institutions of the
LDCs capable of performing research on and development of new
technologies or adapting industrialised countries' technologies to meet their own needs.

E.   Afforestation

The declining availability of traditional fuels is
one of the critical energy problems facing the developing
world. Not only is firewood a very important fuel source,
becoming more scarce and expensive, but the side effects of
deforestation on food production and the environment carry
with them high economic costs. The burning of animal dung and
crop wastes is resulting in the loss of soil nutrients and
declining food and wood production. Finding alternative
sources of energy, therefore, will not only alleviate the
energy problem but also help increase food production and
contribute towards the checking of desertification. If the
conditions of rural energy are neglected and ignored the
result could be serious ecological problems with far reaching
implication of global dimensions.

Assistance is required for programs of afforestation,
fuelwood plots, improved stoves, and better charcoal kilns.

Aid agencies can provide funds, technical advice, technicians, and volunteers to help with forestry programs. They can help find and develop substitutes for firewood. They can also help develop better and efficient stoves, find ways of efficient charcoal production, and undertake research to develop and test new varieties of fast growing wood and perhaps other biomass forms of fuel.

F. Energy Conservation

Although energy waste in the developing countries is not as great as in the industrial nations, there is the need to conserve. The problem is generally one of a lack of skills and capital to improve the level of efficiency. While the poor can least afford to consume energy wastefully, they can also least afford the cash investment that is needed to make energy productivity more efficient. Aid agencies can contribute to energy conservation. For example, they can sponsor studies of energy losses inherent in current practices, finance and undertake surveys of plant layout and equipment, finance the development of more efficient equipment, and train nations in all aspects of conservation.

To a great extent, the developing countries have weathered the increases in oil prices in the 1970s and the resulting recession better than was feared. In spite of all the problems, the LDCs, by and large, have been successful in avoiding disasters so far. They have been able to adjust more easily than anticipated. But many experts doubt that they can in future continue to adjust as easily and avoid economic damage.

In the long run, the developing countries will have to make fundamental structural adjustments to the energy problems. Governments will have to reassess their development strategies, people will have to change their consumption patterns, and changes will have to be made in the economic structure. In addition to increasing the domestic production of energy and finding alternative energy sources, these countries will have to restructure their export and import sectors, adopt more energy efficient patterns of development, and be more self-reliant. Each country will have to make a clear and thorough analysis of its problems and priorities and chart out its long-term adjustment programs accordingly.

However, since such structural adjustments are difficult and costly to make, there is an urgent need for massive international assistance. The international community should provide help not only for the sake of the OIDCs, but because it is in the self-interest of every nation to do so.

4. IMPROVED INTERNATIONAL COOPERATION ON ENERGY

Such topics as food, health, communications, and environment are given careful and systematic attention at the international level by one or more international bodies. Some experts in the energy field have urged that a special international organisation be created to do the same for energy. Whether additional machinery is needed is not a suitable subject for this framework report. However, it may be helpful to identify the kinds of problems in the field of energy that are not adequately manageable at the national level but need attention at the international level, either by existing or possibly by new bodies.

A. A Forum for Southern Views on Energy

The industrialised countries of the North have found it useful to consult with one another frequently on the subject of energy. There are consulting and cooperative arrangements on oil supply, on RD&D on new technologies, on conservation, and, of course, on nuclear power (often involving only the nuclear nations). The South is excluded from most of these arrangements. OIDCs need to be included in a world-wide forum where they may express their views on subjects like energy waste in the North, the management of oil pricing systems, nuclear rules imposed by the IAEA or unilaterally by the nuclear power countries, and the global allocation of energy RD&D funds.

B. Third World Oil Supply Security

One of the important functions of the IEA is to maintain a contingency plan for dealing with politically caused oil supply shortages. Under that plan, members undertake to restrain consumption, build contingency stocks, and share continued oil flows in case of a shortfall. There is no such plan for the oil importing developing countries. An international agency could be asked to establish such a plan or at

least to monitor the IEA plan to ensure that, in the event of
a crisis, it does not harm the interests of these countries.

C. World Energy Balance Sheet

        In the field of world food supply, it has been very
useful for the FAO to sort out and publish, from time to time,
a balance sheet on world food.   A similar service in the
international energy field would be useful.   Such a service
would assemble known data on current and potential energy
supply, demand, costs, investment levels, technologies, and
national and sub-national needs. It would prepare analytical
think pieces on such topics as international energy balances
and emerging energy problems for the guidance of the nations
of the world.

D. Finance For Renewable Energy Development Within the
    Third World

        Just as there is an agency (IAEA) to promote nuclear
energy, so there might be a special international solar (or
renewable) energy assistance program.   Essentially, it would
support fact gathering, site testing of DRE equipment,
training, and institution building; and it would finance or
subsidise the distribution of the more promising DRE equipment
based on site test results and other data.

E. Exchange of Information on RD&D Results for DRE
    Technologies

        The existing network of researchers on international
food issues might serve as a model for the world of DRE
research.   Already, our contacts with researchers in many
Third World countries make clear their feeling of isolation
and their need for a systematic means of keeping up with the
work of other researchers. One task for international energy
machinery may be to establish and monitor such an information
exchange mechanism.

CHAPTER IV: A FRAMEWORK FOR ENERGY POLICIES
IN OIL IMPORTING DEVELOPING CONUNTRIES

In this chapter we examine the main energy supply
options for OIDCs in the medium term, i.e., during the next
10-15 years. These include oil, gas, coal, nuclear, hydro and
geothermal power.

In Section 1 supply options for external energy are
considered. The main conclusion is that trade in oil will
decline in importance but will or may be partly substituted by
coal, gas, and electricity. In particular, there may be
increasing exchanges of gas and electricity among bordering
countries or entire regions.

In Section 2 supply options for domestic energy are
reviewed in light of what is known or inferred regarding
OIDCs' energy potential. The main conclusion is that with
adequate policies most OIDCs, particularly those which are
medium-sized or larger, could become much more self-sufficient
and in some cases exporters of energy. This is because they
contain within their territories energy resources which are
significant for their medium-term needs. An analysis is made
source by source.

In Section 3 an attempt is made to project how the
situation of energy dependency could change over the next
10-15 years. OIDCs are grouped by degree of energy self-
sufficiency now and in the future. At the same time, a second
type of classification is attempted in terms of the main kinds
of external assistance which these countries may need to
overcome their problems. These are divided into: i)
technical assistance from official institutions, ii) financial
assistance from official institutions, iii) foreign private
investment and know-how, and iv) financial assistance from
private banks.

1. EXTERNAL SUPPLY OPTIONS

A. Oil

During 1950-73 the bulk of new energy supplies for
the non-communist world, particularly Western Europe, Japan,

and the OIDCs, was provided by rapidly growing oil production from a small group of OXDCs, members of OPEC.

Oil was abundant, convenient, and required relatively low investments for its production, transport, processing, and use. Furthermore, it was sold at a price lower than that of coal, becoming a significant factor in the unprecedentedly rapid economic expansion which Europe, Japan, and many Third World countries experienced during the period. However, this was at the risk of becoming simultaneously excessively dependent on oil and on imports for the energy needs of their economies.

Since the Middle East war of 1973 and more so since the Iranian revolution of 1979, a fundamental change has taken place. Briefly, this change consists in the adoption by OPEC members of very determined conservation policies. These are aimed at lengthening the life of their oil resources and increasing their value to the level of eventual substitutes (e.g., synthetics). The rationale for these policies has been discussed elsewhere. It must be accepted that it is basically sound from their viewpoint. Moreover, it is also in the longer-term interest of the oil consumers. This is because the transition to a non-oil era is unavoidable, needs several decades to be accomplished, and could be more painful if it did not start with enough time for carrying out the search and implementation of acceptable alternatives.

Because of the new policies of OXDCs, oil importers have no effective choice and must accept the following constraints:

i)   There will be little or no increase in oil supplies from OPEC sources. In fact, there may be a gradual decrease.

ii) External oil supplies will stay at a high price. This price is likely to increase even further, until substitutes may be sufficiently available to satisfy the world's additional energy needs, in particular those of developing nations.

iii) Oil supplies and prices will most probably be subject to violent but hopefully short-term fluctuations.

This will result from likely but unpredictable political, social, and technical accidents, due to the intrinsic vulnerabilities of the supply system.

Chapter I indicated that international trade in other energy sources is likely to increase. Some of these sources will be significant to OIDCs and should be kept in mind when analysing energy options.

B. Gas

Natural gas can be moved by sea in the form of LNG or by land in pipelines. Regarding LNG, the high investment costs of liquefaction, transport, regasification, and distribution make this option of little interest to most OIDCs. Only large consumers with no cheaper alternatives could choose this option. They may include Brazil, Korea, and Rep. of China (Taiwan), though Brazil in particular could obtain gas by pipeline from neighbouring countries such as Bolivia and Argentina.

The option of importing gas by pipeline may be of much greater interest. It is usually possible to purchase the gas at a lower price than oil (both seller and buyer may lack better viable alternatives), and investments are also considerably lower.

As already noted, situations of this type may arise between Brazil, Bolivia, and Argentina. They may also arise between Uruguay and Argentina, and between Central American countries and Mexico to the north or Colombia to the south. In South Asia it could happen between Pakistan and India, as well as between Bangladesh and India (in both cases India the purchaser). In the Middle East, it could happen between Turkey and Iraq or Iran, and between Egypt, Israel, and Jordan (should peace ever come to that area). In North Africa it could happen between Algeria and Tunisia (taking advantage of the pipeline to Italy). West Africa could eventually be linked by gas pipelines, particularly around Nigeria.

C. Coal

Imports of coal from both industrial (Australia, Canada, South Africa, and US) and developing countries (such as Botswana, Colombia, and Indonesia) may be a very attractive option in terms of cost per unit of energy, particularly for power generation and industrial uses (cement, glass, etc.). Security of supply and attractive prices might be obtainable on the basis of long-term contracts. In some cases, especially for large consumers, it could make sense for OIDCs to buy coal mines in foreign countries, as some European countries are doing in the US. Brazil in fact has tried to have an equity position in Colombian coal developments. Korea and Rep. of China could seek the same in such countries as Australia and Indonesia.

Coal trade development in OIDCs will require careful planning, as the infrastructure for unloading, transporting, and burning coal is generally non-existent and costly. In this sense, trade in coal has some of the characteristics of LNG; moreover, coal has greater flexibility and lower investment.

D. Nuclear Fuels

There are a number of OIDCs (e.g., Argentina, Brazil, India, Korea, Pakistan, Philippines, Rep. of China), which are or may become users of nuclear energy in the 1980s. Most of them will need to import nuclear fuel, because they lack either the raw material or the enrichment facilities. The nuclear option is expensive and technologically complex. At the present time, it is available and competitive with oil --and in some instances coal--only for very large power plants, at least 600 MW if not higher. This means that only a few, though some of the largest, developing countries would be justified, on economic grounds alone, to go for this option.

Contrary to the case in which a country possesses gas or coal resources, the availability of domestic uranium resources is not sufficient to justify following the nuclear option. Uranium represents a minor proportion of the cost of nuclear power, and it is more logical to consider it as a possible source of export revenues (as oil) rather than a source of domestic energy.

E. Power

Another possibility is to import electric energy from neighbouring countries. In some cases, it may be to import other countries' large surpluses which cannot be used locally (e.g., ongoing projects to export from Paraguay to Argentina and Brazil; and possibly Nepal to India). In other cases, it may be through better regional planning (e.g., the interconnected system under review by the Central American countries, which allows optional generation and transmission line scheduling).

The conclusions of this section are that:

i) OIDCs could face very tight supplies of foreign oil. They could be competing with the rest of the world (and among themselves) for very limited additional global supplies. Unless they can secure special treatment from suppliers on a government-to-government basis, the competition will be largely on a market-determined basis, and the stronger buyers will more likely be favoured. There is serious danger that OIDCs will get relatively less and pay relatively more than the industrial countries and CPEs.

ii) OIDCs should therefore investigate and pursue other less constrained external sources of energy, especially coal, gas, nuclear, or hydropower. In particular, gas and electricity from neighbouring countries, brought in by pipeline and transmission lines, may prove quite attractive and equally beneficial to the importer and exporter.

iii) Nevertheless, development of domestic supplies and efficient use of energy are the main options to be pursued. Imported oil, which was in the past and is still the most important source for many OIDCs, cannot be expected to support their future energy needs.

This leads us to examine the domestic energy resources of OIDCs and the policies which they may adopt to develop them. The issue of energy efficiency and conservation was discussed in Chapter III.

2. DOMESTIC SUPPLY OPTIONS[*]

The pre-1973 availability of low-cost oil from external sources provided little incentive for the exploration and exploitation of domestic resources. Generally speaking, most countries concentrated in the area of hydroelectric generation, which was usually competitive, especially for the supply of urban and industrial markets. Coal development outside India has been very limited and has mostly been a carry-over of the era before World War II. As for oil and gas, efforts by the international oil industry were concentrated in a few exceptionally promising areas with a clear potential for exports. In the OIDCs, the work was done essentially by national oil companies, in part because of these countries' dissatisfaction with the level of effort and investment which foreign companies appeared able and willing to make at various critical points in time. These foreign companies were, of course, pursuing a global optimisation and moved to countries which offered better geological prospects as well as financial terms. This was what happened in some countries of Latin America (e.g., Argentina, Brazil, Chile) as well as India and Pakistan.

For these reasons, the crisis of 1973 caught OIDCs generally weak and unprepared to face effectively the new situation, in terms of organisation, management, and technical skills, as well as knowledge of their potential energy resources. Part of this gap could have been covered by international development banks and other aid organisations, but these also were initially unequipped in terms of staff and policy to be very effective. Only in 1977 was the World Bank able to start a proper response in this area, to be followed later by others.

In view of these national and official aid weaknesses, it was clear that any quick response to the crisis must turn to external sources for the financial and policy means to secure the necessary skills. These skills are for

---

[*] Issues regarding rural non-commercial energy in developing countries have been discussed in Chapters II & III.

the most part available only in the industrial world's energy companies, particularly in the areas of oil, gas, coal, and nuclear development. In trying to secure these skills, OIDCs are competing i) with pressures in industrial countries for increased domestic efforts, ii) with claims and requests of OPEC countries, iii) with other established exporters which have more negotiating strength and leverage, and iv) among themselves.

Many OIDCs appear to be unaware of this situation or unable to cope with it: some for ideological reasons, others because of political divisions and weaknesses, and others because of explicit opposition or more frequently effective foot-dragging by their national oil companies, which would like to maintain their predominant role, no matter what the cost in risks and delays to the country as a whole. Even if most OIDCs adopt optimal policies a) in the long-term to attain a national implementation capability, and b) in the short- and medium-term to accelerate energy exploration and development, they would still face very serious obstacles, for reasons which are worth repeating:

i)   modest development and export prospects relative to OXDCs,

ii) weak local infrastructure, physical and human, and

iii) investors' concern with political instability and non-commercial risks.

To overcome these obstacles needs enlightened, pragmatic, and stable government policies. It also requires (until these policies become credible for countries with poor records) the sort of de facto international guarantee which can be given by institutions including the World Bank and other development banks as "third parties."

It is taking a long time for these ideas to gain ground in all the parties involved: OIDCs, development institutions, and industry. But there are signs that progress is finally being made.

As for the past period of 1973–78, it is clear that the efforts of industry have been concentrated in the industrialised countries and that, relative to these, the work carried out in the OIDCs is minimal.

Let us now look more specifically at the energy development options of OIDCs. In general, with very few exceptions (islands or very small countries), OIDCs are endowed with a variety of actual or potential energy sources. This is shown in Table IV-1, which list countries with oil, gas, coal, and geothermal potential. In addition, Table IV-2 gives quantitative information on their hydroelectric potential; it shows that most of the potential is still only planned or unused. A brief but more detailed discussion of this potential is given below, regarding type of sources and key development problems.

A. Oil and Gas

Oil and gas are found geologically in sedimentary basins. The map below shows the approximate area of the world's known sedimentary basins, indicating which of them are currently producing oil and gas. It assumes that, if a country has a sedimentary basin in its territory, there is a possibility of finding oil and gas. This assumption, while generally correct, does not hold in every case. To some extent, the evaluation of the oil potential of any given area is a subjective judgement by individual petroleum geologists; hence the wide diversity of estimates of undiscovered oil and gas in any particular country.

Most developing countries' sedimentary areas are relatively unexplored, compared with those of the industrialised countries. One measure is the density of drilling, in terms of the number of wells drilled per thousand square kilometres of prospective area. This type of statistical analysis makes no distinction between the relative oil potential of different sedimentary basins; this potential covers a very wide range and is open to subjective judgement as the size of a country's prospective area.

Nevertheless, if used with caution, the drilling density provides a useful yardstick for estimating the intensity of exploration. The estimates in Table IV-3 serve to illustrate the great disparity in exploration effort, in particular between industrialised countries and non-OPEC developing countries.

TABLE IV-1: CHARACTERISATION OF NON–OPEC DEVELOPING COUNTRIES BASED ON THEIR POTENTIAL ENERGY RESOURCES

Net Oil Exporters	Oil &/or Gas Producers	Potential Oil and/or Gas Producers		
Angola	Afghanistan	Benin	Honduras	Papua New Guinea
Bahrain	Argentina	Chad	Ivory Coast	Senegal
Bolivia	Bangladesh	Costa Rica	Jamaica	Sierra Leone
Brunei	Barbados	Cyprus	Jordan	
Congo	Brazil	Dominican Rep.	Kenya	
Egypt	Burma		Korea	Somalia
Malaysia	Cameroon	Eq. Guinea	Lebanon	Sri Lanka
Mexico	Chile	Ethiopia	Liberia	Sudan
Oman	Colombia	Fiji	Mali	Surinam
Peru	India	Gambia	Madagascar	Tanzania
Syrian AR	Morocco	Ghana	Mauritania	Togo
Trinidad & Tobago	Pakistan	Guatemala	Mauritius	Upper Volta
	Philippines	Guinea-Bissau	Mozambique	
Tunisia	Thailand		Nepal	Uruguay
Zaire	Turkey	Guinea Rep.	Nicaragua	Vietnam
	Yugoslavia	Guyana	Niger	Yemen, AR
		Haiti	Panama	Yemen, PDR

Potential Geothermal Producers	Coal-Endowed	Indigenous Energy[a] Resource Deficient
Cameroon	Argentina	Cyprus
Chile	Bangladesh	Dominican Rep.
Colombia	Botswana	Gambia
Costa Rica	Brazil	Haiti
El Salvador	Chile	Jamaica
Ethiopia	Colombia	Jordan
Guatemala	India	Lebanon
Kenya	Mexico	Mauritius
Malawi	Madagascar	Singapore
Nicaragua	Mozambique	Upper Volta
Philippines	Peru	
Rep. China	Rep. Korea	
Tanzania	Swaziland	
Turkey	Turkey	
Uganda	Vietnam	
Yemen, AR	Zambia	

Note: [a]Proven and probable indigenous commercial energy resources, which are at present competitive with imported oil, are small relative to commercial energy demand in these countries.

Source: World Bank Staff Working Paper No. 350, August 1979.

213

TABLE IV-2: HYDROPOWER CAPACITY IN DEVELOPING COUNTRIES

Countries	Gross Theoretical Capability (TJ[a])	Capacity Operating (MW)	Under Construction (MW)	Planned (MW)	Unused (MW)
Afghanistan	n.a.	n.a.	n.a.	n.a.	n.a.
Angola	252,002	284	80	300	9,000
Argentina	8,755,279	1,393	4,212	36,323	9,125
Bangladesh	n.a.	80	50	100	1,087
Brazil	2,399,536	15,297	24,225	16,537	44,567
Chile	805,321	1,454	950	6,595	6,781
Colombia	4,644,004	1,900	1,150	23,350	23,600
Costa Rica	802,807	214	270	1,635	4,881
Egypt	n.a.	2,445	n.a.	2,440	n.a.
El Salvador	15,120	97	135	940	n.a.
Ethiopia	819,876	n.a.	n.a.	1,390	7,602
Ghana	n.a.	948	n.a.	140	527
Guatemala	46,008	96	n.a.	1,100	n.a.
Honduras	n.a.	69	n.a.	n.a.	n.a.
India	777,602	6,750	6,800	56,450	n.a.
Ivory Coast	230,402	225	n.a.	555	n.a.
Malaysia	n.a.	296	348	341	334
Mexico	n.a.	3,885	3,030	17,975	n.a.
Mozambique	180,002	90	3,700	2,500	5,000
Pakistan	n.a.	2,173	1,125	n.a.	31,171
Peru	n.a.	1,389	n.a.	n.a.	n.a.
Philippines	70,543	641	2,085	n.a.	4,778
Rwanda	n.a.	41	n.a.	128	n.a.
Spain	557,440	11,355	2,326	8,835	6,808
Syria	n.a.	204	n.a.	n.a.	n.a.
Rep. China	105,448	1,365	27	321	n.a.
Thailand	244,113	910	780	6,573	13,602
Tunisia	69	29	n.a.	n.a.	25
Turkey	1,570,485	19,577	n.a.	n.a.	n.a.
Uruguay	n.a.	252	1,890	300	465
Yugoslavia	396,004	4,247	910	9,500	2,300
Zaire	n.a.	597	289	n.a.	32,000
Zambia	757	910	n.a.	n.a.	n.a.

Note: [a]One tera joule (TJ) : 2.8 x 10^5 Kwh.

Source: World Bank Staff Working Paper No. 350, August 1979, based on World Energy Conference data.

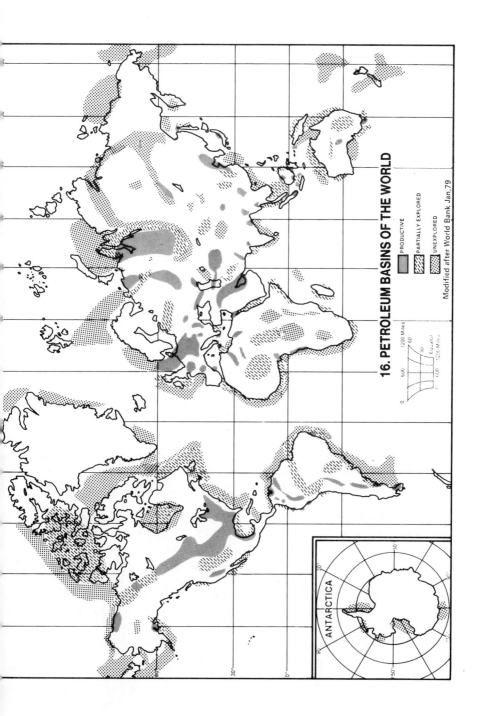

16. PETROLEUM BASINS OF THE WORLD

PRODUCTIVE
PARTIALLY EXPLORED
UNEXPLORED

Modified after World Bank Jan.79

0   600   1200 Miles
0   600   1200 Miles

ANTARCTICA

TABLE IV-3:   OIL EXPLORATION DRILLING DENSITY, 1976

	Petroleum Prospective Area (million sq. miles)	Drilling Density (wells per '000 sq.miles of pro- spective area)
Developed & Developing	30.5	109
Industrialised Countries	9.0	290
of which: US	(3.1)	(780)
Non-OPEC Dev'g Countries	12.9	7
of which: Oil-importing	(8.6)	(5)
OPEC Countries	4	20

Note: The relatively low density in OPEC countries is due
        the very favourable geological conditions (larg
        individual fields), which do not apply elsewhere.

Source: Grossling, Window on Oil, 1977.

        Table IV-4 lists those non-OPEC countries a) whi
are considered to have some possibility of finding addition
oil and gas reserves, and b) in the case of those where no di
coveries have yet been made, where exploration may be justified.

        Most of the OIDCs which are listed in the first thr
columns (with prospects fairly good or better) are already pro
ducers or should become producers in the near future. This gro
includes some of the largest, most populated as well as the mo
seriously affected oil-importing countries. Many of them have
long way to go before solving their problems, even if they ha
recently improved their policies (e.g., Brazil, Pakista
Philippines, Thailand). In most cases, these countries ha
adopted a positive attitude to foreign participation.

TABLE IV-4:   DEVELOPING COUNTRIES: POTENTIAL FOR OIL AND GAS DISCOVERIES

	Good to Very Good	Good	Fairly Good	Fair	Poor to Moderate
COUNTRY INCOME GROUPING					
South Asia					
Low		Bangladesh Burma India Pakistan		Sri Lanka	Nepal
E. Asia & Pacific					
High	Brunei[b]				Singapore
Middle:					
Upper					Hong Kong
Intermediate	Malaysia[b]			Rep.Korea	
Lower			Papua N.Guinea Philippines[a] Thailand[a]		
Low			Vietnam		Laos
Europe, Mid East & N. Africa					
High	Bahrain[b] Oman [b]				
Middle:					
Upper		Yugoslavia			
Intermediate	Syria[b] Tunisia[b]	Turkey			
Lower	Egypt[b]	Morocco		Jordan	
Low		Afghanistan		Yemen AR Yemen PDR	
East Africa					
Middle:					
Intermediate					Mauritius
Lower				Mozambique	Botswana
Low		Zaire[b]	Tanzania	Ethiopia Madagascar Somalia	Comoro Is Kenya Lesotho Malawi Uganda

(Continued)

COUNTRY INCOME GROUPING	Good to Very Good	Good	Fairly Good	Fair	Poor to Moderate
West Africa					
High					
Middle:					
Intermediate				Sao Tome & Principe	
Lower	Angola[b] Congo[b]	Cameroon[b]	Ivory Coast Ghana[b] Benin	Equatorial Guinea Togo Senegal	
Low			Chad[a]	Central African Rep. Gambia Guinea Mali Niger Sierra Leone	Upper Volta
Latin America & Caribbean					
Middle:					
Upper	Mexico[b] Trinidad & Tobago[b]	Argentina Brazil Barbados		Surinam Uruguay Jamaica	
Intermediate	Peru[b]	Colombia Chile	Guatemala	Guyana Paraguay Dominican Rep. Nicaragua Costa Rica	
Lower		Bolivia		Panama Honduras	
Low				Haiti	
Number of Countries	13	15	10	30	10

Notes: [a]Will join the list of oil/gas producers shortly.
          [b]Includes non-OPEC OXDCs.

Source: World Bank Staff Working Paper No. 350, August 1979.

The situation is more difficult for countries with only fair or poor prospects. It is in these countries, particularly those with low-income per capita, where good government policies and front-end support for exploration by international aid may be most critical to get them started. It is also in those countries that it is most important to investigate a) alternatives to oil and b) if alternatives do not exist, options for economic growth which will minimise energy needs and/or allow foreign exchange to be earned for oil imports.

B. Gas

The utilisation of natural gas in a developing country has become economically far more attractive as crude oil prices increase. But it often presents a number of severe problems which call for policy decisions. While natural gas itself is a highly desirable fuel for both domestic and industrial use, it must be transported, in most cases by pipeline. Hence the market needs to be sufficiently large and concentrated, to justify the cost of constructing not only the gas processing plant, but also the pipeline to supply it.*

To provide a market of adequate size, it is necessary to have a grouping of large fuel consumers such as thermal power generating stations, cement plants, nitrogenous fertiliser plants, and similar energy-intensive plants. While many developing countries have such plants, they are rarely grouped in the same area. In most developing countries there is no demand for space heating. It is often necessary to develop the market for natural gas at the same time as the transport facility, because an underused pipeline is an uneconomic investment. Further investment costs are incurred if associated gas is used from oil fields, because this must be collected from dispersed sources of supply, treated, and compressed before it is put in the pipeline.

---

* Natural gas can be liquefied by refrigeration and transported in this form, but the cost makes it only feasible at present for large export-oriented plants. A liquefaction plant for 500 million cubic feet of gas per day costs about $1 billion, and ocean tankers to ship it cost as much again.

Furthermore, natural gas competes in many cases with fuel oil or hydropower for the same market, so that natural gas development may actually increase problems in other parts of the economy. It is, therefore, not uncommon to find unexploited natural gas resources in countries which are having difficulty in obtaining foreign exchange to pay for oil imports. Frustrating as this may be, there is no easy solution to the problem at the present time. Nevertheless, developing countries having natural gas reserves should make a serious attempt to use them.

For the above reasons, gas development for domestic use presents more similarities with coal or hydroelectric development than with oil. The role of government rather than foreign investment becomes paramount. Consequently, the financial and technical assistance of development institutions is very important.

Of the oil-importing countries listed in Table IV–4, the ones where domestic gas development may be of greatest interest are Argentina, Bangladesh, Chile, Colombia, India, Pakistan, Tanzania, and Thailand.

C. Coal

Coal was the main fuel of the industrial world until the early 1950s. It has not played this role in OIDCs, because they began for the most part to industrialise in the oil era. Knowledge of OIDCs' coal resources is very inadequate.

The World Energy Conference in 1977 estimated the world's economically and technically recoverable coal reserves to be 636 billion metric tons, of which only 10% may be located in developing countries.

A larger proportion of these reserves may be recoverable in the future than is estimated at present. Botswana, Brazil, India, Indonesia, and Swaziland account for more than 60% of presently recoverable coal reserves in developing countries. Table IV–5 lists coal reserves in developing countries. In many countries the full extent of coal resources has never been determined, and evaluating these should receive high priority in those countries where coal is known to exist.

TABLE IV-5: COAL RESERVES AND RESOURCES OF DEVELOPING COUNTRIES

	GEOLOGICAL RESOURCES	TECHNICALLY AND ECONOMICALLY RECOVERABLE RESERVES			DEGREE OF EXPLORATION[a]
	mm tce[b]	mm tce[b]	% World Resources	% World Recoverable Reserves	
TOTAL	230,360	65,219	2.28	10.25	
AFRICA	115,338	7,220	1.14	1.13	
Algeria	20				L
Angola	500				L
Benin	n.a.				L
Botswana	100,000	3,500	0.99	0.55	L–M
Burundi	n.a.				L
Cameroon	500				M
Egypt	80				M
Ethiopia	n.a.				L
Madagascar	92		0.02	0.15	M
Malawi	14				M
Morocco	96				M
Mozambique	400	80	—	0.01	M
Niger	n.a.				L
Nigeria	180	90	—	0.01	M
Sierra Leone	n.a.				L
Somalia	n.a.				L
Swaziland	5,000	1,820	0.05	0.29	M
Tanzania	360				M
Tunisia	n.a.				L
Zaire	73				L
Zambia	228	5	—	—	L–M
Zimbabwe	7,130	755	0.07	0.12	M
ASIA	72,466	38,583	0.72	6.06	
Afghanistan	85	—	—	—	L
Bangladesh	1,649	519	0.02	0.08	
Brunei	1	—	—	—	L
Burma	286	1	—	—	M
Cambodia	n.a.	n.a.	0.06	0.25	L
Rep. China	680	—		—	M
India	56,799	33,700	0.56	5.30	M–H
Indonesia	3,723	1,430	0.04	0.22	L
Iran	385	193	—	0.03	M
Rep. Korea	921	386	0.01	0.06	M
Pakistan	1,375	—	—	—	M
Philippines	87	—	—	—	L–M
Thailand	78	—	—	—	M
Turkey	3,268	793	0.03	0.12	M
Vietnam	3,000	—	—	—	M
LATIN AMERICA	31,692	10,951	0.31	1.73	
Argentina	384	290	—	0.05	L
Bolivia	n.a.				M
Brazil	10,082	8,098	0.0	1.27	L–M
Chile	4,585	162	0.5	0.03	M
Colombia	8,318	443	0.8	0.07	L
Costa Rica	n.a.				L
Ecuador	22				M
Guatemala	n.a.	n.a.	...	...	L
Honduras	n.a.				L
Mexico	5,448	875	0.05	0.14	M
Panama	n.a.				L
Peru	1,122	105	0.01	0.02	M
Venezuela	1,630	978	0.02	0.15	M
EUROPE					
Yugoslavia	10,927	8,465	0.11	1.33	H

Notes: [a]Degree of Exploration:
   H – Well established reserve estimates, well defined geology.
   M – Some exploration programs have been documented.
   L – Few exploratory programs.
   [b]mm tce=million metric tons of coal equivalent.

Source: World Bank Staff Working Paper No. 350, August 1979.

World coal production in 1977 was 2,774 million tons, equivalent to about half the energy equivalent of oil output. Of this total, 176 million tons were mined in developing countries.

Ten of these, namely Brazil, Chile, Colombia, Mexico, Pakistan, Republic of China, Republic of Korea, Turkey, Vietnam, and Yugoslavia between them account for 96% of coal output in developing countries. Table IV-6 shows actual and forecast coal production in developing countries. It is evident that there is considerable scope for increasing production of coal in developing countries, since 21 of them are reported to have deposits of coal.

Coal production costs vary over a wide range. Open-cast mining is invariably much cheaper than underground mining. Low-grade coals often cannot be exploited economically except by the open-cast method. Mining costs on a worldwide basis in 1978 averaged $10-15 per ton for open-cast mines, and $20-30 per ton for underground mines. For a good grade of steam coal, this would compare with a cost of $14-20 per ton of fuel oil equivalent for open-cast coal and $27-40 per ton of fuel oil equivalent for coal from underground mines.

Exploration for coal is less costly than for oil, but nevertheless represents a risk outlay. It is carried out by means of geological surveys, assisted by geophysical methods and drilling to prove the thickness, continuity, and grade of the coal away from the outcrop.

Except in the few cases where a potential for competitive coal exports exists (e.g., Botswana, Colombia and Swaziland), it is unlikely that foreign investment would be interested in playing a role in coal development. This will have to take place under the direction and with the financing of the OIDCs, for which they will need maximum technical and financial assistance from development institutions.

Small-scale coal mining for local use does not present many problems. But a large-scale development to support industrial growth presents many. First and foremost is the cost of developing the mines and the need for infrastructure, such as transport and community facilities for miners and

TABLE IV-6: COAL PRODUCTION PROSPECTS OF DEVELOPING COUNTRIES

	Recoverable[a] Reserves	1977	Production 1980	1985	1990	Annual Growth Rate 1977-85	1985-90
	(Million tce[b])		(Million tce[b])			(%)	(%)
WORLD	636,364	2,773.7	3,160	3,861	4,802	4.2	4.4
INDUSTRIAL COUNTRIES	324,341	1,134.4	1,265	1,476	1,752	3.3	3.5
CPEs	246,304	1,463.4	1,662	2,089	2,610	4.6	4.5
DEVELOPING COUNTRIES	65,219	175.9	233.1	304.1	440.4	7.1	7.6
Africa	7,220	5.0	8.3	15.4	31.9	14.8	17.1
Algeria	(20)[c]	...[e]	...[e]	...[e]	...[e]	–	–
Angola	(500)[c]	–	–	–	2.0	–	–
Botswana	3,500	0.2	0.2	0.3	5.0	5.2	75.5
Burundi	n.a.	...[e]	...[e]	...[e]	...[e]	–	–
Cameroon	(500)[c]	–	–	–	–	–	–
Egypt	(80)[c]	–	–	–	–	–	–
Madagascar	(92)[c]	–	–	1.0	2.0	–	–
Malawi	(14)[c]	–	–	–	–	–	–
Morocco	(96)[c]	0.6	0.9	1.0	1.1	6.6	1.9
Mozambique	80	0.4	1.0	2.0	3.0	22.3	9.4
Nigeria	90	0.3	0.3	1.0	3.0	16.2	24.6
Swaziland	1,820	0.1	0.5	1.5	5.0	28.6	27.2
Tanzania	(360)[c]	...[e]	...[e]	2.0	3.0	–	8.5
Zaire	(73)[c]	0.1	0.1	0.1	0.1	0.0	0.0
Zambia	5	0.8	1.3	1.9	2.5	11.4	5.6
Zimbabwe	755	2.5	4.0	4.6	5.2	7.9	2.5
Asia	38,583	136.1	171.5	211.2	288.7	5.7	6.3
Afghanistan	(85)[c]	0.2	0.2	0.6	1.0	14.7	20.1
Bangladesh	519	–	–	–	2.0	–	–
Brunei	(1)[c]	–	–	–	–	–	–
Burma	(280)[c]	...[e]	...[e]	...[e]	...[e]	–	–
China, Rep.	(680)[c]	2.9	4.0	5.0	6.0	5.7	4.5
India	33,700	99.7	125.0	145.0	190.0	4.8	5.6
Indonesia	1,430	0.2	0.2	3.5	12.0	42.2	27.4
Iran	193	0.9	1.0	1.5	1.5	6.6	0.0
Korea, Rep.	386	28.3	19.0	22.0	25.0	3.1	2.6
Malaysia	(75)[c]	–	–	–	2.0	–	–
Pakistan	(1,375)[c]	1.0	1.5	2.0	3.0	9.1	8.5
Philippines	(87)[c]	0.3	0.3	1.6	4.0	23.3	20.1
Thailand	(78)[c]	0.2	0.5	2.0	6.0	13.4	–
Turkey	793	7.4	9.8	13.0	16.2	7.3	5.9
Vietnam	(3,000)[c]	6.0	10.0	15.0	20.0	12.1	24.6

(continued)

TABLE IV-6:   COAL PRODUCTION PROSPECTS OF DEVELOPING COUNTRIES

(Continued)

	Recoverable[a] Reserves	Production				Annual Growth Rate	
		1977	1980	1985	1990	1977-85	1985-90
	(Million tce[b])	(Million tce[b])				(%)	(%)
Latin America	10,951	15.0	23.8	39.3	73.8	12.6	13.4
Argentina	290	0.5	2.3	3.5	7.5	27.5	16.5
Brazil	8,098	3.5	6.4	10.0	20.0	13.9	14.9
Chile	162	1.2	2.0	2.5	7.5	9.6	24.6
Colombia	443	3.7	5.0	10.0	20.0	13.2	14.9
Ecuador	(22)[c]	–	–	–	–	–	–
Haiti	(7)[c]	–	–	–	0.3	–	–
Honduras	(0.2)[c]	–	–	–	–	–	–
Mexico	875	6.0	6.7	8.0	9.3	3.7	3.1
Peru	105	...[e]	0.2	0.3	0.4	...[d]	5.9
Venezuela	978	0.1	1.2	5.0	8.8	63.1	12.0
Europe							
Yugoslavia	8,465	19.8	29.5	18.2	46.0	9.3	3.8

Notes: [a]Data on recoverable reserves are not available for the following countries: Benin, Ethiopia, Niger, Sierra Leone, Somalia, Tunisia, Laos, Bolivia, Guatemala, and Panama.

[b]tce: metric tons of coal equivalent

[c]Figures in parenthesis represent geological resources, since no reserve data are available.

[d]Annual growth rate in excess of 50% due to very low 1977 production base;

[e]Output below 0.1 million tce in 1977.

Source: World Bank Staff Working Paper No. 350, August 1979.

their families. Table IV-7 gives some representative costs
for coal mine development. Large-scale transport of coal is
effected for the most part by rail. Water transport is very
suitable for this type of traffic, but it is rare in developing countries to find a situation where this is feasible. The
cost of building a railroad and handling facilities to
transport the coal is very high. Therefore, if developing
countries propose to develop coal as an industrial fuel, they
should seriously consider setting up industrial development at
the coal field, rather than transporting the coal to existing
population centres.

Many low-grade coals can be improved in quality by
mechanical washing to reduce ash content, and by partial car-
bonisation to reduce water content, sulphur, and the volatile
matter which gives rise to most of the smoke from coal burning. Such smokeless fuels can often be compressed into briquettes, which are easier to transport than the original raw
coal and which provide a useful fuel for domestic purposes and
light industry. In developing countries suffering from shortages of domestic fuel and consequent deforestation, serious
consideration should be given to exploiting coal deposits to
make smokeless fuel briquettes as a substitute. The briquett-
ing potential of each coal deposit needs to be determined
separately, by experiment, so that an appropriate technical
process can be used. Many of the failures reported in this
type of project result from lack of proper investigation of
the properties of the coal before purchasing the plant.

D. Synthetics

There has been much discussion about the production
of synthetic liquid fuels from coal, in consequence of the
higher prices of refined petroleum products. While coal
itself can substitute for fuel oil in most industrial applications, the manufacture of synthetic liquid fuels from coal
offers one of the few possibilities of substitution for
petroleum fuels in the transport sector, i.e., for gasoline
and diesel fuel. The technology is fairly well known, having
been used extensively in Germany during World War II. The
only plants operating at present are located in South Africa,
although there are a number of pilot plants in the US. The
problem is less one of technology, although the plants have
had considerable start-up problems, than of cost. It is

TABLE IV-7: COAL PRODUCTION AND MINE INVESTMENT COSTS
IN SELECTED COAL-PRODUCING COUNTRIES

	Mining Technology	Coal Type	Minehead Production Cost		Incremental Mine Incremental Cost
			Existing Mine	New Mine	
			(US$ per ton-1978)		(US$ per ton-1978)
DEVELOPED COUNTRIES					
Australia	S	B,C,L	12–15	8–15	30–40
Canada	U	B,C	20–45	n.a.	40–50
	S	S,B,L	6–15	n.a.	20–30
France	U	B	80–95	80–90	n.a.
		L	35–45	n.a.	
FR Germany	U	B,C		70–100	70–85
		L	10–25		
S. Africa	U	B,C	10–12	n.a.	30–35
	S	B,C	8–10	n.a.	n.a.
United Kingdom	U	B,C	45–75	n.a.	70–80
United States	U	B,C	20–30	n.a.	40–55
	S	B,L	8–15	n.a.	10–35
CPEs					
PR China	U	B,C	12–20	n.a.	25–35
	S	B,L	6–12	n.a.	5–10
Czechoslovakia	U	B,C	30–40	n.a.	60–70
DR Germany	S	L	8–12	n.a.	15–25
Poland	U	B,C	18–25	n.a.	50–60
	S	L	5–10	n.a.	15–20
Soviet Union	U	B	18–25	n.a.	30–40
	S	L	5–10	n.a.	15–20
DEVELOPING COUNTRIES					
Argentina	U	B	40–45	n.a.	50–60
Brazil	U/S	B	15–25	12–18	25–50
Colombia	U	B,C	5–22	n.a.	n.a.
	S	B	n.a.	25–30	50–60
India	U	B,C	12–25	n.a.	30–35
	S	B,L	20–22	n.a.	n.a.
Indonesia	U	B	35–40	n.a.	n.a.
	S	B	18–20	30–35	50–60
Rep. Korea	U	A	20–25	n.a.	35–40
Mexico	U	B,C	15–20	n.a.	45–55
Pakistan	U	B	20–30	n.a.	n.a.
Philippines	U	B	8–21	18–20	30–70
Thailand	S	L	n.a.	7–12	30–35
Venezuela	S	B	n.a.	20–25	50–55
Yugoslavia	U	S,B,L	20–25	n.a.	25–30
	S	S,B,L	11–16	n.a.	10–20

Legend: Mining Technology
U = underground mine
S = surface mine

n.a. = not available

Coal Type
A = anthracite
B = bituminous
C = coking coal
S = sub-bituminous
L = lignite

Source: World Bank Staff Working Paper No. 350, August 1979.

TABLE IV-8: SPOT STEAM PRICE TRENDS FOR SELECTED COUNTRIES, 1977-80[a]

COUNTRY/ PORT	SPECIFICATIONS			FOB VALUE (US$/metric ton)			
	000s BTU/lb	Sulphur (%)	Ash(%)	July 1977	July 1978	July 1979	Aug. 1980
A. SUPPLY							
United States							
Ashtabula/Conneaut	12.5	2.00	12.0	25.50	34.30	33.45	n.a.
Hampton Roads/Norfolk	12.0	1.00	12.0-13.0	30.90	39.90	36.40	44.55
Baltimore	12.5-12.0	1.00	12.0-12.5	24.50	33.30	37.90	41.35
Duluth	9.5	0.60	27.0[b]	18.10	27.40	27.30	n.a.
Poland							
Gdansk/Swinoujscie	11.8	1.00	15.0-12.0	21.60	26.50	26.55	n.a.
				–	–		
S. Africa							
Richards Bay	11.3-11.9	1.00	15.0	21.60	20.10	20.20	31.50[c]
	11.0	1.00	15.5	–	–	–	29.55
India							
Hadia/Pradip	11.2	.60	16.0	19.60	21.10	21.15	n.a.
Australia							
Newcastle/Port Kembla	12.0	1.00	13.0	24.50	29.90	30.00	44.05
	11.5	1.00	15.5	–	–	–	41.35
B. DEMAND							
N.W. Europe							
Amsterdam, Rotterdam	11.0	1.00	12.0	30.40	30.40	36.40	n.a.
Antwerp, France	12.0	1.00	12.5	37.20	35.80	55.10	54.15
Spain	11.2	1.50	17.0	29.90	30.90	37.90	56.60
	11.7	1.00	23.5	30.90	31.90	32.00	59.05
United Kingdom	10.8	1.00	17.0	30.90[c]	30.90[c]	31.00[c]	n.a.
	11.5	1.75	14.0	–	–	–	54.60
FR Germany	11.3	1.30-1.35	13.0-13.5	38.20	34.30	42.10/ 51.20	59.05
PR China	11.5	1.00	16.0	35.80	35.80	35.90	n.a.
	11.3	1.00	13.0	33.80	33.80	33.95	n.a.
	12.0	1.80	16.5	–	–	–	62.50

Notes: [a]Price quotes are for spot sales, defined as single shipments or volumes to be delivered within one year.

[b]Moisture included.

[c]Contract quote.

Source: Coal Week.

TABLE IV-9: HISTORICAL COAL TRADE VALUES FOR SELECTED COUNTRIES, 1972-76[a]

(US$ per metric ton)

Producing Countries:

Year	Australia fob	Australia W.Europe cif	Australia Japan cif	Poland fob	Poland W.Europe cif	Poland Japan cif	Canada fob	Canada W.Europe cif	Canada Japan cif
1972	6-9	20	18	–	22-24	24	–	13	21
1973	7-9	18-22	20	–	22-25	24	13	–	22
1974	16-17	26	30	–	32-39	39	–	–	31
1975	16-26	40	39	–	42-57	57	18-32	36	48
1976	14-31	45-48	51	–	36-59	59	20-33	–	58

Producing Countries:

Year	F.R. Germany fob	F.R. Germany W.Europe cif	F.R. Germany Japan cif	Mozambique fob	Mozambique W.Europe cif	Mozambique Japan cif	South Africa fob	South Africa W.Europe cif	South Africa Japan cif
1972	23-37	31-55	–	–	–	17	–	7	19
1973	24-39	36-37	–	–	–	–	–	24	18
1974	44-50	42-44	–	–	–	37	–	30-40	34
1975	59-64	54-65	84	–	–	47	15	28-50	43
1976	72	44-70	–	–	–	43	21	30-32	41

Producing Countries:

Year	United Kingdom fob	United Kingdom W.Europe cif	United Kingdom Japan cif	Soviet Union fob	Soviet Union W.Europe cif	Soviet Union Japan cif	United States fob	United States W.Europe cif	United States Japan cif
1972	–	12-35	–	–	14-18	21	21	23-30	29
1973	–	12-29	–	–	14-17	21	23	24-29	30
1974	–	37-44	–	–	19-32	33	48	42-53	63
1975	29-41	40-56	–	–	30-58	50	59	50-73	73
1976	32-46	44-53	–	–	32-48	52	58	48-59	68

Note: [a]Values are calculated on a tonnage basis without consideration of quality differences.

Source: World Bank Staff Working Paper No. 350, August 1979.

228

reported that, provided the cost of coal at the plant is below $10 per ton, it should be possible to produce synthetic automotive fuel from coal at around $40 to $50 per barrel which is already competitive.

The main problems from the viewpoint of developing countries are the massive investment cost and complex technology. It takes around $3 billion and a coal input of 40,000 tons per day for an output of 4,400 tons of gasoline/ diesel oil per day (37,500 b/d). The process does not require a high quality coal feedstock. But the size of coal reserves needed to support a single plant of this capacity (around 500 million tons) and the plant's high cost do limit the number of developing countries which can contemplate the production of synthetic automotive fuels from coal, unless future technological improvements can both reduce the plant's cost and improve its conversion efficiency.

E. Hydropower

This is one of the earliest forms of primary energy to be exploited, and simple primitive water-wheels may still be found in many countries. Because of the rise in oil prices, there has been renewed interest in small hydro plants (micro-hydro and mini-hydro are terms for installations having less than 1 megawatt of installed capacity) for supplying electric generators. Modern hydroelectric installations have installed capacities in the range of hundreds or thousands of megawatts. The largest hydro plant in the world is under construction at Itaipu in Brazil and will have an installed capacity of 14,000 MW.

Almost all hydro plants require some form of civil engineering work for water storage to increase the availability of energy throughout the year. The cost of this work constitutes the largest part of the investment, and the storage must usually be constructed in its entirety before any energy can be generated. Hydro development is therefore characterised by high initial investment and low running costs. Many hydro installations are dual purpose, providing both power and irrigation water.

Capital costs for hydropower installations vary widely. Including an allowance for transmission and distribution facilities, they range from $850/kilowatt installed for a high-head* installation in Colombia to $2,500/kw for small installations in Africa.   An average cost for developing countries is $1,296/kw of installed generating capacity.

As shown earlier in Table IV-2, the potential for increasing hydropower output in many developing countries is considerable. For example, Africa is estimated to have 22% of world hydropower resources, but only 2% of this has been developed. One problem is that many sites have a potential far in excess of any local market demand for the energy, so that the cost per unit of energy delivered becomes prohibitively high. One solution to this problem is to locate energy-intensive industries, such as aluminum smelters, near the hydro site, as was done with the Volta River development scheme in Ghana. Another solution is to arrange to export the power to neighbouring countries where demand is greater, as was done between Uganda and Kenya.

It is unlikely that foreign investment will play a role in hydropower, unless it is linked to a major export-oriented industrial project (e.g., aluminum). Most OIDCs have local power companies with some experience in hydroelectric power. More important, UNDP and the development banks have strong and long experience in this field; they are ready to play a substantial role in providing technical and financial assistance to those OIDCs which need it most. In effect, the main policy question now is to shift aid resources from those countries which already have strong local institutions (mainly Latin American & Caribbean and some major Asian countries) to those which have weaker ones (mostly African).

F. Geothermal Energy

Geothermal resources consist of underground aquifers containing superheated water and steam at temperatures up to 250˚ Celsius, which are exploited by means of wells. Superheated water and steam from geothermal sources have been used for electric power generation, industrial process heat, and

---

* The hydraulic head is the height of the usefully available column of water above the turbine inlet, which determines water pressure at the turbine.

space heating.   Geothermal hot water resources can also be used for domestic space heating and hot water supply.

The geothermal resources of endowed countries should be evaluated and developed, because baseload electricity generated from high-temperature geothermal resources is likely to be substantially cheaper than electricity produced from fossil fuels.   It is important to note that the exploration and development of high-temperature geothermal resources involve an element of financial risk.

The following developing countries are believed to have geothermal potential:

Mexico	Venezuela	Turkey	Yemen A.R.
Guatemala	Bolivia	Iran	Ethiopia
El Salvador	Chile	India	Kenya
Nicaragua	Argentina	Indonesia	Tanzania
Rwanda	Costa Rica	Philippines	Cameroon
Burundi	St. Lucia	Dominica	Martinique
		Guadeloupe	Solomon Islands

Geothermal energy requires technologies and equipment similar to oil exploration and development, though less costly because of the shallower depth of the geothermal sources. Hence, in principle it is possible to interest foreign investors in this field (e.g., Union Oil in the Philippines). But it is possible and more realistic to undertake geothermal development under local management (usually that of the existing power company), with the assistance of the UN agencies which have pioneered in this field and of the development banks.

G.   Other Options (Oil shale, tar-sands)

The options discussed above are of more immediate interest to OIDCs.   But there are other possibilities which should become economically attractive by the late 1980s, once the technology becomes more proven.   In particular, these include the production of oil products from oil shales and tar-sands.   Developing countries known to have significant oil shale resources are: Brazil, China, Morocco, Thailand, and Zaire.   Smaller resources have been identified in Burma, Chile, Jordan, Turkey, etc.   As for tar-sands (which are al-

ready commercially exploited in Canada), they are known to
occur in large amounts in Ghana, Ivory Coast, Madagascar,
Rumania, Syria, Venezuela, etc.

The main tasks which could be usefully initiated in
these countries are exploration and measurement of resources,
feasibility studies, pilot plants, and testing of alternative
technologies (less capital and more labour-intensive). Unless
exploitation is labour-intensive and small-scale, the investments required will be huge, of the order of 5-10 times those
needed to explore and develop conventional oil. At the same
time, in most countries (possibly excepting Venezuela), the
scale of production will not allow exports. In this sense it
seems that these resources will require financing from
development banks in a manner similar to that provided
for hydropower.

3.   EXTERNAL ASSISTANCE NEEDS

The current energy position of developing countries
is summarised in Table IV-10. Taking into account the options
reviewed in Sections 2 and 3 above, the following position
could be achievable by the late 1980s and early 1990s:

a)   Some countries have good possibilities of becoming oil
     exporters, including: Argentina and Colombia
     (currently 0-25% dependent on oil imports to meet
     their commercial energy needs), Mozambique and
     Pakistan (currently 26-50% dependent), and Burma,
     Cameroon, Chad, Guatemala, Honduras, Madagascar, Niger
     (currently 76-100% dependent).

b)   Some countries could significantly decrease their
     energy imports, including: Chile, Bangladesh
     (currently 26-50% dependent), Afghanistan, Brazil,
     Ghana, and Turkey (currently 51-75% dependent), and
     almost all countries currently 76-100% dependent
     (except Cyprus, Gambia, Haiti, Lebanon, Mauritania,
     and Singapore).

c)   Some large- and medium-sized countries could approach
     self-sufficiency, for example: Bangladesh, Brazil,
     Chile, Ivory Coast, Morocco, Philippines, Sudan,
     Thailand, Turkey, and Vietnam.

TABLE IV-10: AN ENERGY CLASSIFICATION OF DEVELOPING COUNTRIES[a]

OIL-EXPORTING DEVELOPING COUNTRIES		OIL-IMPORTING DEVELOPING COUNTRIES[b] (Net Oil Imports as % of Commercial Energy Demand, 1978)				
OPEC MEMBERS	NON-OPEC MEMBERS	0-25%	26-50%	50-75%	76-100%	
ALGERIA	BAHRAIN	ARGENTINA	CHILE	ALBANIA	Bahamas	Jordan
GABON	BOLIVIA	COLOMBIA	Mongolia	BRAZIL	BARBADOS	Malta
IRAN	MALAYSIA	DR Korea	YUGOSLAVIA	Rep. Korea	Costa Rica	Mauritius
IRAQ	MEXICO	ROMANIA		Lebanon	CUBA	Nicaragua
KUWAIT	OMAN	S. Africa		TURKEY	Cyprus	Panama
LIBYA	PERU				Dominican Rep.	Papua New
QATAR	SYRIAN AR				Fiji	Guinea
SAUDI ARABIA	TRINIDAD				GUATEMALA	Paraguay
U.A.E.	& TOBAGO				Guyana	Portugal
VENEZUELA	TUNISIA				Ivory Coast	Suriname
					Jamaica	Uruguay

COUNTRIES WITH ACTUAL OR POTENTIAL FUELWOOD PROBLEMS[c]

		0-25%	26-50%	50-75%	76-100%	
ECUADOR	ANGOLA	INDIA	BANGLADESH	AFGHANISTAN	Benin	Maldives
INDONESIA	BURMA	Vietnam	Botswana	Burundi	Bhutan	Mali
NIGERIA	CHINA	Zimbabwe	Mozambique	GHANA	Cambodia	Mauritania
	CONGO		PAKISTAN	Malawi	CAMEROON	MOROCCO
	EGYPT		Zambia	Rwanda	Cape Verde Is.	Nepal
	ZAIRE				C. African Rep.	Niger
					Chad	PHILIPPINES
					Comoros	Sao Tome &
					El Salvador	Principe
					Eq. Guinear	Senegal
					Ethiopia	Sierre Leone
					Gambia	Solomon Is.
					Grenada	Somalia
					Guinea	Sri Lanka
					Guinea-Bissau	Sudan
					Haiti	Swaziland
					Honduras	Tanzania
					Kenya	THAILAND
					Lao PDR	Togo
					Lesotho	Upper Volta
					Liberia	W. Samoa
					Madagascar	Yemen AR
						Yemen PDR

POPULATION (million)						
320	1180	820	210	245	395	

Notes: [a]Countries shown in CAPITALS are oil and/or gas producers.
Table based on UN World Energy Statistics 1978 and World Bank
estimates of fuelwood. Population data from World Development
Report 1980.

[b]Excluding countries with 1978 per capita GNP above $3000 and
some countries with population of less than 0.5 million.

[c]Countries where annual consumption of fuelwood is unlikely to be
sustainable at minimum levels through the year 2000, without
damage to the ecology. Many countries not included will have
fuelwood problems in local areas.

Source: World Bank, Energy in the Developing Countries, August 1980.

d) Some smaller countries could become minor exporters by
the end of this period (due to their small energy
consumption), for example: Barbados, Guinea, Guinea-
Bissau, Liberia, Mali, Mauritania, Nicaragua, Papua-
New Guinea, Surinam, Tanzania, Yemen A.R., and Yemen
P.D.R.

For these changes to take place, massive increases in
exploration and development effort and finance are needed, as
well as a quantum jump in official technical assistance. The
type of assistance needed by different countries depends on
their experience in energy development, the strength of their
existing energy and economic institutions and, of course, the
strength of their economies vis-à-vis the financing (particularly the risk capital) needed for an accelerated effort for
energy development.

In financial terms alone, the World Bank estimates
that in the ten years to 1975 the developing countries invested about US$ 12 billion a year (in 1980-$) on average in
commercial energy production and transformation, mostly electricity. This represented about 5% of total investment and
1.3% of GNP.[b] In 1980 their energy investment is an estimated US$ 34 billion. Of this amount, investment in OIDCs is
an estimated $25 billion. It represents some 10% of total in-
vestment and 2.5% of GNP, clearly indicating the economic
adjustment triggered by the 1973 oil crisis.

This trend is expected to continue during the 1980s;
energy investments are envisaged to grow by about 10% p.a.,
twice as fast as GNP. A breakdown by source of OIDCs' energy
investment requirements during the 1980s is given in Table
IV-11. In brief, the World Bank estimates these requirements
at US$450-500 billion (in 1980-$) during the decade, or a
yearly average of $37 billion during the first five years and
$53 billion during the second. Of these amounts, investment
in electric power (including transmission and distribution)
will continue to take about three-quarters. Exploration and
development of petroleum is envisaged to grow from $2.6
billion in 1980 to $3.5 billion p.a. during the first five
years, and $4.7 billion p.a. during the second.

The financing of such a program will make heavy
demands on domestic and foreign saving. But OIDCs face even

TABLE IV-11: OIL-IMPORTING DEVELOPING COUNTRIES: PRINCIPAL INVESTMENT REQUIREMENTS IN COMMERCIAL ENERGY, 1980-90[a]

	Estimate 1980	Annual Average 1981-85	Annual Average 1986-90	Average Growth Rate 1980-90
		(US$ billion in 1980-$)		(% p.a.)
Total: OIDCs	24.6	36.7	53.4	10.9
Electric Power[b]	18.5	27.5	39.7	10.7
Thermal	8.0	11.8	15.4	9.1
Hydro	9.2	13.5	15.1	6.8
Nuclear	1.2	2.1	8.8	30.4
Other	0.1	0.1	0.4	20.3
Coal[c]	0.5	0.7	1.5	15.8
Oil[d]	2.6	3.5	4.7	8.2
Exploration	0.5	1.0	1.5	11.6
Development	2.1	2.5	3.2	4.3
Gas[e]	1.0	1.7	2.7	14.2
Alcohol	0.5	0.9	1.2	12.4
Fuelwood	0.5	0.6	1.3	13.6
Refineries[f]	1.0	1.8	2.3	11.8

Note:

All Developing Countries	34.4	54.4	82.2	12.3

Notes: [a]Based on World Bank's case 1 (Probable) projections.

[b]Includes cost of transmission and distribution. Assume that capacity requirements will grow at same rate as in 1973-78.

[c]Based on investments required to develop coal production from 175 million tce in 1980 to 250 million tce in 1990.

[d]Based on investments required to develop oil production from 2.0 mm b/d in 1980 to 3.6 mm b/d in 1990.

[e]Based on investments required to raise gas production from 1.5 mm b/d o.e. in 1980 to 2.5 mm b/d o.e. in 1990.

[f]Assumes capital requirements will grow at same rate as in recent past.

Source: World Bank, Energy in the Developing Countries, August 1980.

larger oil import bills ($67 billion in 1980 alone)[a].   By
maximising energy production during the decade and by vigorous
conservation, it estimates that OIDCs could cut their oil
import bill in 1990 by $25–30 billion (in 1980–$)[b].

        For its part, the World Bank had planned to expand
its energy lending to $13 billion total (in current–$) during
the next five years. Envisaging that this is insufficient, it
now proposes to lend an additional $12 billion during these
five years.

        The economic rationale for OIDCs' increased invest-
ment in domestic energy sources is very clear: their costs are
expected to be much lower than those of imported energy
(Table IV–12).

        Despite the significant dimension of the financing
problem, it seems to us that the main obstacles to energy
development, which might otherwise be achievable in purely
physical terms, will not be financial. Currently, there is a
growing understanding of the global nature of the energy
crisis. Those OIDCs which adopt realistic energy policies and
the minimum managerial and institutional capabilities will
have access to those official and private sources of know–how
and finance which are necessary to improve their energy
position.

        It is helpful to classify OIDCs according to the type
of external sources of energy development assistance which
will be most important in the 1980s, as follows:

    i. technical assistance from official institutions
          – mainly to create an adequate framework for energy
            development, institutional policy, and basic data;
    ii. financial assistance from official institutions
          – mainly to complement i) above, e.g., surveys,
            training, and to finance in "last resort" such
            areas as exploratory drilling, gas, and hydro
            development in countries where private foreign
            financing is unlikely to be a viable alternative;

TABLE IV-12: DEVELOPED COUNTRIES: COMPARATIVE COSTS OF ENERGY FROM DIFFERENT SOURCES

	Export Cost[a] fob	Transport/ Processing Distribution Cost	Delivered Cost[b]
	(US$ per barrel oil equiv. in 1980-$)		

I. DOMESTRIC PRODUCTION

	Export Cost[a] fob	Transport/ Processing Distribution Cost	Delivered Cost[b]
Crude Oil – Low Cost	5.00	1.00	6.00
– High Cost	12.00	1.00–3.00	13.00–15.00
Natural Gas – Low Cost	0.30	1.95	2.25[c]
– High Cost	2.20	8.80	11.00[c]
Coal – Low Cost	2.00	2.50	4.50
– High Cost	5.00–10.00	10.00	15.00

Refined Petroleum Products
(from Domestic Crude
comparable to Arabian Light)

Gasoline (90R)		)	9.40–21.00
Household Kerosene		)	11.30–25.40
Diesel (53/57)		)2.50	9.40–21.00
Heavy Fuel Oil		)	7.20–17.50
Liquefied Petroleum Gases		)	10.00–25.00

Synthetic Fuels[d]

Gasoline, Diesel from Cracked Fuel Oil[e]	11.00–21.00
Gasoline, Diesel from Coal	40.00–60.00
Ethanol from Sugarcane	25.00–45.00
Methanol from Natural Gas[f]	25.00–45.00
Gasoline from Methanol	25.00–35.00
Shale Oil[g]	25.00–35.00

Renewable Energy[d]

Firewood	8.00–20.00
Charcoal	30.00–80.00
Dung Cakes (India)	5.00–10.00
Solar Heat	50.00–90.00
Geothermal Heat	9.00–11.00

Electric Power

(at 2.4¢–10¢ per kwh)[h]	40.00–166.00

(Continued)

	Export Cost[a] fob	Transport/ Processing Distribution Cost	Delivered Cost[b]
	(US$ per barrel oil equiv. in 1980-$)		
II. IMPORTED FUELS			
Crude Oil			
Arabian Light: June 1980	28.00	2.75[i]	30.75
Products from above (Refined at point of Consumption)			
Gasoline (90R)		)	35.50
Household Kerosene		)	42.60
Diesel (53/57)		)4.00	35.50
Heavy Fuel Oil		)	27.20
Refined Products			
Gasoline (90R)	39.35	4.15[i]	43.50
Household Kerosene	41.50	4.38[i]	45.88
Diesel (53/57)	39.50	4.63[i]	44.13
Heavy Fuel Oil	24.20	3.25[i]	27.45
Liquefied Petroleum Gases			42.50
Liquefied Natural Gas			27.00
Steam Coal	6.00-8.00	3.00-6.00	9.00-14.00

Notes: [a]For domestically produced fuels, wellhead or mined cost is used.

[b]Notional delivered cost to OIDC countries in coastal locations. Tanker rates: clean for white products (diesel and gasoline) and dirty for crude oil and heavy oil.

[c]Natural gas prices were derived from Bank projects and studies in Bangladesh, Pakistan and Thailand.

[d]Cost delivered to consumers near point of production.

[e]Assumes production from fuel oil refined locally from indigenous crude.

[f]Based on gas prices of US$0.40-$1.50 per Mcf (US$2.25-$8.50 per barrel o.e.).

[g]Based on Shell and Bechtel estimates adjusted for inflation.

[h]Cost of electricity used in electric heating devices such as cooking stoves.

[i]Freight rates assume 60,000-ton tanker on Persian Gulf - Far East route. Rates: clean for white products (diesel and gasoline) and dirty for crude oil and heavy oil.

Source: World Bank, Energy in the Developing Countries, August 1980.

 iii. financial assistance from private banks
    - mainly to creditworthy countries with adequate
    management and technical capabilities; and
 iv. foreign investment
    - mainly private investment for a package technical,
    risk capital, and (in some cases) marketing
    capabilities. This is especially important in
    areas such as oil development and LNG. It is not
    aid but profit-oriented and concerned with
    political as well as commercial risks; ignoring
    these constraints would be naive.

 Foreign investment can be expected to play a leading role only in the following types of country situations:

 i. countries with potential for oil exports;
 ii. countries with large potential for gas exports, particularly in the form of LNG to industrial countries;
 iii. countries with medium to large potential for coal exports;
 iv. countries with low-cost energy resources which cannot be exported but can be used industrially to produce exportable goods, e.g., mineral processing; and
 v. countries with large domestic markets for energy, where government policies and overall economic outlook allow withdrawal of investment and net revenues in foreign currency.

 Official development assistance (ODA) is needed to cover many other country situations. In particular:

 i. financial support is needed in almost all cases where domestic energy developments are unlikely to lead to exportable surplus. This includes most development projects for electric power (a typical area of past ODA), coal, geothermal, and gas, as well as oil in countries with modest prospects;
 ii. in middle- and high-income countries, ODA financial support should be complemented to the maximum extent by co-financing with private banks. When possible,

this should also be done in creditworthy low-income
countries, e.g., India;

iii. a much larger share of ODA should be allocated to pre-
development stages of energy investments, as little
help can be expected from private sources; and

iv. ODA is needed to overcome non-financial weaknesses,
such as policy advice, strengthening of planning and
management institutions, and training programs.

In principle, it would be possible from the above
criteria to prescribe the mix of official and private assistance, which would be individually needed and feasible for each
country, type of project, and particular timing. In this
manner, a program for global energy development could be designed, and the requisite human and financial resources could
be quantified. Recent efforts by the World Bank seem to point
in that direction and may provide the basis for a major new
international initiative in this field.

FOOTNOTES AND BIBLIOGRAPHY

INTRODUCTION

a. Mahbub ul Haq. The Third World and the International
    Economic Order. Development Paper 22, Overseas Develop-
    ment Council, Washington, D.C., 1979.

b. Khadija Haq, ed. Dialogue for a New Order. Pergamon
    Press, 1980.

c. UNCTAD. The Developing Countries in the World Economy.
    Paper presented at workshop on "Energy and Development:
    Increasing Third World Collective Self-Reliance", spon-
    sored by OPEC, OPEC Fund and UNCTAD. Vienna, July 1980.

d. J. Amuzegar. A Requiem for the North-South Conference.
    Foreign Affairs. October 1977.

e. Independent Commission on International Development
    Issues. North-South: A Programme for Survival. MIT
    Press. Cambridge, Mass., 1980.

I. THE GLOBAL ENERGY SCENE

a. World Bank. World Development Report 1980. Washington,
    D.C. 1980.

b. Workshop on Alternative Energy Strategies (WAES).
    Energy: Global Prospects, 1985-2000. McGraw-Hill. New
    York, 1977.

c. Exxon Corporation. World Energy Outlook. New York, 1980.

d. Conservation Commission. World Energy Conference. World
    Energy Demand to 2020. IPC Science and Technology Press.
    New York, 1978.

e. IIASA. Energy in a Finite World: a Global Energy
    Systems Analysis. Vienna, January 1981.

f. International Energy Agency. Energy Policies and
    Programmes of IEA Countries: 1979 Review. Paris, 1980.

241

I.(<u>continued</u>):

g. US Congressional Budget Office. <u>The World Oil Market in</u>
    <u>the 1980s: Implications for the United States.</u>
    Washington D.C., May 1980.

h. International Monetary Fund. <u>World Economic   Outlook.</u>
    Washington, D.C., 1980.

i. UNCTAD. <u>Energy and Development: Increasing Third World</u>
    <u>Collective Self-Reliance.</u> Papers at Workshop sponsored
    by OPEC, OPEC Fund and UNCTAD. Vienna, July 1980.

j. World Bank. <u>Energy in the Developing Countries.</u>
    Washington, D.C., 1980.

k. OPEC Papers. <u>Energy in Developing Countries - Present</u>
    <u>and Future.</u> Vienna, October 1980.

l. Shell Briefing Service: <u>Energy in the Developing</u>
    <u>Countries.</u> London, January 1980.

m. OPEC Papers. <u>Domestic Energy Requirements in OPEC Member</u>
    <u>Countries.</u> Vienna, August 1980.

n. Committee on Nuclear and Alternative Energy Systems
    (CONAES). <u>Alternative Energy Demand Futures to 2010.</u>
    National Academy of Sciences. Washington, D.C., 1979.

o. Committee on Nuclear and Alternative Energy Systems
    (CONAES). <u>U.S. Energy Supply Prospects to 2010.</u>
    National Academy of Sciences. Washington, D.C., 1979.

p. <u>Energy in America's Future: The Choices Before Us.</u> A
    study by the Staff of the RFF National Energy Strategies
    Project. Sam H. Schurr, Project Director. Resources for
    the Future. Washington, D.C., 1979.

q. <u>Energy: The next 20 years.</u> Report by a Study Group
    sponsored by the Ford Foundation.   S.H. Landsberg,
    Chairman. Ballinger. Cambridge, Mass., 1979.

I.(continued):

r.   Ait-Laoussine, N. OPEC Oil: Recent Developments and
     Problems of Supply.   Paper at Second Oxford Energy
     Seminar. Oxford, September 1980.

s.   US C.I.A. The Energy Outlook and its Implications for the
     USSR and Eastern Europe. Washington, D.C., February 1980.

t.   PetroStudies. Soviet Oil Production Reform of 1980 and
     Its Potential. Malmoe, Sweden 1980.

u.   World Coal Study (WOCOL). Coal: Bridge to the Future.
     Ballinger. Cambridge, Mass., 1980.

v.   International Energy Agency.   Steam Coal: Prospects to
     2000. Paris, 1978.

w.   President's Commission on Accident at Three Mile Island.
     The Need for Change: the Legacy of TMI. John G. Kemeny,
     Chairman. Washington, D.C., 1979.

x.   International Consultative Group on Nuclear Energy
     (ICGNE). Papers. Rockefeller Foundation. New York, 1980.

y.   International Nuclear Fuel Cycle Evaluation (INFCE).
     Working Group Reports.   International Atomic Energy
     Agency. Vienna, 1980.

z.   UNITAR. "Summary Report of the Conference on Long-Term
     Energy Resources." Special Issue of Important for the
     Future. Vol. 5, no.1. New York, February 1980.

aa. OECD.   Renewable Energy Technologies for Developing
     Countries. Paris, 1979.

Other Relevant Literature

     Bénard, André.   World Oil and Cold Reality.   Harvard
     Business Review. Vol. 58, no.6. November-December 1980.

     Brown, Wm. N. & Herman Kahn. Energy Perspective for 1980s
     & 1990s: A Scenario Based on Guardedly Optimistic Assump-
     tions. Hudson Institute. Croton, New York, July 1980.

I.(continued):

Commission on Energy and raw materials of the French VIIIe Plan. Summary of report. Taking over from Oil. Commissariat Général du Plan. Paris, October 1980.

Independent Commission on International Development Issues (Brandt Commission). North-South: A Program for Survival. MIT Press. Cambridge, Mass., 1980.

Interfutures: Facing the Future; Mastering the Probable and Managing the Unpredictable. OECD. Paris, 1979.

Levy, Walter J. Oil and the Decline of the West. Foreign Affairs. Vol. 58, no. 5. Summer 1980.

National Foreign Assesment Center (CIA). Some Perspectives on Oil Availability for the Non-OPEC LDCs. Washington, D.C., September 1980.

Petro-Canada. International Energy Prospects to 2000-Revisited. Ottawa, July 1979.

Petro-Canada/Petroleos de Venezuela. World Oil Supply Prospects. Ottawa, February 1980.

Petroleum Industry Research Associates. Outlook for World Oil into the 21st Century, with Emphasis on the Period to 1990. Final Report. New York, 1978.

Sewell, John W. et al. The United States and World Development. Agenda 1980. Praeger. For the Overseas Development Council. New York, 1980.

Smith, Gerald C. and Rathjens, George W. Nuclear Energy and Non-Proliferation. Trialogue. Winter/spring no.22. Trilateral Commission. New York, 1979.

Sorensen, Bent. Renewable Energy. Academic Press. London, 1980.

Stobaugh, R. and D. Yergin. Energy Futures. Report of the Energy Project of the Harvard Business School. Harvard University Press. Boston, Mass., 1979.

I.(continued):

    Turner, Louis. Oil Companies in the International System. Royal Institute of International Affairs. London, 1978.

    US Department of Energy. Energy Supply and Demand Balance and Financing Requirements in Non-OPEC Developing Nations. February 1979.

II.   THE PARTIES INVOLVED

II.1 Oil-Importing Developing Countries

a.   Lincoln Gordon. International Energy Arrangements and the Developing Countries. Working paper for meeting of the Ford Foundation Energy/LDC Group. July 1979.

b.   Ted Taylor Associates. Energy Profiles of Selected Countries. (Mimeo.) Washington, D.C., 1977.

c.   James A. Bever. U.S. AID Renewable Energy Project. Paper for Senegal 1978, and personal observation and notes from field visits to West African villages.

d.   Antonio R. Parra. Overview of the Energy Situation in Oil-Importing Developing Countries. Prepared for OPEC Ministerial Committee on Long-Term Strategy. March 1979.

e.   Bernardo Grossling. Window on Oil. The Financial Times Ltd. London, 1977.

f.   U.N. World Energy Supplies, 1973-1978. Statistical Papers Series J. No. 22. New York, 1979.

g.   World Bank. Rural Electrification. Washington, D.C., October 1975.

h.   William Knowland and Carol Winski. Traditional Fuels: Present Data, Past Experience and Possible Strategies. Prepared for U.S. AID. September 1979.

II.1(continued):

i.   This discussion of Africa is adapted from James W. Howe
     and Frances A. Gulick.   Fuelwood and Other Renewable
     Energies in Africa: A Progress Report on the Problem and
     the Response. ODC. Washington, D.C., January 1980.

j.   David French. Firewood in Africa. Prepared for AID/AFR
     Firewood Workshop. June 1978.

k.   Energy in the Development of the Sahel: Situation --
     Perspectives -- Recommendations. CILSS (Club du Sahel).

l.   Reidar Persson. Forecast Resources of Africa: An
     Approach to International Forest Resource Appraisals,
     Part II: Regional Analysis.   pp. 128-132, 144-145.
     Royal College of Forestry.   Stockholm, 1977.   Part I,
     published in 1975, provides a country-by-country summary
     analysis of the status of national forests, including
     details on inventories.

m.   As calculated by F. Weber.   Wood Lot Estimate Guides.
     (Sahel.)   International Resources Development and
     Conservation Services. Boise, Idaho, December 1979.

n.   Bo Ohlsson.   Forestry for Rural Communities: A Case
     Study from Tiro. Supplementary Special Paper.   Ethiopia
     Forestry and Wildlife Development Authority (FAWDA).
     Addis Ababa, Ethiopia, 16 October 1978. Presented at the
     Eighth World Forest Congress. Jakarta, October 1978.

o.   See ODC's various Peace Corps case studies.

p.   Helen Hughes.   Changing Relative Energy Prices, The
     Balance-of-Payments and Growth in Developing Countries.
     Paper presented at EPRI Workshop on Energy and the
     Developing Nations. Palo Alto, California, March 1980.

q.   World Bank. World Development Report, 1980.   Washington,
     D.C., August 1980.

r.   Morgan Guaranty Trust Co.   LDC Prospects and Role of the
     IMF. World Financial Markets. New York, September 1980.

II.1(<u>continued</u>):

s. Workshop on Alternative Energy Strategies (WAES). <u>Energy: Global Prospects, 1985–2000.</u> McGraw–Hill. New York, 1977.

t. IMF Survey. Washington, D.C., January 1980.

u. International Monetary Fund. <u>World Economic Outlook.</u> Washington, D.C., 1980.

v. For example, see Martin M. McLaughlin and staff of Overseas Development Council. <u>The United States and World Development Agenda 1979.</u> Praeger. For the Overseas Development Council. Washington, D.C., 1979.

w. <u>Middle East Economic Survey.</u> Vol. xxiii, No. 19. February 1980.

x. IMF Press Release 80/34. Washington, D.C., April 1980.

y. Independent Commission on International Development Issues. (Brandt Commission.) <u>North–South: A Program for Survival.</u> MIT Press. Cambridge, Mass., 1980. Also James H. Howe and staff of Overseas Development Council. <u>The U.S. and the Developing World: Agenda for Action, 1974.</u> Praeger. For the Overseas Development Council. Washington, D.C., 1974.

z. Jean Louis Waelbroeck. <u>Energy and International Trade Issues.</u> Paper at EPRI Workshop on Energy and the Developing Nations. Palo Alto, California, March 1980.

Other Relevant Literature

Cleveland, Harlan. Ed. <u>Energy Futures of Developing Countries.</u> Aspen Institute for Humanistic Studies. New York, 1980.

Dunkerley, D. et al. <u>Energy Strategies for Developing Nations.</u> Resources for the Future. Washington, D.C., 1981.

Hoffmann, T. & Johnson, B. <u>World Energy Triangle: Strategy for Cooperation.</u> Ballinger. Cambridge, Mass., 1981.

II.2. Oil-Exporting Developing Countries

Relevant Literature

> Al-Chalabi, F. Papers in OPEC Review and OPEC Bulletin.
> Vienna, 1979-80.
>
> Al-Chalabi, F. OPEC and the International Oil Industry:
> A Changing Structure. Oxford University Press. Oxford,
> 1980.

II.3. Industrialised Countries

a. Krapels, Edward N. Oil Crisis Management. Johns Hopkins
   University Press. Baltimore, Maryland, 1980.

b. Conant, Melvin A. The Global Impact of Energy on US
   Security Intents and Commitments. Paper at Fall-Winter
   Seminar Series. National Security Affairs Institute.
   Washington, D.C., December 1979.

c. Canada, National Energy Program, Department of Energy,
   Mines & Resources. Ottawa, November 1980.

d. Commission of the European Communities. Energy Policy
   Communication from the Commission to the European
   Council, 31st March - 1st April 1980). Com (80) 130
   Final. Brussels, 1980.

e. International Energy Agency. Energy Policies and Programs
   of IEA countries. 1979 Review. OECD. Paris, 1980.

f. Lantzke, Ulf. Energy: A Continuing Trilateral Priority.
   Trialogue.   Winter/spring,   no.   22.   Trilateral
   Commission. New York, 1979.

g. Organisation for Economic Cooperation and Development
   (OECD). Economic Outlook no. 27. Paris, July 1980.

h. International Monetary Fund. World Economic Outlook.
   Washington, D.C., 1980.

i. World Bank. World Development Report, 1980. Washington,
   D.C., 1980.

II.3(<u>continued</u>):

j.   European   Economic   Community.   "Energy"   Council.
     <u>Community Energy Objectives for 1990 and convergence of</u>
     <u>the policies of the member states.</u>   Europe Documents
     no.1099. May 20, 1980.

k.   Byer, Trevor A. <u>The End of the Paris Energy Dialogue and</u>
     <u>the Need for an International Energy Institute.</u>   Energy
     Policy. Vol.6, no.4. December 1978.

Other Relevant Literature

     Commission   of   the   European   Communities.   <u>Energy</u>
     <u>Cooperation with Developing Countries and the Role of the</u>
     <u>Community.</u>   Report from the Commission to the Council.
     Com (80) 96 Final. Brussels, 1980.

     Commission of the European Communities.   <u>Measures to</u>
     <u>Mitigate the Effects of Short-Term Oil Supply Problems.</u>
     (Communication from the Commission to the Council) Com
     (80) 247 Final. Brussels, 1980.

     European Communities - European Council. <u>Summary by the</u>
     <u>Presidency fo the proceedings of the European Council.</u>
     European Report no.693.   June 14, 1980.

     European Economic Community.   "Energy" Council.   <u>New</u>
     <u>Lines of Action by the Community in the Field of Energy</u>
     <u>Saving.</u> Europe Documents no.1099. May 20, 1980.

     <u>International Energy Supply: A Perspective from the</u>
     <u>Industrial World.</u>   Working Paper.   International Policy
     Studies. Rockefeller Foundation. March 1978.

     Noreng, Oystein. <u>Oil Politics in the 1980's: Pattern of</u>
     <u>International Cooperation.</u> New York Council on Foreign
     Relations, 1978.

     Sawhill, John C., Hans W. Maull and Keichi Oshima.
     <u>Energy, Managing the Transition.</u> Trilateral Commission
     Task Force. New York, 1978.

II.3(<u>continued</u>):

Smart, Ian. <u>Communicating with the Oil-Exporters: The
Old Trialogue and the New</u>. Trialogue. Winter/Spring no.
22. Trilateral Commission. New York, 1979.

Stobaugh, R. and Yergin, D. <u>Energy Futures</u>. Report of
the Energy Project of the Harvard Business School.
Harvard University Press. Boston, Mass., 1979.

United Kingdom. Department of Energy. <u>International
Energy Questions</u>. U.K. Dept. of Energy. Energy
Commission Paper no. 13.

United Nations Economic Commission for Europe. <u>New
Issues Affecting the Energy Economy of the ECE Region in
the Medium and Long Term</u>. 1978.

III. <u>GLOBAL OPPORTUNITIES</u>

III.I <u>Managing the Remaining Decades of Oil</u>

a. World Bank. <u>A Program to Accelerate Petroleum Production
in the Developing Countries</u>. Washington, D.C., 1979.

b. Committee on Nuclear and Alternative Energy Systems
(CONAES). <u>Alternative Energy Demand Futures to 2010</u>.
National Academy of Sciences. Washington, D.C., 1979.

c. <u>Energy: The Next 20 Years</u>. Report by a Study Group
sponsored by the Ford Foundation. S.H. Landsberg,
Chairman. Ballinger. Cambridge, Mass., 1979.

d. Stobaugh, R. and Yergin, D. <u>Energy Futures</u>. Report of
the Energy Project of the Harvard Business School.
Harvard University Press. Boston, Mass., 1979.

e. <u>Energy in America's Future: The Choices before Us</u>. A
Study by staff of the RFF National Energy Strategies
Project. Sam H. Schurr, Project Director. Resources for
the Future. Washington, D.C., 1979.

III.I(<u>continued</u>):

f. Leach, G. R. et al. <u>A Low Energy Strategy for the United
    Kingdom</u>. International Institute for Development and
    Environment. London, 1979.

g. Beijdorff, A. F. <u>Energy Efficiency</u>. Shell International
    Petroleum Company. London, 1979.

h. International Energy Agency. <u>Energy Policies and Programs
    of IEA Countries. 1979 Review</u>. OECD. Paris, 1980.

i. Exxon Corporation. <u>World Energy Outlook</u>. New York, 1980.

j. Darmstadter, Joel et al. <u>How Industrial Societies Use
    Energy; a Comparative Analysis</u>. Johns Hopkins University
    Press.   For Resources for the Future.   Baltimore,
    Maryland, 1977.

k. <u>International   Comparisons   of   Energy   Consumption</u>.
    Proceedings of a Workshop sponsored by Resources for the
    Future and the Electric Power Research Institute.   Joy
    Dunkerley, Editor. Resources of the Future. Washington,
    D.C., 1978.

l. European Economic Community.   "Energy" Council.   <u>New
    Lines of action by the Community in the Field of Energy
    Saving.</u> Europe Documents no.1099, May 20, 1980.

<u>Other Relevant Literature</u>

    Ehrlich, Everett M.   <u>Oil and Gas Prospects in Non-OPEC
    Less Developed Countries</u>. EPRI Workshop on Energy and
    the Developing Nations. Stanford University. Palo Alto,
    California, March 1980.

    Fallen-Bailey, O.G. and T.A. Byer.   <u>Energy Options and
    Policy Issues in Developing Countries</u>. World Bank Staff
    Working Paper no. 350. Washington, D.C., August 1979.

    Hughart, David.   <u>Prospects for Traditional and Non-
    Conventional Energy Sources in Developing Countries</u>.
    World Bank Staff Working Paper no. 346.   Washington,
    D.C., 1979.

III.I(<u>continued</u>):

Petro–Canada/Petroleos de Venezuela. <u>World Oil Supply Prospects</u>. A Staff Report. February 1980.

Pipes, K. <u>Exploration in Developing Countries</u>. Exxon paper presented at UNITAR Conference. Montreal, 1979.

Socolow, Robert H. <u>The Coming Age of Conservation</u>. Annual Review of Energy, 1977. Vol. 2.

Socolow, Robert H. <u>Resource-Efficient High Technology and the Convergence of North and South</u>. Discussion Paper. Symposium on Social Values and Technological

Vedavalli, R. <u>Petroleum and Gas in Non-OPEC Developing Countries 1976-1985</u>. World Bank Staff Working Paper no. 289. Washington, D.C., 1978.

World Bank. <u>Program to Accelerate Petroleum Production in the Developing Countries</u>. Washington, D.C., 1979.

World Bank. <u>Coal Development Potential and Prospects in the Developing Countries</u>. Washington, D.C., 1979.

World Bank. <u>Energy in the Developing Countries</u>. Washington, D.C., August 1980.

III.2 <u>Managing the Transition from Oil to Other Sources</u>

International Energy Agency. <u>Energy Research, Development and Demonstration in the IEA Countries: A Strategic View</u>. OECD. Paris, 1980.

International Energy Agency. <u>Energy Policies and Programmes of IEA Countries</u>. 1979 Review. Paris, 1980.

IV. <u>FRAMEWORK FOR ENERGY POLICIES IN OIDCs</u>

a. McNamara, R. S. <u>World Bank President's Address to the Board of Governors</u>. Washington, D.C., September 1980.

IV.(<u>continued</u>):

b.   World   Bank.   <u>Energy   in   the   Developing   Countries.</u>
     Washington, D.C., August 1980.

c.   World Bank. <u>World Development Report, 1980.</u> Washington,
     D.C., 1980.

About the

of the Society for International Development

        The North-South Roundtable (NSRT), established in
1978 under the auspices of the Society for International Development, is an unofficial, intellectual forum which brings
together eminent leaders of thought in all walks of life to
discuss and debate global development issues. Members of the
Roundtable participate in its activities in their personal capacities. They come from many continents and countries and are
united by a shared committment to orderly change in human
affairs. The NSRT organizes its deliberations both through its
annual sessions and through periodic, smaller sessions on specific global policy themes. Its various sessions are regarded
not as unique events in themselves but as part of a process of
careful analysis, continuing debate, and attempts to reach common understandings in a very diverse world--all contributing to
a process of orderly structural change within and among nations.

        The Roundtable's main ongoing projects are:

North-South Energy Roundtable: An international task
force to prepare policy studies on the future of energy
to serve as a basis for continuing dialogue leading to
negotiations of a new national and international framework for dealing with energy issues.

<u>Global Round</u>: A programme of study and discussion on
the global round of North-South negotiations, carrying
on from the report of the Brandt Commission.

<u>North-South Food Roundtable</u>: An international task
force to prepare policy studies on world food situation intended to start a process of dialogue on food
issues.

The Society for International Development is an independent nongovernmental organization whose purposes are to provide a forum for collective reflection and to encourage a mutually educating dialogue on development, at all levels. The
Society was founded in 1957 and has evolved into several inter-
locking networks--where individuals and institutions are linked
in different ways around a varied range of activities. The
President of SID is James Grant and its Secretary General is
Ponna Wignaraja. The Society's international headquarters is
in Rome.

<u>North-South Roundtable Secretariat</u>
Khadija Haq, Secretariat Director
1717 Massachusetts Avenue, N.W., Suite 501
Washington, D.C. 20036
Tel. (202) 234-8701

NORTH SOUTH ENERGY ROUNDTABLE PROJECT

Steering Committee

Maurice F. Strong, Chairman   Chairman, International Energy Development Corporation

Kenneth Dadzie   Director General for Development United Nations

James P. Grant   Executive Director, UNICEF

Mahbub ul Haq   Director, Policy Planning, The World Bank

Enrique Iglesias   Executive Secretary, UN Economic Commission for Latin America, & Secretary General, UN Conference on New and Renewable Sources of Energy

Donald Mills   Former Ambassador of Jamaica to the United Nations

Ponna Wignaraja   Secretary General, Society for International Development

Core Group

Salah Al-Shaikhly   Assistant Administrator and Regional Director for Arab States, UNDP

John Foster   Senior Economic Adviser, Petro-Canada

James W. Howe   Director of International Affairs Solar Energy Research Institute, Golden, Colorado

Francisco R. Parra   Executive Director, International Energy Development Corporation, and formerly Secretary General, OPEC

David H. Pollock   Norman Paterson Professor of International Affairs, Carleton University

Consultative Group

Miguel Ozorio de Almeyda	Adviser to the Minister of Scientific and Technological Affairs, Brazil
Vladimir Baum	Director, United Nations Center for Natural Resources, Energy and Transportation
Edward Fried	Senior Fellow, Brookings Institution, Washington, D.C.
Efrain Friedmann	Companía de Petroleos de Chile, (COPEC)
Hans Landsberg	Senior Fellow, Resources for the Future, Washington, D.C.
Arjun Makhijani	Consultant in Energy and Development Field
Olof Murelius	Energy Coordinator, Swedish International Development Agency, and United Nations Division of Natural Resources and Energy
Ignacy Sachs	Director, International Centre for Research on Environment and Development
John Sewell	President, Overseas Development Council, Washington, D.C.
Janez Stanovnik	Executive Secretary, United Nations Economic Commission for Europe
Carlos Suarez	Professor, Instituto de Economía Energética, Fundación Bariloche
Carl Tham	M.P., Special Counsellor of the Swedish Foreign Ministry
Ghebru Woldeghiorghis	Executive Secretary, Ethiopian National Energy Committee